Handbook of
Grammar &
Composition

James A. Chapman

A Beka Book®
A MINISTRY OF
PENSACOLA CHRISTIAN COLLEGE
PENSACOLA, FLORIDA 32523-9160

Handbook of Grammar & Composition
Third Edition

A Beka Book Publications, a division of Pensacola Christian
College, is a Christian textbook ministry designed to meet
the need for Christian textbooks and teaching aids. The
purpose of this publications ministry is to help Christian
schools reach children and young people for the Lord and
train them in the Christian way of life.

Staff Credits

Edition Editor: Marie Thompson

Editorial Assistants: Susan Etheridge,
    Erin Zimmerman

Designer: Amy Tedder

CONTENTS

To the Teacher

This *Handbook of Grammar and Composition* provides a complete treatment of those elements necessary for clear and effective writing. The first four sections of the *Handbook* thoroughly teach the rules of grammar, sentence structure, word usage, and mechanics. The final section contains clear, concise instructions for writing compositions and includes sample paragraphs and compositions.

Although the *Handbook* is intended to be used as a textbook, it is also a valuable reference tool which students will wish to keep for future use. The following features have been included to make the text easy to use:

1. a convenient **reference key** on the inside front cover and a chart of **correction symbols** on the inside back cover
2. **marginal tabs** on the pages to help students locate the different sections of the book
3. **numbered grammar rules** to help students find specific rules within a chapter
4. an **extensive index** to help students locate specific references quickly

Parts 1–4 of the *Handbook* have been arranged so that they can be taught in order, but the teacher may vary the order if he prefers to do so. The sections in part 5 can be assigned at any time throughout the year.

A Beka Book Publications also provides workbooks for use with this handbook. The preface to each workbook and the structure of the workbooks themselves suggest an effective course of study for one year.

Part 1

Grammar
for
Composition

Language, as well as the faculty of speech, was the immediate gift of God.
Noah Webster

Despite all its deviations and excrescences, English does have a structure, a logic at its center, a set of principles, a consistency matching that of the orderly mind. Of this structure grammar is the working diagram and teachable plan—reason enough why, to the worker in prose, grammar remains indispensable.
Wilson Follett

1 Basic Definitions

Gram. 1.1

1.1 A *sentence* **is a group of words that expresses a complete thought and can stand alone. Every grammatical sentence must have a subject and a predicate.**
The sun is our most important source of heat and light.

1.2 **The** *subject* **of a sentence is that part about which something is said.**
*The **words** of the Lord are pure words.*

1.3 **The** *predicate* **of a sentence is that part which says something about the subject.**
The words of the Lord ***are*** *pure words.*

Parts of Speech

1.4 A *verb* **is a word that** *shows action,* **links** **another word to the subject,** *helps* **another verb, or merely** *indicates existence.*
God *created* all things. (shows action)
Jesus *is* God. (links *God* to the subject *Jesus*)
Only Christ *can* give you peace. (helps the verb *give* to make a statement)
Christ, our mediator, *is* in heaven. (merely indicates the existence of Christ)

1.5 A *noun* **is a word that names a person, place, thing, or idea.**
persons—*Gwen, wife, companion, secretary*
places—*Wales, kitchen, airport, city*
things—*rocket, pliers, canary, trestle*
ideas—*harmony, compassion, righteousness, excellence*

1.6 A *pronoun* **is a word that takes the place of a noun.** (*I, you, he, him, she, her, it, they, us, that, who, whom, mine, yours, everyone, nobody,* etc.)
They recognized *him* as *one* with *whom they* could win.

1.7 **An** *adjective* **is a word that modifies a noun or a pronoun.** It answers the questions *what kind, which one, how many, how much,* or *whose.* (A modifier makes the meaning of another word more specific by describing or limiting that word.)

2

diligent worker (what kind)   *this* article (which one)
six reporters (how many)   *sufficient* rest (how much)
her apron (whose)   *Jan's* cookbook (whose)

1.8 **An *adverb* is a word that modifies a verb, an adjective, or another adverb.** It answers the questions *where, when, how, how often, to what extent.*

stand *there* (where)   speak *now* (when)
proceed *cautiously* (how)   *seldom* comes (how often)
partially finished
   (to what extent)

1.9 **A *preposition* is a word that shows how a noun or a pronoun is related to some other word in the sentence.** (*above, against, behind, between, by, in, of, on, to,* etc.)

The men lounged *on* benches *outside* the country store.

1.10 **A *conjunction* is a word (or word group) that joins words, phrases, or clauses.** (*and, but, or, neither—nor, not only—but also, as if, so that, although, because, if,* etc.)

Gail *and* Jess are on the newspaper staff.
They work on the staff *in order that* they may gain experience in journalism.

1.11 **An *interjection* is an exclamatory word that is not grammatically related to the other words in a sentence.**

Hey! Where are you going with that?
Oh, I didn't know they were coming.

1.12 **You cannot tell what part of speech a word is until you determine its function in a sentence. The same word may function as several different parts of speech.**

Lightning struck a pine *tree* in our back yard. (noun)
The *tree* surgeon lopped off low-hanging branches.
   (adjective)
Our dog *trees* squirrels when other dogs cannot.
   (verb)

Phrases and Clauses

1.13 A *phrase* **is a group of related words that does not contain a subject and a verb. The phrase is used as a single part of speech.**

> Grant is the boy *in the red shirt.* (prepositional phrase used as an adjective)

1.14 A *clause* **is a group of related words that contains both a subject and a verb.**

> Grant is the boy *who is wearing the red shirt.* (*Who* is the subject; *is wearing* is the verb.)

1.15 **An** *independent clause* **expresses a complete thought and can stand alone as a sentence.**

> *He* that keepeth his mouth *keepeth his life.*

1.16 A *dependent* **(subordinate)** *clause* **contains a subject and a verb but does not express a complete thought and cannot stand alone as a sentence.**

> He *that keepeth his mouth* keepeth his life.

Kinds of Sentences

1.17 **There are** *four kinds of sentences* **classified according to structure (***simple, compound, complex, compound-complex***).** In the examples below, independent clauses are enclosed within brackets and dependent clauses within parentheses.

1.18 A *simple sentence* **contains one independent clause and no dependent (subordinate) clauses.**

> [A righteous <u>man</u> <u>hateth</u> lying.]

1.19 A *compound sentence* **contains two or more independent clauses but no dependent (subordinate) clauses.**

> [The <u>wicked</u> <u>shall be</u> cut off from the earth], and [the <u>transgressors</u> <u>shall be rooted</u> out of it.]

1.20 A *complex sentence* **contains one independent clause and one or more dependent (subordinate) clauses.**

> (If <u>thou</u> <u>faint</u> in the day of adversity), [thy <u>strength</u> <u>is</u> small.]

1.21 A *compound-complex sentence* contains two or more independent clauses and one or more dependent (subordinate) clauses.

> [The <u>heart</u> of him (<u>that</u> <u>hath</u> understanding) <u>seeketh</u> knowledge], but [the <u>mouth</u> of fools <u>feedeth</u> on foolishness.]

1.22 There are four kinds of sentences classified according to their purpose: *declarative, imperative, interrogative, exclamatory.*

1.23 A *declarative sentence* makes a statement. It ends with a period.

> The beginning is the most important part of the work.
>
> —*Plato*

1.24 An *imperative sentence* gives a command or makes a request. It ends with a period or an exclamation point.

> Never make the same mistake twice.   Pay the price!

The subject of an imperative sentence is the word *you,* understood but not expressed. The first sentence means, *You* never make the same mistake twice. The second means, *You* pay the price!

1.25 An *interrogative sentence* asks a question. It ends with a question mark.

> O death, where is thy sting?

1.26 An *exclamatory sentence* shows sudden or strong feeling. It ends with an exclamation point.

> How excellent is Thy lovingkindness, O God!

2 Sentence Parts

2.1 A *sentence* is a group of words that expresses a complete thought and can stand alone.

2.2 Every grammatical sentence must have a *subject* (expressed or understood) and a *predicate.*

> ▶ Note. Experienced writers sometimes use sentences like these:
>
> Thanks!   Nonsense!   Quiet!   This way, please.
> Good work!   Away with such a fellow!

As to grammatical form, such expressions are not full sentences; but as to meaning, they are equivalent to sentences because they express a relatively complete thought and can stand alone. However, the word *sentence* in this book refers to the grammatical sentence.

Gram.
2.3

2.3 **The *subject* of a sentence is that part about which something is said; the *predicate* of a sentence is that part which says something about the subject.**

2.4 **The *simple subject* is the subject without any modifiers.**

The *actions* of men are the best interpreters of their thoughts. —*Locke*

2.5 **The *complete subject* is the subject plus all of its modifiers.**

The actions of men are the best interpreters of their thoughts.

2.6 **The *simple predicate* is the verb (1.4) without any complements or modifiers.**

The actions of men *are* the best interpreters of their thoughts.

▶ Note. A simple predicate may be a group of words, called a *verb phrase*. A *verb phrase* consists of a main verb and one or more helping verbs.

The haters of the Lord *should have submitted* themselves unto Him.

2.7 **The *complete predicate* is the verb (1.4) plus any complements and modifiers.**

The actions of men *are the best interpreters of their thoughts.*

▶ Note. Hereafter the word *subject* will refer to the simple subject, and the word *verb* will refer to the simple predicate.

2.8 **A *complement* is a word or group of words that completes the meaning begun by the subject and verb (2.22–2.31).**

2.9 **The following is an outline of the elements that make up a grammatical sentence.**

1. Subject (always necessary)
2. Verb (always necessary)
3. Complement (often necessary, but not always)
4. Modifiers of subject, verb, or complement (not necessary, but usually present)
5. Miscellaneous elements (See 3.63–3.72.)

6

Locating Sentence Parts

2.10 **To locate the subject and verb** of a sentence, follow this general procedure: First find the verb (2.11). Then ask *who* or *what* before the verb in order to find the subject. Remember that the subject will never be in a prepositional phrase (5.3).

> A man of knowledge increaseth strength. (*Increaseth* is the verb. *Who* or *what* increaseth? *Man* increaseth. *Man* is the subject. *Knowledge* cannot be the subject because it is the object of the preposition *of.*)

Gram. 2.13

Locating the Verb

2.11 **To locate the verb,** look for a word that shows action. If you do not find an action word, look for a word from the lists below. The following words are almost always verbs (main verbs [3.5] or helping verbs [3.12]).

Linking, Helping, or Existence		Action or Helping		Helping		Action or Linking		
am	were	have	do	shall	may	taste	look	grow
is	be	has	does	will	might	feel	appear	remain
are	being	had	did	should	must	smell	become	stay
was	been			would	can	sound	seem	
					could			

2.12 **A *verb phrase* (3.4) is often *interrupted* by other words.** Be careful to locate all the helping verbs that go with the main verb.

> My Spirit *shall* not always *strive* with man.

2.13 **When looking for verbs, do not mistake a verbal for a verb.** A verbal is a verb form and has many of the characteristics of a verb, but it does not function as a verb: it functions as a noun, as an adjective, or as an adverb. (Verbals are explained in section 4.) You can easily distinguish a verb from a verbal if you will remember that a verb must always have a subject and that the subject of a verb must be in the nominative case (11.2–11.4).

> They *hid* under the porch. (*Hid* is the verb because it has a subject, *they,* which is in the nominative case.)
> The boys, *hiding* under the porch, were discovered. (*Hiding* is a verbal. It has no subject at all. It functions as an adjective, modifying *boys.*)

7

We *expected* them *to arrive* early. (*Expected* is the verb because it has a subject, *we,* which is in the nominative case. *To arrive* is a verbal because although it has a subject, *them,* the subject is not in the nominative case. See 11.7.)

Locating the Subject

2.14 **To locate the subject** of a sentence, follow the procedure as explained under 2.10, but be aware of certain peculiarities of word order (2.15–2.21).

2.15 **The subject of a sentence normally comes before the predicate, but sometimes the *predicate* or *part of the predicate* comes *before the subject.*** When any part of the predicate comes before the subject, the sentence is in *inverted order.* (See 2.16–2.19.)

2.16 **In interrogative sentences, the subject is usually between the parts of a verb phrase.** It is easier to find the subject and verb if you change the question into a declarative sentence.

Will you go with us? (interrogative sentence)
You will go with us. (changed into a declarative sentence)

2.17 **The word *here,* which begins some sentences, is rarely the subject.** The subject usually follows the verb in sentences of this type.

Here is the final report.

2.18 **Some sentences begin with prepositional phrases (5.3). Remember that subjects cannot be in prepositional phrases.** In this example, the word *porch* cannot be the subject.

On the back porch lay a rusty shotgun.

2.19 **Some sentences begin with the words *there* or *it.* These words are usually expletives (3.72), not subjects.** In such sentences, look for the subject after the verb. Observe that in the following examples the words *there* and *it* are not grammatically necessary.

There was given me a reed like unto a rod. (A reed like unto a rod was given me.)
It is wise to be diligent. (To be diligent is wise.)

▶ Note. The words *there* and *it* have other uses. *There* may be used as an adverb: There sat Billy. (*There* modifies the verb *sat.*) *It* may be used as an indefinite subject in such sentences as the following: It is raining. It is early. It is warm.

2.20 **The *subject* of an *imperative sentence* is the word *you*, understood but not written.**

> Go not in the way of evil men. (*Who* go? You.)
> (You) Go not in the way of evil men.

2.21 **The subject almost always comes *before* its appositive (3.24).**

> Mr. Jones, our new mayor, is doing a good job.
>   (*Mayor* is the appositive.)
> Our new mayor, Mr. Jones, is doing a good job. (*Mr. Jones* is the appositive.)

[For diagrams of subject and verb see 8.1, 8.9, 8.10.]

Complements

2.22 Many times a subject and a verb are sufficient to express a complete thought.

> The mail must be delivered.
> The machine suddenly stopped.

2.23 However, sometimes a subject and a verb are not sufficient to express a complete thought. A third part is needed, called a *complement*. **A complement completes the meaning begun by the subject and verb.** The following subject-verb combinations require a third part to complete the meaning. Can you supply a word to complete each of these sentences?

> Tony was ...   Bill threw...   Marie always seems ...

Complements of the Verb

2.24 **Those complements that are concerned in some way with the action of a verb are called *objects: direct object, indirect object,* and *objective complement.***

2.25 **The *direct object* is a substantive (a noun or its equivalent, 3.22) that receives the action of a verb or shows the result of that action.** It answers the questions *whom* or *what* after the verb.

> Jim hit the *ball.* (Jim hit *what?* The answer is *ball;* therefore *ball* is the direct object. *Ball* receives the action of the verb.)

9

We dug a *hole.* (We dug *what?* The answer is *hole;* therefore *hole* is the direct object. *Hole* shows the result of the action.)

2.26 **The *indirect object* is a substantive (a noun or its equivalent) that tells *to whom* or *for whom,* or *to what* or *for what* the action of the verb is done.** The indirect object (when present) precedes the direct object.

The Sunday school superintendent gave *Emily* an award. (Superintendent gave *what?* Superintendent gave *award. Award* is the direct object. Superintendent gave *to whom* an award? Superintendent gave to *Emily* an award. *Emily* is the indirect object.)

▶ Note. In many instances you can say the same thing by using either an indirect object or a prepositional phrase (5.3). Just remember that these are two different grammatical constructions. If the word *to* or *for* precedes the substantive, you know that the substantive is the object of a preposition, not an indirect object.

We gave *God* the glory. (*God* is the indirect object.)
We gave the glory *to God.* (*God* is the object of the preposition *to.*)

2.27 **The *objective complement* is a noun or an adjective (or the equivalent of either) that is sometimes needed in addition to the direct object to complete the sense of the verb.** If the objective complement is a noun or a noun equivalent, it will explain or rename the direct object. If the objective complement is an adjective, it will modify the direct object. The objective complement usually follows the direct object.

We made Scott *treasurer.* (The noun *treasurer* renames the direct object *Scott.* Notice that without the complement *treasurer* the sense of the verb is incomplete. To say "We made Scott" is quite different from saying "We made Scott treasurer.")
We consider Scott *dependable.* (The adjective *dependable* describes the direct object *Scott.*)

▶ Note 1. You can usually identify an objective complement by inserting "to be" between the direct object and the word you think is the objective complement. If the "to be" fits naturally in this position, you are probably correct in thinking that the second word is an objective complement.

> We made Scott (to be) treasurer.
> We consider Scott (to be) dependable.

▶ Note 2. Objective complements are usually used with verbs such as these: *make, consider, name, choose, elect, appoint, render, leave, think, find.*

[For diagrams of complements of the verb see 8.4–8.6.]

Subject Complements

2.28 **Those complements that refer to the subject and at the same time complete the predication begun by a linking verb (3.10) are called *subject complements: predicate nominative* and *predicate adjective.***

2.29 **The *predicate nominative* is a substantive (a noun or its equivalent) that follows a linking verb and renames or explains the subject.** This substantive means the same thing or person as the subject.

> Mr. Hurley is our *coach.* (*Coach* is a noun that means the same person as the subject, *Mr. Hurley.*)

2.30 **The *predicate adjective* is an adjective that follows a linking verb and modifies the subject.**

> The plains are *desolate.* (*Desolate* modifies the subject *plains.*)

2.31 **Because subject complements always follow verbs that may function as linking verbs, it is helpful to know the following list of verbs that are commonly used as *linking verbs.***

am	were	taste	look	grow
is	be	feel	appear	remain
are	being	smell	become	stay
was	been	sound	seem	

[For diagrams of subject complements see 8.7–8.8.]

2.32 **The following is a summary of the basic patterns of English sentences.**

S.	V.
Fred	shouted.

S.	V.	M.
Fred	shouted	loudly.

(continued on next page)

11

S.   V. ⟶ D.O.
The pilot   gave   a demonstration.

S.   V. ⟶ I.O. ⟶ D.O.
The pilot   gave   us   a demonstration.

S.   V. ⟶ D.O.   O.C. (adjective)
The demonstration   made   the spectators   dizzy.

S.   V. ⟶ D.O.   O.C. (noun)
They   made   him   an instructor.

S.   V.   P.N.
Don   is   the pilot.

S.   V.   P.A.
Don   is   skillful.

Compound Sentence Parts

2.33   **Any part of a sentence may be compound.**

2.34   **A *compound subject* consists of two or more subjects connected by *and, or,* or *nor.* These subjects are used with the same verb.**

> Hell and destruction are before the Lord. (The two parts of the subject are used with the same verb, *are.*)

2.35   **A *compound verb* consists of two or more verbs connected by *and, or, nor,* or *but.* These verbs are used with the same subject.**

> Then I saw and considered it well. (The two parts of the verb are used with the same subject, *I.*)

▶ Note. A sentence may contain both a compound subject and a compound verb.

> Paul and Barnabas went to the people and preached Christ crucified.

2.36   ***Direct objects, indirect objects,* and *objective complements* may be compound.**

> God created the *heaven* and the *earth.* (compound direct object)
> The quarterback threw *Ray* and *Jim* long passes. (compound indirect object)
> Malaria rendered the soldier *weak* and *helpless.* (compound objective complement)

2.37 ***Predicate nominatives*** **and** ***predicate adjectives*** **may be compound.**

Some early men of great faith were *Job, Enoch,* and *Noah.* (compound predicate nominative)

A good quarterback must be *courageous* and *intelligent.* (compound predicate adjective)

[For diagrams of compound sentence parts see 8.9–8.13.]

3 Parts of Speech

Words are generally classified into eight parts of speech: *verb, noun, pronoun, adjective, adverb, preposition, conjunction,* and *interjection.* These terms are applied to words according to their function within a sentence. The principal words in a sentence are the verb, noun, and pronoun. Adjectives and adverbs support the principal words by describing them. Prepositions and conjunctions connect the parts of a sentence in various ways. The interjection is an independent element that serves no grammatical function in a sentence.

Verb

3.1 **A verb is a word that** *shows action,* **links** **another word to the subject,** *helps* **another verb, or merely** *indicates existence.* It is the main word of a sentence or clause.

Dad *painted* the house. (shows action)

The coffee *was* hot. (links *hot* to the subject *coffee*)

Mike *will* cut the lawn. (helps the verb *cut* to make a statement)

The actors *are* on the stage. (merely indicates the existence of *actors*)

3.2 **The action of a verb may be either** *physical* **or** *mental.*

kick, swallow, speak, close, swing, build, eat (physical action)

believe, ponder, consider, imagine, realize, hope (mental action)

3.3 **Sometimes the verb is a single word; other times the verb is made up of two or more words called a** *verb phrase.*

3.4 **A** *verb phrase* **consists of a main verb (3.5) plus one or more helping verbs (3.12).**

Any excuse *will serve* a tyrant. —*Aesop*

13

3.5 **A _main verb_ is the word that contains the central meaning of a verb phrase.** It is always the last word in the phrase. (In the example above, the word _serve_ is the main verb.)

3.6 **A verb must be distinguished from a verbal (4.1).** A verb can make an assertion (a predication); a verbal cannot. (See also 2.13.)

> Drew _ran_. (_Ran_ is a verb: it makes an assertion.)
> Drew _running_ (_Running_ is a verbal: it does not make an assertion.)

3.7 **Verbs may be called _transitive, intransitive, linking_ (copulative), or _helping_ (auxiliary) according to their use in sentences.**

3.8 **_Transitive_ is the term applied to a verb (or verbal) that requires a receiver of its action in order to express a complete thought.** The word _transitive_ means "passing over." Therefore, if the action of the verb (or verbal) passes over to a receiver, that verb (or verbal) is called "transitive."

> The pitcher _threw_ the ball. (The direct object _ball_ receives the action of the verb.)
> Mr. Gray _reseeded_ his lawn. (The direct object _lawn_ receives the action of the verb.)
> _Renting_ a car is easy. (The direct object _car_ receives the action of the verbal.)

▶ Note. In the active voice (10.32), the direct object receives the action; in the passive voice the subject receives the action.

> Phil _hit_ the ball into left field. (The direct object _ball_ receives the action.)
> The ball _was hit_ into left field. (The subject _ball_ receives the action.)

3.9 **_Intransitive_ is the term applied to a verb (or verbal) that does not require a receiver of its action in order to express a complete thought.**

> Their plot _failed._
> The train _stopped_ abruptly.
> The ball _sailed_ over the fence.

3.10 **_Linking_ (or copulative) is the term applied to a verb that links a word in the predicate to the subject.** The word linked to the subject will be a noun, a pronoun, or an adjective (or the equivalent of one of these) that identifies or describes the subject.

> Mr. Brown *is* our coach. (The verb *is* links the noun *coach* to the subject *Mr. Brown.* The word *coach* identifies *Mr. Brown.*)
>
> The general's strategy *was* effective. (The verb *was* links the adjective *effective* to the subject *strategy.* The word *effective* describes *strategy.*)

3.11 **Certain verbs are commonly used as *linking verbs.*** The verb *be,* including all of its forms, is the most common linking verb: *am, is, are, was, were, be, being, been.* (Any verb that ends with *be* or *been* is a form of the verb *be: have been, has been, had been, shall be, will be, might have been,* etc.)

The following are also often used as linking verbs: *taste, feel, smell, sound, look, appear, become, seem, grow, remain, stay.* (There are other verbs that can be used as linking verbs, but since the others have meanings similar to the verbs listed here, you should be able to recognize the others if you know only these.)

▶ Note. The forms of *be* are intransitive (not linking) when the verb means "to exist."

> God *is.* (God "exists.")
>
> There *are* no pears on the tree. (No pears "exist" on the tree.)

3.12 ***Helping* (or auxiliary) is the term applied to a verb that helps the main verb to make a statement.** You will observe in section 10 that helping verbs aid in forming the tense, voice, and mood of other verbs.

> No man *can* serve two masters. (The verb *can* helps the transitive verb *serve* to show action.)
>
> I *will* dwell in the house of the Lord forever. (The verb *will* helps the intransitive verb *dwell* to show action.)
>
> The hope of the righteous *shall* be gladness. (The verb *shall* helps the linking verb *be* to link *gladness* to the subject *hope.*)
>
> There *will* be rewards for faithfulness. (The verb *will* helps the intransitive verb *be* to indicate existence.)

3.13 The following verbs are commonly used as *helping verbs.*

am	were	have	do	shall	may
is	be	has	does	will	might
are	being	had	did	should	must
was	been			would	can
					could

3.14 Although some verbs may normally be transitive, intransitive, linking, or helping, there are a few verbs that can be classified invariably as one or the other. In order to apply one of these terms to a verb, one must determine its function within a particular sentence. Notice in the following examples that the same verb may be used in various ways.

Terri *plays* the piano. (transitive—*piano* is the direct object.)
Terri *plays* well. (intransitive)

He *sounded* the bell. (transitive—*bell* is the direct object.)
The bell *sounded* early. (intransitive)
The bell *sounded* ominous. (linking—the adjective *ominous* is linked to the subject *bell*.)

She *has* a cat. (transitive—*cat* is the direct object.)
She *has* bought a canary. (helping—*has* helps the main verb *bought.*)

They *are* tourists. (linking—the noun *tourists* is linked to the subject *they.*)
They *are* in France. (intransitive—*are* means "to exist.")

Noun

3.15 A *noun* is a word that names a person, place, thing, or idea.

persons—*doctor, sister, Harold, clerk*
places—*Europe, Colorado, garden, store*
things—*rock, pencil, hammer, car*
ideas—*beauty, gladness, courage, determination*

3.16 A *common noun* names a person, place, thing, or idea but does not say which particular one.

man   state   airplane   horse   hope

3.17 A *proper noun* **names a particular person, place, or thing and always begins with a capital letter.**

John Calvin   Nebraska

Percheron   *Southern Cross*

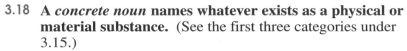

Gram.
3.24

3.18 A *concrete noun* **names whatever exists as a physical or material substance.** (See the first three categories under 3.15.)

house   earth   book   grass   Jeff   Canada

3.19 An *abstract noun* **names a quality, state, activity, or general idea.** (See the fourth category under 3.15.)

strength   honor   mercy   goodness   progress

3.20 A *collective noun* **names a group or a collection.**

herd   team   swarm   flock   orchestra   club

3.21 A *compound noun* **is two or more words used as a single noun.** Some are written as separate words; some are hyphenated; some are solid. (Consult your dictionary.)

Matthew Henry   barbershop

Life of Cromwell   mother-in-law

3.22 *Substantive* **is another term that may be used to refer to any word, phrase, or clause that functions as a noun or as a noun equivalent (3.23).** The term *substantive,* of course, includes nouns and pronouns.

3.23 **The following are examples of** *noun equivalents* **(substantives).**

Jogging is good exercise. (gerund, 4.3)

To die is gain for the Christian. (infinitive, 4.4)

After lunch is a good time to doze. (phrase, 5.6)

That our team is superior is evident. (clause, 6.5)

3.24 An *appositive* **is a substantive (3.22) that follows another substantive to explain or identify it.** The two substantives are equivalent and have the same grammatical relationship with the other elements in the sentence.

Nehemiah, the king's *cupbearer,* rebuilt the walls of Jerusalem. (*Cupbearer* is an appositive that identifies the noun *Nehemiah.*)

a. An appositive *may be compound.*

The home run hitters *Babe Ruth* and *Roger Maris* played for the Yankees.

Gram.
3.25

b. An *appositive phrase* **is an appositive with all its modifiers.**

> Moses, *the uncompromising leader of the Israelites,* defied the powerful king of Egypt.

c. Nonessential appositives and appositive phrases are *set off by commas.* (Appositives that follow proper nouns are usually nonessential.)

> Harry, *our next-door neighbor,* is a kind man.
> Our next-door neighbor *Harry* is a kind man.
> Did you like the story *"The Boys' Ambition"* by Mark Twain?

[For diagram of an appositive see 8.42.]

Pronoun

3.25 **A *pronoun* is a word that takes the place of a noun.**

> Alex Dunbar is our bus driver. *He* knows every rider by name. (The pronoun *He* takes the place of the noun *Alex Dunbar.*)

3.26 **An *antecedent* is the word for which a pronoun stands.**

> Alex Dunbar is our bus driver. He knows every rider by name. (*Alex Dunbar* is the antecedent of the pronoun *He.*)

▶ Note. The antecedent is not always stated within the same sentence.

> Was *she* at *her* house? (The antecedent of *she* and *her* is not stated.)

3.27 **There are various kinds of pronouns: *personal, reflexive, intensive, interrogative, demonstrative, indefinite, relative.***

3.28 ***Personal pronouns* show by their form whether reference is made to the *speaker* (first person), to the *person spoken to* (second person), or to the *person spoken about* (third person).**

Personal Pronouns

	Singular	Plural
First Person:	*I, me, my, mine*	*we, us, our, ours*
Second Person:	*you* (thou, thee), *your* (thy), *yours* (thine)	*you* (ye), *your, yours*
Third Person:	*he, him, his, she, her, hers, it, its*	*they, them, their, theirs*

18

▶ Note. The forms in parentheses are archaic forms often used in Biblical or poetic language and in prayers.

Gram.
3.36

3.29 *Compound personal pronouns* **are those personal pronouns to which the suffix** *-self* **(or the plural** *-selves*) **is added.** (*myself, yourself, thyself, himself, herself, itself, ourselves, yourselves, themselves*)

▶ Note. Do not use the incorrect forms *hisself* or *theirselves*.

3.30 **Compound personal pronouns have two uses:** *reflexive* **and** *intensive.* The forms are the same for both uses.

3.31 *Reflexive* **is the term applied to a compound personal pronoun that "reflects" the action of the verb back to the subject.**

They can defend *themselves.*
He hit *himself* on the thumb with a hammer.

3.32 *Intensive* **is the term applied to a compound personal pronoun that is used for emphasis.**

They *themselves* can defend the fort.
Mr. Smith *himself* did the work.
or Mr. Smith did the work *himself.*

3.33 **Compound personal pronouns should be limited to the reflexive and intensive uses explained in 3.31 and 3.32.** They should not be used in the place of personal pronouns.

Bethany and *myself* will be there to help. (incorrect)
Bethany and *I* will be there to help. (correct)
Should I return the forms to Lindsay or to *yourself?* (incorrect)
Should I return the forms to Lindsay or to *you?* (correct)

3.34 *Interrogative pronouns* **are used to ask a question.** (*who, whom, whose, which, what*)

3.35 *Demonstrative pronouns* **point out the person or thing referred to.** (*this, that, these, those*)

3.36 *Indefinite pronouns* **do not definitely point out persons or things and do not usually have antecedents.** (*each, either, neither, one, everyone, everybody, no one, nobody, anyone, anybody, someone, somebody, both, few, several, many, some, any, none, all, most*)

3.37 *Relative pronouns* are used to introduce dependent clauses. (*who, whom, whose, which, that*)

3.38 Many of the words called pronouns in 3.28–3.37 may also function as adjectives. Some of them function only as adjectives. (See 3.48 and 11.9.)

Adjective

3.39 An *adjective* is a word that modifies a noun or a pronoun. It answers the questions *what kind, which one, how many, how much,* or *whose.* (A modifier makes the meaning of another word more specific by describing or limiting that word.)

  cheerful giver (what kind) *those* apples (which ones)

  six points (how many) *abundant* grace (how much)

  his puppy (whose) *Hannah's* Bible (whose)

3.40 A *proper adjective* is either a word formed from a proper noun (3.17) or a proper noun used as an adjective. A proper adjective begins with a capital letter.

Proper nouns	Proper adjectives
Hawaii	*Hawaiian* pineapple (formed from proper noun)
Easter	*Easter* parade (proper noun used as adjective)

3.41 Although most adjectives come before the words they modify as in the examples above, some adjectives come *after* the words they modify.

  Peter was *impetuous.* (predicate adjective)

  Doug, *skilled* and *cautious,* is an excellent driver. (appositive adjectives)

  They painted the barn *red.* (objective complement)

3.42 Several adjectives may modify the same word.

  The *long, slow* drive will be *tiring.*

3.43 The words *a, an,* and *the* are the most frequently used adjectives. They are called *articles.* (Do not confuse *an* with *and. And* is a conjunction; *an* is an adjective.)

3.44 The *indefinite* articles *a* and *an* refer to someone or something as merely one among others of the same class. Use *a* before words that begin with a *consonant sound: a* clock, *a* feud, *a* unicycle. Use *an* before words that begin with a *vowel sound: an* elephant, *an* ox, *an* hour.

Gram.
3.49

> ▶ Note. Among the examples above, *a* is used before a vowel (a *u*nicycle) because the word *unicycle* begins with a consonant *sound* (yoo); and *an* is used before a consonant (an *h*our) because the word *hour* begins with a vowel *sound.* Remember that it is the beginning *sound* of the noun that determines which article to use.

3.45 The *definite* article *the* refers specifically to someone or something as distinguished from others of the same class.

The tree in my yard is over two hundred years old.

3.46 A *participle* is a verb form used as an adjective. (See 4.2.)

The *cheering* crowds encouraged our team.

3.47 An *infinitive* is a verb form that may be used as an adjective. (See 4.4.)

The team *to beat* is the Eagles.

3.48 The following kinds of words which may normally be called nouns or pronouns can also function as adjectives.

> nouns—*Brad's* cycle, *Lydia's* purse, *Eskimo* family, *July* vacation
> possessive pronouns—*my, your, his, her, its, our, their*
> demonstrative pronouns—*this, that, these, those*
> interrogative pronouns—*which, what, whose*
> indefinite pronouns—*each, either, neither, one, some, any, all, most, both, few, several, many*
> relative pronouns—*which, whose*

3.49 The part of speech of any word is determined by its function within a sentence. Notice how the same word may be used as a noun or a pronoun in one sentence and as an adjective in another.

> *Madeline* cleaned her room. (noun)
> *Madeline's* room is neat. (adjective)

We camped near the *prairie.* (noun)
Prairie soil is especially dark and fertile. (adjective)

Your room is larger than *his.* (possessive pronoun)
His room is smaller than yours. (adjective)

That is an interesting painting. (demonstrative pronoun)
That painting is interesting. (adjective)

What happened to the vase? (interrogative pronoun)
What evidence have you found? (adjective)

Some of the cups are missing. (indefinite pronoun)
Some people eat raw honey. (adjective)

The cat *which* you see was given to us. (relative pronoun)
She knew *which* answer to give. (adjective)

Adverb

3.50 **An *adverb* is a word that modifies a verb, an adjective, or another adverb.** It answers the questions *where, when, how, how often, to what extent.* (A modifier makes the meaning of another word more specific.)

look *there* (where)   work *now* (when)

spoke *softly* (how)   *seldom* sings (how often)

partially completed (to what extent)

3.51 **The word *not* or its contraction *n't* is a frequently used adverb.**

3.52 **Adverbs modify *verbs* most of the time.** An adverb that modifies a verb may be *before or after* the verb it modifies; it may be *in the middle of a verb phrase* that it modifies; or it may be *at the beginning of the sentence,* nowhere near the verb it modifies.

Granddad *often* takes a brisk walk after meals.

The water dripped *slowly* from the faucet.

Ray will *not* arrive until Friday.

Anxiously, the father of the injured child paced the floor.

To locate adverbs, first find the verb. Then ask the questions that adverbs answer.

> Anxiously, the father of the injured child paced the floor. (*Paced* is the verb. Paced *how? Anxiously. Anxiously* is the adverb that answers the question *how.* Father paced *anxiously.*)

Many adverbs are formed by adding -ly to adjectives: cautious*ly,* loud*ly,* hurried*ly,* careful*ly.* However, not all words that end in -*ly* are adverbs. Some are adjectives: *manly, scraggly, costly, friendly.* Some frequently used adverbs do not end in -*ly;* therefore, when identifying adverbs, do not depend on the -*ly* ending. Use the procedure mentioned above to locate adverbs.

3.53 **Adverbs also modify *adjectives*.** When adverbs modify adjectives, they are located *immediately* before those adjectives and usually tell *how* or *to what extent.*

> Grandmother makes *especially* good pickles. (*Good* is an adjective because it modifies the noun *pickles. Especially* is an adverb because it modifies the adjective *good,* telling *to what extent* the pickles are good.)

3.54 **Adverbs occasionally modify *other adverbs*.** When adverbs modify other adverbs, they are located *immediately before* those adverbs and usually tell *how.*

> Nick approached the beehive *somewhat* cautiously. (*Cautiously* is an adverb because it modifies the verb *approached. Somewhat* is an adverb because it modifies the adverb *cautiously,* telling *how* cautiously Nick approached.)

3.55 **Infinitives may be used as adverbs. (See 4.4.)**

> He does not practice enough *to be* a really great player.
>
> She ran outside *to greet* her father.

3.56 **Some nouns may be used as adverbs.**

> She is arriving *Saturday.*   I am going *home.*

[For diagrams of adjectives and adverbs see 8.2 and 8.11.]

Preposition

**Gram.
3.57**

3.57 **A *preposition* is a word that shows how a noun or a
pronoun is related to some other word in the sentence.**

> Lynn sat *on* the barrel.
> Lynn lay *beside* the barrel.
> Lynn climbed *into* the barrel.
> Lynn crawled *through* the barrel.
> Lynn jumped *over* the barrel.

The prepositions *on, beside, into, through,* and *over* show
how the word *Lynn* is related to the noun *barrel.*

Frequently Used Prepositions					
aboard	among	between	from	over	underneath
about	around	beyond	in	past	until
above	at	but	into	since	unto
across	before	by	like	through	up
after	behind	down	near	throughout	upon
against	below	during	of	to	with
along	beneath	except	off	toward	within
amid	beside	for	on	under	without

3.58 **Some prepositions are *compound.*** They consist of more
than one word, but they function the same as a single-word
preposition.

Compound Prepositions			
according to	by way of	in spite of	out of
as for	except for	instead of	regardless of
because of	in front of	on account of	with regard to

3.59 **A *prepositional phrase* consists of a preposition, its noun
or pronoun object, and any modifiers of the object.**

prep.   obj.

The moonlight shone ***through*** the open *window.*

3.60 **The *object of a preposition* is the noun or pronoun that
completes a prepositional phrase.** A preposition must
always have an object.

prep.   obj.

He maketh me to lie down ***in*** green *pastures.*

3.61 A preposition may have a *compound object*.

prep.　obj.　　obj.

What fellowship is there **between** *light* and *darkness?*

**3.62 Many of the words in the preposition list under 3.57
can also be used as adverbs.** It is easy to tell the difference. Prepositions have objects; adverbs do not.

> We all went *aboard.* (adverb—no object)
> We all went *aboard* the C5A transport. (preposition—
> *transport* is the object.)

[For diagrams of prepositional phrases see 8.3.]

Conjunction

**3.63 A *conjunction* is a word (or word group) that joins
words, phrases, or clauses.**

**3.64 There are two main classes of conjunctions: *coordinat-
ing* and *subordinating*.**

**3.65 *Coordinating conjunctions* join words, phrases, or
clauses of *equal* grammatical rank.** These are common
coordinating conjunctions: *and, but, or, nor, for, yet.*

> They also serve who only *stand* **and** *wait.* —*Milton*
> (conjunction joining words)
> *In quietness* **and** *in confidence* shall be your strength.
> (conjunction joining prepositional phrases)
> *Knowledge puffeth up,* **but** *charity edifieth.* (conjunc-
> tion joining independent clauses)

These coordinating conjunctions are used in pairs:
either—or, neither—nor, both—and, not only—but also.
These conjunctions are called *correlative conjunctions*.

> The explorers are **either** *studying maps* **or** *watching
> for landmarks.*

**3.66 *Subordinating conjunctions* join clauses of *unequal*
grammatical rank; that is, they join dependent clauses
to independent clauses.** These are common subordinating
conjunctions: *after, although, as, as if, as much as, as long
as, as soon as, because, before, if, in order that, lest, since,
so that, than, that, though, unless, until, when, whenever,
where, wherever, whether, while.*

> ***Though** He slay me,* yet will I trust in Him.

25

Interjection and Other Independent Elements

Gram.
3.67

The interjection is usually classified as the eighth part of speech. Although the interjection may be classified as one of the parts of speech, it should be understood that the interjection and a number of other expressions are actually independent sentence elements.

3.67 **An *independent element* is a word or group of words that has little or no grammatical function in the sentence in which it appears.**

3.68 **An *interjection* is an exclamatory word that is not grammatically related to the other words in a sentence.**
Ouch! Get off my injured foot!
Oh, we are sorry that you cannot come.
Aha! We have found you.

► Note. An exclamation point is often used after an interjection, but a comma may be used after a mild interjection. If you punctuate an interjection with an exclamation point, capitalize the next word.

Words commonly used as other parts of speech may be used as interjections.
Behold! Listen! Excellent! Nonsense! My! Certainly!

3.69 **A noun of *direct address* is an independent element that names the person or persons to whom a sentence is directed.** It is set off by commas.
Have you filed your income tax return, *Jason?*

3.70 **A *parenthetical expression* is a comment or an explanation inserted into an already grammatically complete sentence.** Such expressions are usually set off by commas, dashes, or parentheses. The following are some examples:
at any rate, I think, I suppose, in fact, in my opinion, on the contrary, on the other hand, to tell the truth.
He went there, *I am sure,* to be helpful.

► Note. Parenthetical expressions should be disregarded when analyzing the grammatical structure of a sentence.

3.71 **A *nominative absolute* is an independent element that consists of a substantive (3.22) followed by and modified by a participle or a participial phrase (5.7).** The construction is called *absolute* because it serves no grammatical function in the sentence. The term *nominative* is used because the substantive modified by the participle is normally in the nominative case.

> *Everything considered,* our vacation was superb. (*Everything* is the substantive; *considered* is the participle that modifies it. Notice that the substantive *everything* serves no function in the sentence of which it is a part.)

> He just stood there, *his face clearly revealing his disappointment.* (*Face* is the substantive; *revealing* is the participle that modifies it. The substantive *face* serves no function in the sentence.)

Gram 4.2

3.72 **An *expletive* is a word that does not function grammatically in a sentence but plays an important rhetorical role.** Expletives help to get a sentence smoothly underway. The words *there* and *it* are commonly used for this purpose.

> *There* is no other answer to the problem. (This sentence means "No other answer to the problem exists." The word *there* is an expletive.)

> *It* is easy to see why he was misunderstood. (This sentence without the expletive reads "Why he was misunderstood is easy to see.")

▶ Note. For other uses of *there* and *it,* see note under 2.19.

[For diagrams of independent elements see 8.43–8.47.]

4 Verbals

4.1 **A *verbal* is a verb form that is not used as a verb, but rather as a noun, adjective, or adverb.** A verbal retains many of the characteristics of a verb; for example, it can have complements and modifiers. It differs from a verb in that it cannot make an assertion (3.6). The three kinds of verbals are the *participle,* the *gerund,* and the *infinitive.*

4.2 **A *participle* is a verb form used as an *adjective.*** It modifies a noun or a pronoun. Present participles end in *-ing.* Past participles often end in *-d, -ed, -t,* or *-en.*

> *Working* rapidly, we completed the task in record time. (*Completed* is the verb. Notice that *completed* has a subject, *we,* and the subject is in the nominative case. *Working* is the participle; it is used as an adjective to modify the pronoun *we.*)

The poor horse, *ridden* to exhaustion, could barely stand. (*Could stand* is the verb; *ridden* is the participle.)

They were trapped in an *abandoned* mine. (*Were trapped* is the verb; *abandoned* is the participle.)

4.3 **A *gerund* is a verb form used as a *noun*.** Like nouns, gerunds can be used as subjects, direct objects, predicate nominatives, objects of prepositions, and appositives. The gerund ends in *-ing*.

Jogging is a popular exercise. (*Is* is the verb. *Jogging* is a gerund, used as the subject.)

Our pastor enjoys *preaching*. (*Enjoys* is the verb. *Preaching* is a gerund, used as the direct object.)

Faith comes by *hearing* the Word of God. (*Comes* is the verb. *Hearing* is a gerund, used as the object of a preposition.)

Her favorite chore was *feeding* the chickens. (*Was* is the verb; *feeding* is a gerund, used as the predicate nominative.)

His problem, *idolizing* rock stars, was resolved when he trusted Christ. (*Was resolved* is the verb; *idolizing* is a gerund, used as an appositive.)

4.4 **An *infinitive* is a verb form used as a *noun, adjective,* or *adverb*.** Like nouns, infinitives can be used as subjects, direct objects, predicate nominatives, objects of prepositions, and appositives. The infinitive is usually, but not always, preceded by the word *to*.

To learn self-discipline is *to conquer* one's self. (*To learn* is used as the subject; *to conquer* is used as a predicate nominative.)

Kelsey likes *to listen* to opera. (*To listen* is used as the direct object.)

He gave me advice about how *to begin*. (*To begin* is the object of the preposition *about*.)

God's command, *to dress* modestly, must not be ignored. (*To dress* is an appositive.)

They have a truckload of tomatoes *to sell*. (*To sell* is used as an adjective to modify the noun *tomatoes*.)

He studied *to show* himself approved unto God. (*To show* is used as an adverb to modify the verb *studied*.)

5 The Phrase

5.1 A *phrase* is a group of related words that does not contain a subject and a verb. The phrase is used as a single part of speech.

adjective

prep. adj. n.

Cindy's house is the one │ with two gables. │ (*With two gables* is the phrase. The three words in the phrase are used together to modify the pronoun *one;* therefore, the group of words is used as a single part of speech: an adjective.)

5.2 According to their *function* within a sentence, phrases are classified as *noun, adjective,* or *adverb.* According to *structure,* phrases may be classified into four main groups: *prepositional, participial, gerund,* and *infinitive.*

Prepositional Phrase

5.3 A *prepositional phrase* consists of a preposition (3.57), its noun or pronoun object, and any modifiers of the object.

We gave them a crate *of fresh fruit.*

The students *in my science class* are going to take a field trip.

The object of a preposition may be *compound.*

The book of *poems* and *stories* was exceptional.

5.4 **A prepositional phrase that modifies a verb, an adjective, or an adverb is functioning as an *adverb.*** An adverb phrase often answers the questions *where, when, how, why,* or *to what extent.*

In 1862, the Homestead Act was passed. (The adverb phrase modifies the verb *was passed,* telling *when.*)

My uncle is becoming bald *on top.* (The adverb phrase modifies the adjective *bald,* telling *where.*)

Our guests arrived early *in the morning.* (The adverb phrase modifies the adverb *early,* telling *when.*)

5.5 **A prepositional phrase that modifies a noun or a pronoun is functioning as an *adjective.*** An adjective phrase answers the questions *what kind, which one, how many, how much,* or *whose.*

A mower *with a grass catcher* is a real time saver. (The adjective phrase modifies the noun *mower,* telling *what kind.*)

29

5.6 **A prepositional phrase may occasionally function as a** *noun.*

Right *after dinner* will be a good time. (The noun phrase *after dinner* functions as the subject of *will be*.)

Participial Phrase

5.7 A *participial phrase* **consists of a participle (4.2) together with any complements and modifiers. The participial phrase functions as an** *adjective.*

Observe the following things in the examples below:
- Participles can have complements just as a verb can.
- Participles can be modified by single adverbs or prepositional phrases.
- The entire participial phrase is used as an adjective.

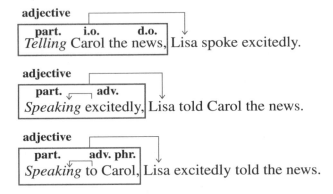

Gerund Phrase

5.8 A *gerund phrase* **consists of a gerund (4.3) together with any complements and modifiers. The gerund phrase functions as a** *noun.*

Observe the following things in the examples below:
- Gerunds can have complements just as a verb can.
- Gerunds can be modified by single adverbs or prepositional phrases.
- The entire gerund phrase is used as a noun (*s., d.o., p.n., o.p.,* or *ap.*).

subject

> **ger.**   **d.o.**   **prep. phrase**
> *Writing* your assignments in a notebook   is a good
> practice.

direct object

> We all enjoy | **ger.**   **d.o.**
> *eating* homemade ice cream.

predicate nominative

> **ger.**   **d.o.**   **prep. phrase**
> The problem is | *applying* the mind to the task.

object of preposition

> **ger.**   **i.o.**   **d.o.**
> We can protect our eyes by | *giving* them proper rest.

appositive

> **ger.**   **adv.**   **prep. phrase**
> A new habit, | *studying* quietly without any music,
> improved his grades.

Infinitive Phrase

5.9 An *infinitive phrase* consists of an infinitive (4.4) together with any complements and modifiers. The infinitive phrase may be used as a *noun,* an *adjective,* or an *adverb.*

5.10 An infinitive phrase that serves as a subject, a direct object, a predicate nominative, an object of a preposition, or an appositive is functioning as a *noun.*

Observe the following things in the examples below:
- Infinitives sometimes have subjects, and these subjects are in the *objective* case (second example).
- The word *to* is sometimes omitted before the infinitive (fourth example).
- The entire infinitive phrase is used as a noun (*s., d.o., p.n., o.p.,* or *ap.*).

31

subject

inf.	i.o.	d.o.

To tell Mrs. Flap your plans │ is to tell the world.

direct object

s.   in͝f. ┌── adv.   prep. phrase

The people wanted │ him *to speak* frankly about the issue.

predicate nominative

in͝f.   d.o.   adv.

His sound advice was │ *to practice* the fundamentals daily.

object of preposition

in͝f.   adv.

She does nothing but │ *talk* incessantly.

appositive

inf.   p.a.

Their goal, │ *to become* the very best, │ is admirable.

5.11 **An infinitive phrase that modifies a noun or pronoun is functioning as an *adjective*.**

A truck *to deliver the produce* must be obtained. (The adjective phrase modifies the noun *truck*.)

Billy was the only one *to complete the assignment*. (The adjective phrase modifies the pronoun *one*.)

5.12 **An infinitive phrase that modifies a verb, an adjective, or an adverb is functioning as an *adverb*.** An adverb phrase often answers the questions *where, when, how, why,* or *to what extent*.

We exercise *to maintain good health*. (The adverb phrase modifies the verb *exercise*.)

Hegel's philosophy is difficult *to state simply*. (The adverb phrase modifies the adjective *difficult*.)

He does not practice enough *to be a really great player*. (The adverb phrase modifies the adverb *enough*.)

[For diagrams of verbal phrases see 8.15–8.23.]

Kinds of Phrases

5.13 Refer to the following chart to help you distinguish the various kinds of phrases. Phrases may be classified into six kinds: *prepositional, participial, gerund, infinitive, appositive,* and *nominative absolute.* These phrases (except for the nominative absolute) function as a *noun,* an *adjective,* or an *adverb.*

Gram 6.5

KIND	FUNCTION	FORM
prepositional	*noun, adjective,* or *adverb*	preposition + noun or pronoun object
participial	*adjective*	verb form ending in *-ing, -d, -ed, -t,* or *-en.*
gerund	*noun* (s., d.o., p.n., o.p., ap.)	verb form ending in *-ing*
infinitive	*noun* (s., d.o., p.n., o.p., ap.), *adjective,* or *adverb*	*to* + a verb form
appositive	*noun*	ordinary noun, gerund, or infinitive
nominative absolute	no grammatical function	noun or pronoun modified by a participle or participial phrase

6 The Clause

6.1 A *clause* is a group of words that contains both a subject and a verb. It is used as part of a sentence.

6.2 An *independent clause* expresses a complete thought and can stand alone as a sentence.
He read the book that a friend had recommended.

6.3 A *dependent* (subordinate) *clause* does not express a complete thought and cannot stand alone as a sentence.
Evan has not decided *whether he will accept the position.*

6.4 Dependent (subordinate) clauses are classified as *noun, adjective,* or *adverb.*

Noun Clause

6.5 A dependent clause that functions as a noun within a sentence is called a *noun clause.* Some common noun functions are subject, direct object, predicate nominative, object of a preposition, and appositive.

Gram. 6.6

6.6 **Noun clauses are introduced by signal words such as the following:** *that, whether, if, who, whom, whose, which, what, when, where, why, how, whoever, whomever, whichever,* **and** *whatever.*

Observe the following things in the examples below:
- Every clause has a subject and a verb and may have complements and modifiers.
- The entire noun clause is used as a noun (*s., d.o., p.n., o.p.,* or *ap.*).
- The signal words *that, whether,* and *if* are merely introductory connectives; they serve no other function. (See examples 1 and 5 below.)
- The other signal words in the list above are introductory connectives, but they also serve a grammatical function within the dependent clause. (See examples 2, 3, and 4 below.)

subject

s.	v.	adv. phrase

Whether we travel by train or plane | has not been decided.

direct object

s.	v.	p.a.

We did | *whatever* was necessary.

predicate nominative

d.o.	s.	v.	adv.

Painting portraits is | *what* she enjoys most.

object of preposition

adv.	s.	v.	adv.

He said nothing about | *where* he would go next.

appositive

s.	v.

The idea | *that* he could succeed | carried him through.

6.7 **Sometimes the introductory word *that* is omitted when the noun clause is used as a direct object.**

They thought (that) *Thursday was a holiday.*

Adjective Clause

6.8 **A dependent clause that modifies a noun or a pronoun is called an *adjective clause*.**

This is the day *which the Lord hath made.*

6.9 **Adjective clauses are introduced by words called *relatives*.** *Who, whom, which, that* are relative pronouns. *Whose* (and occasionally *which*) are relative adjectives. *When* and *where* are relative adverbs.

6.10 **A relative (1) serves a grammatical function within its own dependent clause; (2) joins the dependent clause that it introduces to another clause; and (3) refers to an antecedent in another clause.** (The antecedent is the noun or pronoun being modified by the adjective clause.)

God, ***Who*** *created the universe,* also controls it. (***Who*** is the subject of *created.*)

That is a battle *about **which** much has been written.* (***Which*** is the object of the preposition *about.*)

A Chopin nocturne was the first piece ***that*** *he played.* (***That*** is the direct object of *played.*)

A hemophiliac is one | ***whose*** *blood does not clot.* (***Whose*** is an adjective, modifying the noun *blood.*)

We just passed a place | ***where*** *we could have eaten breakfast.* (***Where*** is an adverb, modifying the verb *could have eaten.*)

▶ Note. Sometimes the relative pronoun is omitted, but this understood pronoun still serves its usual functions.

The flight *I needed* was canceled. (The understood pronoun *that* functions as the direct object of the verb *needed.*)

35

Adverb Clause

6.11 **A dependent clause that modifies a verb, an adjective, or an adverb is called an *adverb clause.*** Adverb clauses usually answer the questions *where, when, how, why, to what extent,* or *under what condition.*

Gram. 6.11

> We will leave *when the storm subsides.* (modifies the verb *will leave*)
>
> He is certain *that his request will be granted.* (modifies the adjective *certain*)
>
> Their boat rides smoother *than ours does.* (modifies the adverb *smoother*)

6.12 **Adverb clauses are introduced by *subordinating conjunctions: after, although, as, as if, as much as, as long as, as soon as, because, before, if, in order that, lest, since, so that, than, that, though, unless, until, when, whenever, where, wherever, whether, while.***

6.13 **Essential parts of an adverb clause may properly be omitted if no misunderstanding will occur. Such a clause is called an *elliptical clause.***
> Scott can swim better *than I* (can swim).

6.14 **Introductory adverb clauses are set off by commas. Adverb clauses at the end of a sentence do not require commas unless they are nonessential. (See 42.10b.)**
> *If any man love the world,* the love of the Father is not in him.
>
> Never answer a letter *while you are angry.*

Distinguishing Dependent Clauses

6.15 All dependent clauses have introductory words (see 6.6, 6.9, and 6.12). Sometimes these words are understood but not stated. These introductory words may help you locate dependent clauses, but they usually do not help you determine whether the clause is noun, adjective, or adverb. To decide this, you must figure out how the clause functions in the sentence. These functions are stated in 6.5, 6.8, and 6.11. The following suggestions (6.16 and 6.17) will enable you to easily distinguish some clauses that often give students difficulty.

6.16 Adjective clauses are often introduced by words that can also introduce noun clauses or adverb clauses (*who, whom, whose, which, when, where*). A clause is an adjective clause if its introductory word has an antecedent in the other clause. Words that introduce noun clauses or adverb clauses do not have antecedents.

> Select a time *when we can meet.* (*When* introduces an adjective clause that modifies the noun *time.* *When* has the antecedent *time* in the main clause.)
>
> I do not know *when we can meet.* (*When* introduces a noun clause that is used as a direct object. *When* has no antecedent.)
>
> We can meet *when you have time.* (*When* introduces an adverb clause that modifies the verb *can meet.* *When* has no antecedent.)

Gram. 7.2

6.17 An *adjective clause* can be confused with a *noun clause used as an appositive* whenever the clauses are introduced with *that.* One can easily determine the difference by substituting the word *which* for *that.* If *which* can be sensibly substituted, the clause is an adjective clause.

> The suggestion *that we leave early* was well received. (noun clause—*which* cannot be sensibly substituted for *that.*)
>
> The suggestion *that we contributed* was well received. (adjective clause—*which* can be sensibly substituted for *that.*)

[For diagrams of clauses see 8.24–8.36.]

7 Kinds of Sentences

7.1 According to their structure, sentences may be classified as *simple, compound, complex,* or *compound-complex.*

Simple Sentences

7.2 A *simple sentence* contains one independent clause (6.2) and no dependent (subordinate) clauses (6.3). Both subject and verb may be compound (2.34–2.35).

> <u>Malice</u> <u>drinks</u> one half of its own poison. —*Seneca*
> (This is a *simple* sentence with a simple subject and a simple verb—S   V.)

Good <u>words</u> <u>are</u> worth much and <u>cost</u> little. —*Herbert*
(This is a *simple* sentence with a compound verb—
S   V and V.)

<u>Ignorance</u> and <u>pride</u> <u>keep</u> constant company. (This is
a *simple* sentence with a compound subject—
S and S   V.)

The <u>people</u> and the religious <u>leaders</u> <u>cast</u> Stephen out
of the city and <u>stoned</u> him. (This is a *simple* sentence with a compound subject and a compound
verb—S and S   V and V.)

Compound Sentence

7.3 **A *compound sentence* contains two or more independent clauses (6.2) but no dependent (subordinate) clauses
(6.3).** Compound sentences may be joined by (1) a comma
and coordinating conjunction or (2) a semicolon. (*And,
but, or* are the most commonly used coordinating conjunctions.)

<u>God</u> <u>heals</u> ⎡, and⎤ the <u>doctor</u> <u>takes</u> the fee. —*Franklin*
(SV ⎡, and⎤ SV)

<u>Genius</u> <u>begins</u> great works ⎡;⎤ <u>labor</u> alone <u>finishes</u>
them. —*Joubert* (SV ⎡;⎤ SV)

▶ Note. If a sentence is compound, there will be a subject
and a verb to the left of the comma and coordinating
conjunction (or semicolon) and a subject and a verb to
the right of the comma and coordinating conjunction (or
semicolon).

Complex Sentence

7.4 **A *complex sentence* contains one independent clause
(6.2) and one or more dependent (subordinate) clauses
(6.3).**

⎡If <u>sinners</u> <u>entice</u> thee,⎤ <u>consent</u> <u>thou</u> not.
(one independent clause and one dependent clause
= complex sentence)

⎡If <u>you</u> <u>wish</u> to be held in esteem,⎤ <u>you</u> <u>must associate</u>
only with those ⎡<u>who</u> <u>are</u> estimable.⎤ —*Bruyere*
(one independent clause and two dependent clauses
= complex sentence)

▶ Note. Remember that dependent clauses always have introductory words (sometimes understood) that join them to an independent clause (*who, whom, whose, which, that, what, after, although, as, as if, because, since, when, whenever, where, wherever, whether, while,* etc.)

Gram. 7.6

7.5 **In some complex sentences containing a noun clause, the independent clause is not obvious because the noun clause is a part of the independent clause.**

[Who bravely dares] must sometimes risk a fall.

(*Who bravely dares* is the dependent clause. *Who bravely dares must sometimes risk a fall* is the independent clause. *Who bravely dares* is the subject of the verb *must risk.*)

Compound-Complex Sentence

7.6 **A *compound-complex sentence* contains two or more independent clauses (6.2) and one or more dependent (subordinate) clauses (6.3).**

Many [that are first] shall be last [, and] the last shall be first.

(two independent clauses and one dependent clause = compound-complex sentence)

He [who receives a benefit] should never forget it [;] he [who bestows] should never remember it.

—Charron

(two independent clauses and two dependent clauses = compound-complex sentence)

We judge ourselves by [what we feel capable of doing][;] others judge us by [what we have done.]

—Longfellow

(two independent clauses and two dependent clauses = compound-complex sentence)

▶ Note. It is two or more *independent clauses* that make any sentence *compound.* It is one or more *dependent clauses* that make any sentence *complex.* When you have *both* of the above, you have a compound-complex sentence.

[For diagrams of kinds of sentences see 8.37–8.41.]

8 Diagraming

**Gram.
8.1**

Drawing a diagram can be a great help in recognizing the arrangement and the relationships of words in a sentence.

Simple Sentence

8.1 **Subject and Predicate.** (Draw a horizontal line and divide it with a vertical line. The complete subject [2.5] goes to the left of the vertical line; the complete predicate [2.7] goes to the right of the vertical line.)

Dogs bark.   *Stop.*

| Dogs | bark | | x | Stop |

► Note. The *x*'s used in the diagrams throughout this section indicate implied words or an ellipsis. The *x* here stands for the word *you,* which is the understood subject in an imperative sentence.

8.2 **Single-word modifiers (adjective and adverb).** (Place on slanted lines attached to the line on which the modified word is located.)

The diver ascended *gradually.*

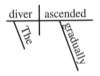

An unusually heavy rainfall swept *in very suddenly.*

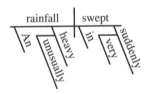

40

8.3 **Prepositional phrase modifiers.** 5.3 (The slanted line, on which the preposition is placed, drops slightly below the horizontal line, on which the object of the preposition is placed.)

a. **Prepositional phrase used as an adjective.**
The girl *with blond hair* was elected.

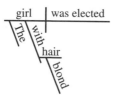

b. **Prepositional phrase used as an adverb, modifying the verb.**
In 1862, the Homestead Act was passed.

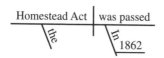

c. **Prepositional phrase used as an adverb, modifying an adverb.**
Our guests arrived early *in the morning.*

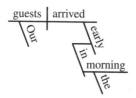

Complements of the Verb

8.4 **Direct object.** 2.25 (Separate the direct object from the verb with a vertical line that stops at the base line.)
Samson defeated the *Philistines.*

Gram. 8.5

8.5 **Indirect object.** 2.26 (Draw the lines the same as for a prepositional phrase, 8.3.)

Marty handed *Glen* the baton.

```
Marty | handed | baton
            \ Glen      \the
```

8.6 **Objective complement.** 2.27 (Draw a line slanting toward the direct object and verb.)

We elected Scott *treasurer.*

```
We | elected | Scott \ treasurer
```

Subject Complements

8.7 **Predicate nominative.** 2.29 (Draw a slanted line pointing toward the subject.)

Ray is the *soloist.*

```
Ray | is \ soloist
            \the
```

8.8 **Predicate adjective.** 2.30 (Draw a slanted line pointing toward the subject.)

The oranges are *ripe.*

```
oranges | are \ ripe
  \The
```

Compound Sentence Parts

Following are diagrams of only some of the sentence parts that may be compound, but from these examples you can determine how to diagram all the others.

8.9 **Compound subject.** 2.34

Football, wrestling, and *basketball* demand much stamina.

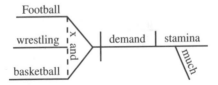

8.10 Compound subject and compound verb. 2.34–2.35

Boxing and *fencing* *must be* carefully *planned* and *supervised.*

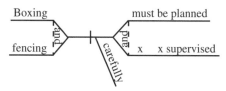

8.11 Compound adverb.

The pastor spoke *simply* but *powerfully.*

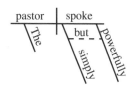

8.12 Compound indirect object. 2.36

Mother read *Gwen* and *Emily* a Bible story.

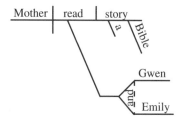

8.13 Compound predicate nominative. 2.37

His accompanists are *Cheryl* and *Terri.*

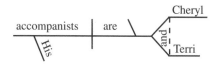

43

Participle

(The lines are drawn as for a prepositional phrase [8.3] except that the slanted line does not extend below the horizontal line. The participle begins on the slanted line and curves around, ending on the horizontal line. The slanted line represents the adjective nature of the participle; the horizontal line represents its verb nature.)

8.14 Participle without complements or modifiers. 4.2

The *grinning* boy unwrapped the large package.

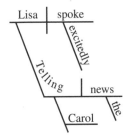

8.15 Participial phrase containing direct and indirect object. 5.7

Telling Carol the news, Lisa spoke excitedly.

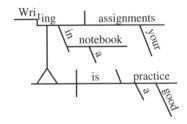

Gerund

(The gerund is placed on a broken line. The upper part represents the noun nature of the gerund; the lower part represents its verb nature. When the gerund is used as a part of the sentence that is diagramed on the base line, put it and all of its parts upon a support.)

8.16 Gerund phrase as subject. 5.8

Writing your assignments in a notebook is a good practice.

8.17 **Gerund phrase as direct object.** 5.8

We enjoy *eating homemade ice cream.*

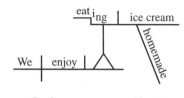

8.18 **Gerund phrase as predicate nominative.** 5.8

The problem is *applying the mind to the task.*

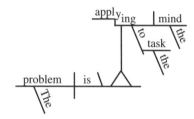

8.19 **Gerund phrase as object of preposition.** 5.8

We can protect our eyes by *giving them proper rest.*

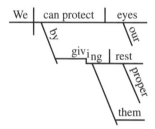

8.20 **Gerund phrase as appositive of the subject.** 5.8

A new habit, *studying quietly without any music,*
improved his grades.

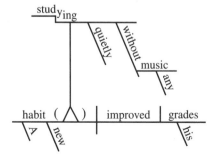

Infinitive

(Draw the lines exactly as you do for a prepositional phrase [8.3]. Put the *to* on the slanted line and the infinitive on the horizontal. When the infinitive functions as a noun, diagram the infinitive and all of its parts upon a support.)

8.21 **Infinitive phrase as noun.** 5.10

a. Subject

To tell Mrs. Flap your plans is to tell the world.

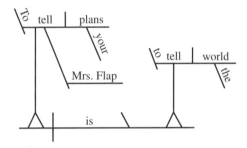

b. Direct object

The people wanted *him to speak frankly about the issue.*

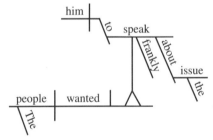

c. Predicate nominative

His sound advice was *to practice the fundamentals daily.*

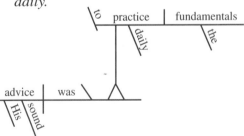

d. Object of preposition

She does nothing but *talk incessantly.*

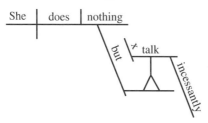

e. Appositive

Their goal, *to become the very best,* is admirable.

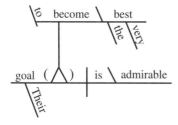

8.22 Infinitive phrase as adjective. 5.11

A truck *to deliver the produce* must be obtained.

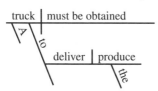

8.23 Infinitive phrase as adverb. 5.12

The fruit is ripe enough *to eat.*

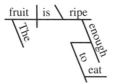

Noun Clause

Gram.
8.24

(The introductory words *that, whether,* and *if* are diagramed on a short horizontal line above the noun clause and connected to the clause with a dotted line. Other introductory words are diagramed within the clause, according to their function.)

8.24 Noun clause as subject. 6.6

Whether we travel by train or plane has not been decided.

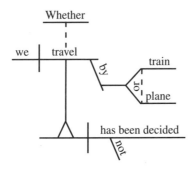

8.25 Noun clause as direct object. 6.6

They thought *Thursday was a holiday.*

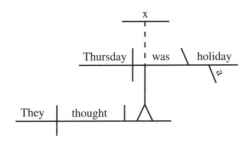

8.26 Noun clause as predicate nominative. 6.6

Painting portraits is *what she enjoys most.*

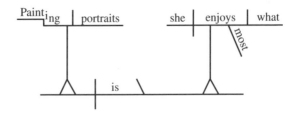

8.27 Noun clause as object of preposition. 6.6

He said nothing about *where he would go next.*

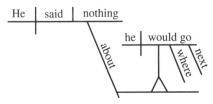

8.28 Noun clause as appositive. 6.6

The idea *that he could succeed* carried him through.

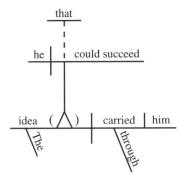

Adjective Clause

(Diagram the independent clause first. Then diagram the adjective clause below the independent clause. Draw a dotted line from the relative to the noun or pronoun that the clause modifies.)

8.29 Adjective clause introduced by the relative pronoun *who*. 6.8–6.10

God, *Who created the universe,* also controls it.

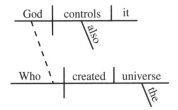

**Gram.
8.30**

8.30 Adjective clause introduced by the relative pronoun *which.* 6.8–6.10

That is a battle *about which much has been written.*

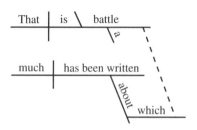

8.31 Adjective clause introduced by the relative pronoun *that* (understood). 6.8–6.10

The flight *I needed* was canceled.

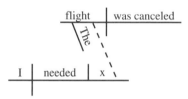

8.32 Adjective clause introduced by the relative adjective *whose.* 6.8–6.10

A hemophiliac is one *whose blood does not clot.*

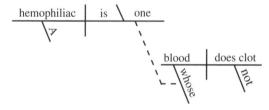

8.33 Adjective clause introduced by the relative adverb *where.* 6.8–6.10

We just passed a place *where we could have eaten breakfast.*

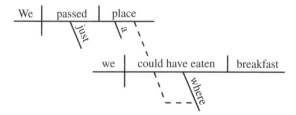

Adverb Clause

(Diagram the independent clause first. Then diagram the adverb clause below the independent clause. Draw a dotted line from the verb in the dependent clause to the word modified in the independent clause. Write the subordinating conjunction on the dotted line. Use an *x* to indicate each omission in an elliptical clause.)

Gram. 8.36

8.34 Adverb clause modifying a verb. 6.11–6.14
   If the blind lead the blind, both shall fall into the ditch.

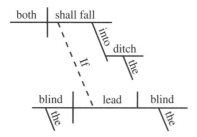

8.35 Adverb clause modifying an adjective. 6.11–6.14
   He is certain *that his request will be granted.*

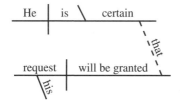

8.36 Adverb clause modifying an adverb. 6.11–6.14
   Scott can swim better *than I.*

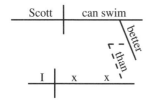

Compound Sentence

Gram.
8.37

(A compound sentence is diagramed like two simple sentences, the first one placed above the second one. If the clauses are joined by a semicolon, leave the connecting line blank or put an *x* to indicate an understood *and* or *but.*)

8.37 Compound sentence connected by the conjunction *or*. 7.3

Give according to your means, or God will make your means according to your giving. —*Hall*

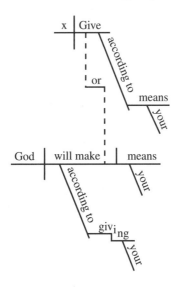

8.38 Compound sentence connected by semicolon. 7.3

Bad men excuse their faults; good men will leave them. —*Johnson*

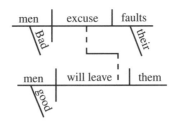

Complex Sentence

(All of the diagrams under numbers 8.24–8.36 are of complex sentences.)

8.39 Complex sentence containing an adjective clause and an adverb clause. 7.4–7.5

Books are but wastepaper unless we spend in action the wisdom we get from thought.

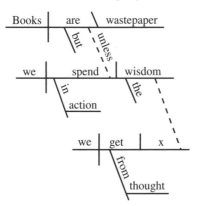

Compound-Complex Sentence

(Compound-complex sentences are diagramed by putting the independent clauses underneath each other in the same order as they appear in the sentence. The dependent clauses are placed below the words they modify.)

8.40 Compound-complex sentence containing two adjective clauses. 7.6

They that know God will be humble; they that know themselves cannot be proud. —*Flavel*

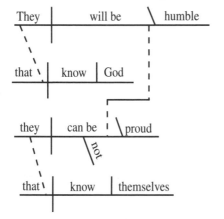

53

8.41 Compound-complex sentence containing one adverb clause. 7.6

Our prayer and God's grace are like two buckets in a well; while the one ascends, the other descends.

—*Hopkins*

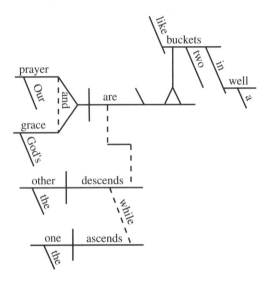

Appositive and Independent Elements

8.42 Appositive phrase. 3.24 (An appositive is placed immediately after the word it explains or identifies and is enclosed in parentheses. See also 8.20, 8.21e, 8.28.)

Herod, *the king of Judea,* sought the death of Christ.

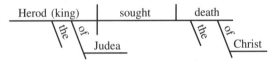

(Independent elements are diagramed separate from the rest of the sentence.)

8.43 Interjection. 3.68

Aha, we have found you.

Aha

| We | have found | you |

8.44   Noun of direct address. 3.69

Greg, have you met your new teachers?

8.45   Parenthetical expressions. 3.70

He went there, *I am sure,* to be helpful.

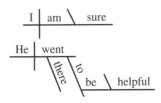

8.46   Nominative absolute. 3.71

Everything considered, our vacation was superb.

8.47   Expletives, *there* **and** *it.* 3.72

There is no other answer to the problem.

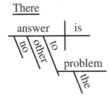

It is easy to see why he was misunderstood.

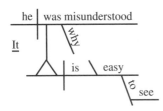

9 Agreement

Subject-Verb Agreement

Gram. 9.1

9.1 **The verb of a sentence must agree with its subject in number.** Number is that form of a word which indicates whether one (singular) or more than one (plural) is meant.

9.2 *Singular subjects* take *singular verbs; plural subjects* take *plural verbs. Nouns* ending in *s* are usually *plural; verbs* ending in *s* are usually *singular.*
The *boy works* hard. (singular)
The *boys work* hard. (plural)

9.3 **The number of a subject is *not affected by phrases* between the subject and the verb.**
The *row* of bushes *was* planted to form a privacy screen. (singular)
The *boats* by the dock *need* repair. (plural)
Coach Brock, together with his players, *is* leaving for the tournament. (singular)
The *stereo,* including headphones and speakers, *was* on sale. (singular)

9.4 **The verb agrees with the subject *not the predicate nominative.***
One of his favorite snacks *is* peanuts. (The predicate nominative *peanuts* is plural, but that has no effect on the subject-verb agreement.)

▶ Note. It is often better to avoid this agreement problem by rewording the sentence.

9.5 **If a sentence *asks a question* or begins with *there* or *here,* you must be careful to locate the subject and make the verb agree with it.** (*There* and *here* are rarely subjects.)
What *is* the *title* of your project?
There *are* thirty-five *pages* in this chapter.
Here *are* the *ingredients* for the recipe.

9.6 *Titles* **of literary works, works of art, organizations, cities, and countries are usually singular even if they are plural in form.**
Pickwick Papers is a novel written by Charles Dickens.
The Massacre of the Innocents by Giovanni Pisano *was* used to adorn a pulpit in Italy.

General Motors *is* a huge corporation.
Grand Rapids is located in western Michigan.

9.7 **The following words are usually *singular* although plural in form: *mumps, measles, rickets, molasses, news, stamina.***

Measles was once a dreaded disease.
Rickets is caused by a lack of vitamin D.
The *news* keeps us informed of world events.

9.8 **_Collective nouns_ may be either singular or plural.** A collective noun names a group and is singular in form (examples: *jury, team, class, family*). A collective noun is *singular* when the group is thought of as a *unit;* a collective noun is *plural* when the group is thought of as *individuals acting separately.*

The *jury has* been dismissed. (singular)
The *jury were* unable to agree among themselves. (plural)

▶ Note. A collective noun, of course, can take a plural form to refer to more than one group of the same kind (*juries, teams, classes, families*).

Federal and petit *juries* often *have* twelve members. (plural)

9.9 **Expressions stating *amounts* (fractions, measurements, money, time) may be either singular or plural.** They are *singular* when the amount is considered a *unit.* They are *plural* when the amount is regarded as *separate parts.*

Two thirds of the milk *was* spilled on the floor. (singular)
Two thirds of the peanuts *were* gone. (plural)
Fifty dollars for a bicycle *is* reasonable. (singular)
Fifty dollars were placed in separate envelopes and distributed. (plural)

9.10 **Words that end in *-ics* may be singular or plural depending on their meaning.**

a. When words that end in *-ics* refer to a *course of study* or to a *science,* they are considered *singular.*

Civics was his best subject in high school.
Dramatics is a course offered during the junior year.
Mathematics is a pure science.
Ethics is the science of human conduct.

Gram. 9.11

b. When words that end in -*ics* *do* *not* refer to a course of study or to a science, they are considered *plural*. (Sometimes they refer to qualities, behavior, or physical activity.)

> His *economics were* responsible for his business success.
> *Gymnastics are* performed before large audiences now.
> His *ethics are* not what they should be.

9.11 *Compound subjects* **joined by *and* take a plural verb.**

> *Jack* and *Joe were* here today.

▶ Note. Sometimes subjects joined by *and* refer to only one person or are considered as one thing. Use a singular verb in this situation.

> Our *quarterback* and team *captain is* Jared Johnson. (Jared is both quarterback and captain.)
> *Spaghetti* and *meatballs is* a delightful meal. (Spaghetti and meatballs is only one dish.)

9.12 **When a *compound subject* is joined by *or, nor, either— or, neither—nor,* the verb agrees with the nearer subject.**

> Either her *helpers* or the *librarian is* there to assist you. (The subject closer to the verb is singular; therefore, the verb is singular.)
> Either the *librarian* or her *helpers are* there to assist you. (The subject closer to the verb is plural; therefore, the verb is plural.)

9.13 **These *indefinite pronouns* are *singular* and take a singular verb: *each, either, neither, one, everyone, everybody, no one, nobody, anyone, anybody, someone, somebody.***

> *Everyone* in the room *is* working toward a definite goal.
> *Each* of the visitors *was* taken on a tour of the campus.
> *Neither* of the contestants *was* well prepared.

9.14 **These *indefinite pronouns* are *plural* and take a plural verb: *both, few, several, many.***

> *Many* of the flowers *are* in full bloom.
> *Several* of the workers *are* receiving safety awards.

9.15 **These *indefinite pronouns* may be either *singular* or *plural: some, any, none, all, most.*** To determine the number of these words, look at the context of the sentence.

Some of the harvest *was* completed by November.
Some of the crops *were* frozen.
All of the land *was* cultivated.
All of the seeds *were* carefully planted.

9.16 ***Doesn't, isn't,* and *wasn't* are *singular* and must be used with singular subjects. *Don't, aren't,* and *weren't* are *plural* and must be used with plural subjects.** (Exception: Use *don't* with the pronouns *I* and *you.*) Most errors occur when *don't* is used incorrectly with *he, she,* or *it.*

He don't play football any more. (incorrect)
He doesn't play football any more. (correct)

It don't matter to him. (incorrect)
It doesn't matter to him. (correct)

9.17 **In expressions like *one of those who, one of those which,* and *one of those that,* the relative pronouns *who, which, that* do not refer to the word *one,* but rather to the plural object of *of.* (See also 9.25.)**

She is one of those girls who *love* competition. (The relative *who* refers to the plural object *girls,* not to the word *one.* Therefore, *who* is plural and takes a plural verb. For these expressions, it helps to turn the sentence around: Of those girls who love competition, she is one.)

This is one of those assignments that *seem* impossible. (i.e., Of those assignments that seem impossible, this is one.)

Pronoun-Antecedent Agreement

9.18 **A pronoun must agree with its antecedent (3.26) in number, gender, and person.** (Its case is determined according to its function within a given statement.)

NUMBER

9.19 **A pronoun must agree with its antecedent in *number*.** If the antecedent is singular, the pronoun referring to it must be singular; if the antecedent is plural, the pronoun referring to it must be plural.

**Gram.
9.20**

9.20 Use *singular* pronouns to refer to the singular indefinite pronouns: *each, either, neither, one, everyone, everybody, no one, nobody, anyone, anybody, someone, somebody.*

> *Each* of the girls came armed with *their* own ideas. (incorrect)
> *Each* of the girls came armed with *her* own ideas. (correct)

9.21 Use *plural* pronouns to refer to the plural indefinite pronouns: *both, few, several, many.*

> A *few* filled *their* nets with fish.

9.22 The indefinite pronouns *some, any, none, all, most* may be referred to by *singular* or *plural* pronouns, depending on the sense of the sentence.

> *Most* of the trees have lost *their* leaves. (plural)
> *Most* of the castle retains *its* splendor. (singular)

9.23 Pronouns that refer to *compound antecedents* joined by *and* are usually plural.

> *Bobby* **and** *Kenneth* visited *their* parents during the holidays.

9.24 Pronouns that refer to *compound antecedents* joined by *or* or *nor* usually agree with the nearer antecedent.

> Neither Mark **nor** his *brothers* have received *their* passports.
> Neither Mark **nor** *Tom* has received *his* passport.

9.25 A *relative pronoun* (who, which, that) agrees with its antecedent in number and so determines number in its own clause. (See also 9.17.)

> Molly is the *girl* **who** *is* willing to lend *her* own books. (The relative pronoun *who* is singular because it refers to *girl;* therefore, the singular forms *is* and *her* are used to agree with *who.*)
> Those are the *girls* **who** *are* willing to lend *their* own books. (The relative pronoun *who* is plural because it refers to *girls;* therefore, the plural forms *are* and *their* are used to agree with *who.*)

GENDER

9.26 A pronoun must agree with its antecedent in *gender.*

9.27 Antecedents of *masculine* gender (male sex) are referred to by *he, him, his.*

> *Mr. Wilson* put some papers into *his* briefcase.

9.28 **Antecedents of *feminine* gender (female sex) are referred to by *she, her, hers.***
The *bride* tossed *her* bouquet toward the unmarried girls.

Gram. 10.1

9.29 **Antecedents of *neuter* gender (no sex) are referred to by *it, its.***
The *tree* lost all *its* leaves.

9.30 **Antecedents of *common* gender (sex not known) are referred to by *he, him, his.*** It is understood that the masculine pronouns include both male and female.
Each *speaker* maintained *his* poise. (correct)
not Each *speaker* maintained *their* poise. (incorrect)
not Each *speaker* maintained *his* or *her* poise. (awkward)

9.31 **Antecedents that are names of animals are generally referred to by the neuter pronouns unless the writer wishes to indicate special interest in the animal, in which case the masculine pronouns are often used. When a feminine role is naturally suggested, the feminine pronouns are used.**
The *tiger* paced back and forth in *its* cage (or *his* cage).
A *tigress* teaches *her* cubs how to kill for food.

PERSON

9.32 **A pronoun must agree with its antecedent in *person* (3.28).**
We can bring *our* picnic table. (first person)
Will *you* ask *your* mother for that recipe? (second person)
Alex gave *his* speech first. (third person)

10 Correct Use of Verbs

Principal Parts

10.1 **Verbs have four principal parts: the *present* (present infinitive), the *present participle,* the *past* (past indicative), and the *past participle.*** All other forms of any verb (with a few exceptions) can be derived from these principal parts.

10.2 **All verbs may be classified as *regular* or *irregular* verbs, depending on the way the past and past participle are formed.**

10.3 ***Regular verbs* form the *past* and *past participle* by adding *-ed, -d,* or *-t* to the *present.***

burn, burn*ed,* burn*ed,* or burn*t*   move, move*d,* move*d*
mean, mean*t,* mean*t*

10.4 ***Irregular verbs* form the *past* and *past participle* in irregular ways.** (Any verb that does not form its past and past participle by adding *-ed, -d,* or *-t* to the present is an irregular verb.)

come, came, come   drive, drove, driven
see, saw, seen   set, set, set

10.5 ***Both regular and irregular verbs* form the *present participle* by adding *-ing* to the *present.***

walk, walk*ing*   pray, pray*ing*
draw, draw*ing*   eat, eat*ing*

10.6 **Sometimes *spelling changes* must be made before adding *-ing* or *-ed* to verbs.**

a. For verbs ending in silent *e,* drop the *e* before adding *-ing.*

tape, tap*ing*   hope, hop*ing*
take, tak*ing*   write, writ*ing*

(Some exceptions: cano*e*ing, ho*e*ing, sho*e*ing, sing*e*ing)

b. For verbs ending in *y* preceded by a consonant, change the *y* to *i* before adding *-ed.*

supply, suppl*i*ed   deny, den*i*ed
cry, cr*i*ed   spy, sp*i*ed

c. For verbs ending in a single consonant preceded by an *accented* short vowel, double the final consonant before adding *-ing* or *-ed.*

confer, confe*rr*ing, confe*rr*ed
but marvel, marve*l*ing, marve*l*ed

10.7   Following are the principal parts of some common irregular verbs. The present participle has been omitted because its formation is invariable: it always ends in *-ing.* The helping verb *have* has been included with the past participle to remind you that the past participle is always used with a helping verb.

Gram 10.7

Irregular Verbs

Present Tense	Past Tense	Past Participle	Present Tense	Past Tense	Past Participle
beat	beat	(have) beaten	pay	paid	(have) paid
begin	began	(have) begun	ride	rode	(have) ridden
bite	bit	(have) bitten	ring	rang	(have) rung
blow	blew	(have) blown	rise	rose	(have) risen
break	broke	(have) broken	run	ran	(have) run
bring	brought	(have) brought	say	said	(have) said
build	built	(have) built	see	saw	(have) seen
burst	burst	(have) burst	set	set	(have) set
buy	bought	(have) bought	shake	shook	(have) shaken
choose	chose	(have) chosen	shine	shone, shined[2]	(have) shone, shined[2]
come	came	(have) come	show	showed	(have) shown
do	did	(have) done	shrink	shrank	(have) shrunk
draw	drew	(have) drawn	sing	sang	(have) sung
drink	drank	(have) drunk	sink	sank	(have) sunk
drive	drove	(have) driven	sit	sat	(have) sat
eat	ate	(have) eaten	speak	spoke	(have) spoken
fall	fell	(have) fallen	spring	sprang	(have) sprung
fly	flew	(have) flown	steal	stole	(have) stolen
freeze	froze	(have) frozen	swear	swore	(have) sworn
get	got	(have) got, gotten[1]	swim	swam	(have) swum
give	gave	(have) given	swing	swung	(have) swung
go	went	(have) gone	take	took	(have) taken
grow	grew	(have) grown	tear	tore	(have) torn
hold	held	(have) held	think	thought	(have) thought
know	knew	(have) known	throw	threw	(have) thrown
lay	laid	(have) laid	wear	wore	(have) worn
lead	led	(have) led	weep	wept	(have) wept
leave	left	(have) left	win	won	(have) won
lie	lay	(have) lain	wring	wrung	(have) wrung
lose	lost	(have) lost	write	wrote	(have) written

[1]The first form is the form used in British English; both forms are used in America.

[2]*Shine, shined, shined* are the principal parts when *shine* means "to polish."

Gram. 10.8

10.8   **Do not confuse the *past tense* with the *past participle.*** Never use helping verbs with the past tense. Always use helping verbs with the past participle.

> Curtis *drawn* the best sketch. (past participle used without helping verb—incorrect)
> Curtis *drew* the best sketch. (correct)
> Curtis *has drew* the best sketch. (past used with helping verb—incorrect)
> Curtis *has drawn* the best sketch. (correct)

10.9   **Do not use such incorrect forms as the following: *attackted, brung, busted, clumb, drownded, drug* (for *dragged*), *et, aten, growed, snuck, stoled, throwed, thunk.***

> Mike *brought* (not *brung*) back bushels of apples in his truck.
> Caitlin has already *eaten* (not *aten*) her meal.
> Bill has *grown* (not *growed*) into a fine young man.
> Jake *stole* (not *stoled*) second base.
> We *thought* (not *thunk*) a long time before making the purchase.

10.10   **The following verbs are often used incorrectly: *come, do, give, go, see.***

> The hostages *came* (not *come*) home after 444 days in captivity.
> Ben *did* (not *done*) his work well.
> They *had given* (not *had gave*) fair warning.
> We *had gone* (not *had went*) there before.
> Who *saw* (not *seen*) Jerry at the mall?

10.11   **Three pairs of verbs are especially troublesome: *sit* and *set, rise* and *raise, lie* and *lay.*** In order to use these verbs correctly, you must learn the principal parts and the definitions of these words.

Sit and Set

10.12   **The verb *sit* means "to be seated." Its principal parts are *sit, sitting, sat, (have) sat.* The verb *sit* is usually *intransitive:* it has *no receiver* for its action.**

> I always *sit* in the bleachers at football games.
> The visiting teams *are sitting* with their coaches.
> We *sat* there until the game was over.
> The Dawsons *have sat* in the same section for every game.

10.13 **The verb** *set* **means "to put or place something." Its principal parts are** *set, setting, set, (have) set.* **The verb** *set* **is usually** *transitive:* **it has a** *receiver* **for its action.**

Gram.
10.15

Laura *sets* the *plates* on the table. (*Plates* receives the action of the verb.)

They *were setting* the *jars* on the shelf. (*Jars* receives the action of the verb.)

He *set* the gas *cap* on the ground. (*Cap* receives the action of the verb.)

Her *plants have been set* outside the door. (*Plants* receives the action of the verb.)

▶ Note. The following examples illustrate some special meanings of the verbs *sit* and *set:* he *sits* his horse well; the hen *sets;* the sun *sets;* concrete *sets; set* your watch.

Rise and Raise

10.14 **The verb** *rise* **means "to go up" or "to get up." Its principal parts are** *rise, rising, rose, (have) risen.* **The verb** *rise* **is** *intransitive:* **it has** *no receiver* **for its action.**

Rise and say the pledge to the flag.

The water in the river *is rising* rapidly.

The weather balloon *rose* to a height of 10,000 feet.

The sun *has risen,* and we must depart.

10.15 **The verb** *raise* **means "to lift something" or "to push up something." Its principal parts are** *raise, raising, raised, (have) raised.* **The verb** *raise* **is** *transitive:* **it has a** *receiver* **for its action.**

Raise the *flag* when the trumpet sounds. (*Flag* receives the action of the verb.)

They *are raising* the *drawbridge* for the sailboat. (*Drawbridge* receives the action of the verb.)

She *raised* her *voice* when the jet flew overhead. (*Voice* receives the action of the verb.)

Potatoes have been raised by Maine farmers for generations. (*Potatoes* receives the action of the verb.)

Lie and Lay

10.16 Gram. 10.16 **The verb *lie* means "to recline." Its principal parts are *lie, lying, lay, (have) lain.* The verb *lie* is *intransitive:* it has *no receiver* for its action.**

> She *lies* down for twenty minutes at noon time.
>
> Our dog *is lying* in the shade.
>
> He *lay* in the shade all afternoon.
>
> The ship *has lain* at anchor for two weeks.

10.17 The verb *lay* means "to put or place something." Its principal parts are *lay, laying, laid, (have) laid.* The verb *lay* is *transitive:* it has a *receiver* for its action.

> *Lay* down your *rifle* before checking the targets. (*Rifle* receives the action of the verb.)
>
> They *were laying* the *carpet* last night. (*Carpet* receives the action of the verb.)
>
> Pastor Vaughn *laid* an open *Bible* before the man. (*Bible* receives the action of the verb.)
>
> Our *sins were laid* on Jesus Christ. (*Sins* receives the action of the verb.)

Tense

10.18 The *tense* of a verb *indicates* the *time* of the action—past, present, or future—or the condition expressed by the verb. There are six verb tenses in the English language: the *present tense,* the *past tense,* the *future tense,* the *present perfect tense,* the *past perfect tense,* and the *future perfect tense.* Study the following list of tense forms to see how the various tenses are formed. Such a listing is called a *conjugation.*

Conjugation of the Verb *See* (Indicative Mood, Active Voice)

Principal Parts

Present	Present Participle	Past	Past Participle
see	seeing	saw	seen

———————————— Present Tense ————————————

	Singular	Plural
First person:	I see	we see
Second person:	you see	you see
Third person:	he, she, it sees	they see

Present progressive: I am seeing, etc.
Present emphatic: I do see, etc.

———————————— Past Tense ————————————

First person:	I saw	we saw
Second person:	you saw	you saw
Third person:	he, she, it saw	they saw

Past progressive: I was seeing, etc.
Past emphatic: I did see, etc.

———————————— Future Tense ————————————
(*will* or *shall* + the present)

	Singular	Plural
First person:	I will (shall) see	we will (shall) see
Second person:	you will see	you will see
Third person:	he, she, it will see	they will see

Future progressive: I shall be seeing, etc.

———————————— Present Perfect Tense ————————————
(*have* or *has* + the past participle)

First person:	I have seen	we have seen
Second person:	you have seen	you have seen
Third person:	he, she, it has seen	they have seen

Present perfect progressive: I have been seeing, etc.

———————————— Past Perfect Tense ————————————
(*had* + the past participle)

First person:	I had seen	we had seen
Second person:	you had seen	you had seen
Third person:	he, she, it had seen	they had seen

Past perfect progressive: I had been seeing, etc.

———————————— Future Perfect Tense ————————————
(*will have* or *shall have* + the past participle)

First person:	I will (shall) have seen	we will (shall) have seen
Second person:	you will have seen	you will have seen
Third person:	he, she, it will have seen	they will have seen

Future perfect progressive: I shall have been seeing, etc.

Present Infinitive: (to) see **Perfect Infinitive:** (to) have seen
Present Gerund: seeing **Perfect Gerund:** having seen
Present Participle: seeing **Perfect Participle:** having seen

Gram.
10.19

10.19 The verb *be* is an important helping (auxiliary) verb. It is used in all six tenses in forming the *progressive tenses* and in forming the *passive voice.* The forms of *be* are listed here for your reference.

Conjugation of the Verb *Be* (Indicative Mood, Active Voice)

Principal Parts

	Present	Present Participle	Past	Past Participle
	be	being	was	been

──────────────── Present Tense ────────────────

	Singular	Plural
First person:	I am	we are
Second person:	you are	you are
Third person:	he, she, it is	they are

──────────────── Past Tense ────────────────

First person:	I was	we were
Second person:	you were	you were
Third person:	he, she, it was	they were

──────────────── Future Tense ────────────────

(*will* or *shall* + the present)

First person:	I will (shall) be	we will (shall) be
Second person:	you will be	you will be
Third person:	he, she, it will be	they will be

──────────────── Present Perfect Tense ────────────────

(*have* or *has* + the past participle)

First person:	I have been	we have been
Second person:	you have been	you have been
Third person:	he, she, it has been	they have been

──────────────── Past Perfect Tense ────────────────

(*had* + the past participle)

First person:	I had been	we had been
Second person:	you had been	you had been
Third person:	he, she, it had been	they had been

──────────────── Future Perfect Tense ────────────────

(*will have* or *shall have* + the past participle)

First person:	I will (shall) have been	we will (shall) have been
Second person:	you will have been	you will have been
Third person:	he, she, it will have been	they will have been

Present Infinitive: (to) be   **Perfect Infinitive:** (to) have been
Present Gerund: being   **Perfect Gerund:** having been
Present Participle: being   **Perfect Participle:** having been

10.20 **The helping (auxiliary) verb** *do* **is used in forming the** *present emphatic tense* **and the** *past emphatic tense.* The present and past forms of *do* are listed here for your reference. The other tenses of *do* are not listed here because they are seldom, if ever, used as helping verb forms. The other tenses of *do* are formed like any other main verb. (See 10.18.)

Gram.
10.22

Present and Past of the Verb *Do*
(Indicative Mood, Active Voice)

Principal Parts

Present	Present Participle	Past	Past Participle
do	doing	did	done

——— **Present Tense** ———

	Singular	Plural
First person:	I do	we do
Second person:	you do	you do
Third person:	he, she, it does	they do

——— **Past Tense** ———

First person:	I did	we did
Second person:	you did	you did
Third person:	he, she, it did	they did

10.21 **The six tenses indicate the time of the action (or condition) expressed by a verb. The names of the tenses generally represent the actual time of the action (or condition), but not always.** For example, the *present tense* verb in the following sentence refers to an action that will take place in the *future.*
   I *leave* for Tampa tomorrow.

10.22 **Use the** *present tense* **to indicate an action that is occurring (or a condition that exists)** *now,* **at the present time.**
   Mr. Keith *drives* a truck. (simple—customary or habitual action)
   Jack *is* president of his class. (simple—static condition)
   Mr. Baker *is traveling* to Ohio. (progressive—action occurring at the time of writing)
   Some people *do eat* pigs' feet. (emphatic—emphasizes the statement)

▶Note. The present tense has some special uses.

• The present tense is used to indicate a *universal truth,* something that is true at all times.

In Columbus's day, some did not believe that the earth *is* (not *was*) round.

• The present tense, along with an adverbial modifier, may be used to indicate a *future action.*

His plane *arrives* in the morning. (present tense verb + adverb phrase)

10.23 **Use the** *past tense* **to indicate an action that occurred (or a condition that existed) at some definite time in the past.**

He *played* tennis whenever he could find the time. (simple—customary or habitual action)

Jack *was* president of his class. (simple—static condition)

He *was* still *working* at midnight. (progressive— duration of action at a definite time in the past)

He *did work* hard to meet the deadline. (emphatic— emphasizes the statement)

10.24 **Use the** *future tense* **to indicate an action that will occur (or a condition that will exist) in the future.** The future tense may be formed by adding *shall* or *will* to the present tense.

I *shall go* with you. (simple)

I *shall be going* with you each week. (progressive)

▶ Note. Another way to indicate the future is to use a present form of *be* + *going* + an infinitive.

He *is going to get* a degree in physics.

10.25 **Use the** *present perfect tense* **to indicate an action (or condition) that was begun in the past and is completed at the present time or is continuing into the present.** The present perfect indicates that the past action has some connection with the present moment.

Paul *has completed* his science project. (simple— action completed at the present time)

Mr. Clive *has been teaching* math for ten years. (progressive—action continuing into present time)

10.26 Use the *past perfect tense* to indicate an action (or condition) that will be completed before some other past action (or condition).

> Mrs. Stone *had* already *bought* the gifts before the sale started. (simple)
>
> She *had been swimming* for five hours when her crew sighted a shark. (progressive)

10.27 Use the *future perfect tense* to indicate an action (or condition) that will be completed before some other future action (or condition).

> He *will have visited* all the major cities before he returns. (simple)
>
> They *will have been traveling* for nine hours by the time we awake tomorrow. (progressive)

Tense Sequence

10.28 In sentences that have a subordinate element (dependent clause or verbal phrase), be sure that the tense in the subordinate element shows a logical time relationship with the verb of the governing clause.

10.29 **Maintain a logical time relationship between verbs in dependent and independent *clauses.*** Adjust the tense of the verb in the dependent clause to the tense of the verb in the independent clause.

a. **Use the *past perfect* tense to express action that occurred *before* some other past action.**

> After I *had studied* for fifty minutes, I *realized* that I had been studying the wrong assignment. (The *past perfect* tense *had studied* is correct here because the studying occurred *before* the realization.)
>
> When the President *entered,* everyone *rose.* (The past tense *entered* is correct here because the entering and the rising occurred at the *same time.*)

b. **Do not use *would have* as a helping verb form for *had* in conditional clauses introduced by *if.***

> If he *had* (not *would have*) tried harder, he *could have* won.

10.30 **Maintain a logical time relationship between *verbals* and their governing verbs.**

a. Use the *present infinitive (to go, to see,* etc.*)* to express action that occurs at the *same time* as that of the main verb, *or later.*

> We *were* all *hoping to go* (not *to have gone*). (At the time indicated by the main verb, we were hoping *to go,* not *to have gone.*)

b. Use the *perfect infinitive (to have gone, to have seen,* etc.*)* to express action that occurs *before* that of the main verb.

> They *were* relieved *to have crossed* the canyon. (Here the crossing occurred *before* the relief came.)

c. Use the *present participle* to express action that occurs at the *same time* as that of the main verb.

> *Walking* along in the dark, I *stumbled.* (The walking and the stumbling occurred at the *same time.*)

d. Use the *perfect participle* to express action that occurs *before* that of the main verb.

> *Having studied* hard, I *was* ready for the exam. (The studying *preceded* the readiness.)

Voice

10.31 *Voice* is that property of a transitive verb that tells whether the *subject* is *doing* the action or *receiving* the action described by the verb.

10.32 If the *subject* is *doing* the action, the transitive verb is in the *active voice.* If the *subject* is *receiving* the action, the transitive verb is in the *passive voice.*

> A hornet *stung* Bobby. (active voice)
> Bobby *was stung* by a hornet. (passive voice)

10.33 A verb in the *passive voice* contains a *form of the verb "be" (am, is, are, was, were, be, being, been)* plus the past participle of a main verb. *Shall, will, have, has, had* are used in addition to "be" and the past participle of a main verb in forming the future tense and the perfect tenses. Any verb that contains a form of "be" and a past participle is a passive verb.

> Gold *was found* at Sutter's Mill in California. (form of *be* + past participle = past tense in passive voice)
> Gold *had been found* at Sutter's Mill in California. (had + form of *be* + past participle = past perfect in passive voice)

10.34 **The following is a conjugation of a verb in the passive voice.**

Conjugation of the Verb *See* (Indicative Mood, Passive Voice)

——————————— Present Tense ———————————

	Singular	Plural
First person:	I am seen	we are seen
Second person:	you are seen	you are seen
Third person:	he, she, it is seen	they are seen

Present progressive: I am being seen, etc.

——————————— Past Tense ———————————

First person:	I was seen	we were seen
Second person:	you were seen	you were seen
Third person:	he, she, it was seen	they were seen

Past progressive: I was being seen, etc.

——————————— Future Tense ———————————

First person:	I will (shall) be seen	we will (shall) be seen
Second person:	you will be seen	you will be seen
Third person:	he, she, it will be seen	they will be seen

——————————— Present Perfect Tense ———————————

First person:	I have been seen	we have been seen
Second person:	you have been seen	you have been seen
Third person:	he, she, it has been seen	they have been seen

——————————— Past Perfect Tense ———————————

First person:	I had been seen	we had been seen
Second person:	you had been seen	you had been seen
Third person:	he, she, it had been seen	they had been seen

——————————— Future Perfect Tense ———————————

First person:	I will (shall) have been seen	we will (shall) have been seen
Second person:	you will have been seen	you will have been seen
Third person:	he, she, it will have been seen	they will have been seen

Present Infinitive: (to) be seen **Perfect Infinitive:** (to) have been seen
Present Gerund: being seen **Perfect Gerund:** having been seen
Present Participle: being seen **Perfect Participle:** having been seen

10.35 **When the verb is changed from the active to the passive voice, the object of the verb becomes the subject, and the subject becomes the object of a preposition.**

    s.   d.o.
The water *damaged* their new carpet. (active voice)

    s.   o.p.
Their new carpet *was damaged* by the water. (passive voice)

▶ Note. Sometimes the active subject may be omitted altogether.

Their new carpet *was damaged.* (*Carpet* is a passive subject; the active subject *water* has been omitted in the change from active voice to passive voice.)

10.36 **An indirect object or a direct object that is retained when a verb is changed from active to passive voice is called a *retained object*.**

              i.o.   **d.o.**
My mother gave *me* a *bracelet.* (active voice)

  s.   **r.o.**
I was given a *bracelet* by my mother. (passive voice—The indirect object becomes the subject; the direct object is the retained object.)

              i.o.   **d.o.**
My mother gave *me* a *bracelet.* (active voice)

    s.   **r.o.**
A *bracelet* was given *me* by my mother. (passive voice—The direct object becomes the subject; the indirect object is the retained object.)

▶ Note. A retained object is diagramed the same as a direct object (8.4).

10.37 **An objective complement (2.27) that is retained when a verb is changed from active to passive voice becomes a *subject complement* (predicate nominative or predicate adjective, 2.28).** The passive verb functions as a *linking verb* to join the complement to the subject.

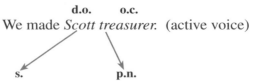

              d.o.   **o.c.**
We made *Scott treasurer.* (active voice)

    s.   **p.n.**
Scott was made *treasurer.* (passive voice—The direct object becomes the subject; the objective complement becomes a predicate nominative.)

d.o.   o.c.
We consider *Scott dependable.* (active voice)

s.   p.a.
Scott is considered *dependable.* (passive voice—The
direct object becomes the subject; the objective
complement becomes a predicate adjective.)

▶ Note. Subject complements that follow passive-voice
verbs are diagramed the same as those that follow linking verbs (8.7–8.8).

10.38 **In writing, use the passive voice sparingly.** Overuse of
the passive voice causes a weak and awkward style. However, there are occasions when the passive is more natural
and emphatic than the active.

**a. Use the passive voice if the *doer* of the action is
*unknown.***

Some products of earlier times *have* now *been replaced.*

Many fine horses *are raised* in the bluegrass pastures
of Kentucky.

**b. Use the passive voice if the object (receiver of the
action) is more important than the doer of the action.**
The context will determine whether the receiver or the
doer is more important.

Hardshell clams *were used* by the American Indians as
money. (The passive construction, which places the
object *hardshell clams* in the subject position, puts
the emphasis on clams rather than on Indians. This
is perfectly natural if the topic of discussion is
clams. If the topic of discussion were Indians, the
active voice would be used: "The American Indians
used hardshell clams as money.")

**c. Use the passive voice if you think it better to leave
the doer of the action unidentified.**

Regrettable things *were said* in the heat of the moment.

Mood

10.39 **The mood of a verb is a grammatical form that indicates the state of mind or the manner in which a state-**

ment is made. **There are three moods in English: the** *indicative,* **the** *imperative,* **and the** *subjunctive.*

10.40 **The** *indicative* **mood states a fact or asks a question.** This is the mood used most of the time.

He always *gives* his tithe.   *Do* you always *give* your tithe?

10.41 **The** *imperative* **mood gives a command or makes a request.**

Close the door.   Please *take* this to the office.

10.42 **The** *subjunctive* **mood expresses an action or condition as a conception of the mind rather than as a reality.**

If I *were* you, I would keep my head down. (I am not you.)

I wish you *were* going with us. (You are not going.)

10.43 **The subjunctive mood has only a few forms which differ from the indicative.** The present subjunctive form of *be* is invariably *be* in all persons, singular and plural; and the past subjunctive form of *be* is invariably *were* in all persons, singular and plural. For all other verbs, the only subjunctive form that is different from the indicative is the third person singular present tense, which drops the *s* or *es* and becomes like all the other forms: he *has* becomes he *have;* he *does* becomes he *do,* he *sees* becomes he *see,* etc.

Subjunctive Mood

Present Tense of *Be*

	Singular	Plural
First person:	(if) I *be*	(if) we *be*
Second person:	(if) you *be*	(if) you *be*
Third person:	(if) he, she, it *be*	(if) they *be*

Past Tense of *Be*

First person:	(if) I *were*	(if) we *were*
Second person:	(if) you *were*	(if) you *were*
Third person:	(if) he, she, it *were*	(if) they *were*

Present Tense of *Have*

First person:	(if) I *have*	(if) we *have*
Second person:	(if) you *have*	(if) you *have*
Third person:	(if) he, she, it *have*	(if) they *have*

Present Tense of *Do*

First person:	(if) I *do*	(if) we *do*
Second person:	(if) you *do*	(if) you *do*
Third person:	(if) he, she, it *do*	(if) they *do*

▶ Note. The other tense forms of *be, have,* and *do* are exactly the same in the subjunctive as they are in the indicative.

10.44 **The following are some common uses of the subjunctive mood.**

    a. **Use the subjunctive mood in dependent clauses to express a condition that is *contrary to fact:* something that is not or could not be true.** Such clauses are often introduced by the word *if.*

> If I *were* you, I would listen to good advice. (I am not you.)
> If he *were* properly disciplined, he would behave. (He is not properly disciplined.)

    b. **Use the subjunctive mood to express a statement following *as if* or *as though.***

> She looked as if she *were* going to cry.

    c. **Use the subjunctive mood in a dependent clause after an independent clause that expresses a *wish,* a *request,* or a *requirement.***

> I wish that he *were* able to go.
> The senator urgently requested that the bill *be* rejected.
> The teacher insists that David *improve* his writing.

    d. **Use the subjunctive mood in a dependent clause that states a *parliamentary motion* or a *legal judgment.***

> I move that the meeting *be* adjourned until tomorrow.
> The court's decision is that the golf course *be* sold to the highest bidder.

11 Correct Use of Pronouns

11.1 Because different functions of pronouns require different forms, one must learn those distinctive forms and know how to use them.

11.2 ***Case* is that form of a noun or pronoun which marks its function in a sentence. There are three cases: *nominative, objective,* and *possessive.***

    ▶ Note. Though nouns may be said to have case, they present no case problems, because the forms are the same in both the nominative and objective cases.

**Gram.
11.3**

11.3 **Following are the case forms of the personal pronouns (3.28) and the relative or interrogative pronoun *who* (3.34, 3.37).** The nominative and objective cases of these pronouns are the ones often misused, the one for the other. (For usage of possessive pronouns see 11.9–11.10.)

Personal Pronouns

Singular

	Nominative Case	Objective Case	Possessive Case
First person:	I	me	my (mine)
Second person:	you	you	your (yours)
Third person:			
Masculine	he	him	his
Feminine	she	her	her (hers)
Neuter	it	it	its

Plural

	Nominative Case	Objective Case	Possessive Case
First person:	we	us	our (ours)
Second person:	you	you	your (yours)
Third person:			
All genders	they	them	their (theirs)

Relative and Interrogative Pronoun *Who*

Singular and Plural

	Nominative Case	Objective Case	Possessive Case
Simple:	who	whom	whose
Compound:	whoever	whomever	whosever

Nominative Case

11.4 **Nominative case pronouns are used as subjects or as predicate nominatives (2.29).** Memorize these nominative case pronouns: *I, he, she, we, they, who, whoever.* (*You* and *it* are in both the nominative case and the objective case.) A pronoun that is used as a predicate nominative will follow a form of the verb *be: am, is, are, was, were, may be, shall be, might have been,* etc.

> *He* and *I* will be in the library. (subject)
> The winner will be *he.* (predicate nominative)

▶ Note. The expression *It is me* or *It's me* is now commonly used in everyday conversation. However, in formal writing follow the rule and write *It is I.*

11.5 A nominative case pronoun is used as the complement of the infinitive *to be* whenever the infinitive does not have a grammatical subject of its own. (See also 11.8.)

He was thought to be *I*. (Since *to be* has no subject of its own, the complement refers to the subject of the verb *was thought,* which is, of course, in the nominative case.)

▶ Note. By exchanging the pronoun complement with the word to which it refers, you can test whether you have chosen the correct pronoun.

He was thought to be *I* = *I* was thought to be he. (correct)

but He was thought to be *me* = *Me* was thought to be he. (incorrect)

Objective Case

11.6 Objective case pronouns are used as direct objects (2.25), indirect objects (2.26), and objects of prepositions (3.60). Memorize these objective case pronouns: *me, him, her, us, them, whom, whomever.* (*You* and *it* are in both the objective case and the nominative case.)

Dad advised *him*. (*Him* is a direct object following the verb *advised*.)

Dad gave *him* advice. (*Him* is an indirect object between the verb *gave* and the direct object *advice*.)

A helicopter circled above *them*. (*Them* is the object of the preposition *above*.)

11.7 The subject of an infinitive is in the objective case.

They wanted *us* to go with them. (*Us* is the subject of the infinitive *to go*. The entire phrase *us to go with them* is the direct object of *wanted*.)

11.8 An objective case pronoun is used as the complement of the infinitive *to be* whenever the infinitive has a grammatical subject of its own. (See also 11.5.)

They thought him to be *me*. (Here the complement refers to the subject of the infinitive which is, of course, in the objective case, 11.7.)

Possessive Case

11.9 Possessive case pronouns show ownership or relationship. (See forms under 11.3.)

a. **The forms** *my, your, her, our,* **and** *their* **are used before nouns and function as** *adjectives.* Some authorities call them possessive adjectives.

b. **The forms** *mine, yours, hers, ours,* **and** *theirs* **function as** *pronouns;* that is, they may be subjects, direct objects, predicate nominatives, etc.

c. **The forms** *his* **and** *its* **may function as adjectives or as pronouns.**

> We used *his* boat and *my* motor on *our* fishing trip. (*His, my,* and *our* function as adjectives. *His* modifies *boat; my* modifies *motor;* and *our* modifies *trip.*)
>
> *His* boat was old, but *mine* was older than *his.* (The first *his* functions as an adjective. *Mine* and the second *his* function as pronouns; that is, they are used as subjects.)

11.10 **The possessive case is used to modify a gerund (4.3).**

> *My* (not *me*) meeting you here is quite a coincidence.

▶ Note. The possessive modifying a gerund is sometimes confused with a participle modifying a noun or pronoun. You can usually tell the difference if you ask yourself whether the *person* performing the activity should receive the emphasis, or whether the *activity* being performed should receive the emphasis.

> We watched *them* (not *their*) *hanging* the lights in the field house. (*Hanging* is a participle modifying the objective case pronoun *them.* The emphasis here is on the people rather than on the activity.)
>
> We appreciate *your* (not *you*) *visiting* us today. (*Visiting* is a gerund modified by the possessive *your.* The emphasis here is on the activity, rather than on the people. Compare the same sentence with a noun substituted for the gerund: We appreciate *your visit.*)

Distinguishing Nominative and Objective Case

11.11 **In order to know which pronoun is correct, you must first determine how the pronoun functions in the sentence or clause. Then you select the pronoun from the correct case.**

He gave the Crandons and (they, them) a huge turkey. [*Crandons and (they, them)* is used as a compound indirect object. Therefore, we must select the objective case pronoun *them.* He gave the Crandons and *them* a huge turkey.]

11.12 **Most problems occur when the pronoun appears in a compound construction.** In such instances it is helpful to try each pronoun alone in the sentence.

The senator praised John and (I, me).
The senator praised *I.* (incorrect)
The senator praised *me.* (correct)
The senator praised John and *me.*

11.13 **If the pronoun is followed by an appositive (3.24), it is helpful to try the pronoun apart from the appositive.**

(We, Us) Christians should do right.
Us should do right. (incorrect)
We should do right. (correct)
We Christians should do right.

11.14 **If the pronoun itself is used as an appositive (3.24), the pronoun appositive must be in the same case as the word to which it refers.**

The fastest runners on the team are the *twins,* Joey and *he.* (The predicate nominative *twins* is in the nominative case; therefore, a pronoun appositive referring to the predicate nominative must be in the nominative case.)

He praised his business *partners,* Frank and *him.* (The direct object *partners* is in the objective case; therefore, a pronoun appositive referring to the direct object must be in the objective case.)

Special Case Problems

11.15 **Using *who, whoever, whom, whomever* can be troublesome.** If you have difficulty determining which of these pronouns to use, the following method will help you.

a. *Identify the clause* in which the pronoun is located and put brackets [ ] around it. Words outside the clause have no effect on the case of a pronoun.

b. *Analyze the clause to determine the use* of the pronoun. First, find the verb. Second, ask *who* or *what* before the verb to find the subject. Third, ask *who* (*whom*) or *what* after the verb to find a complement. Fourth, if the pronoun is neither subject nor complement, it will be the object of a preposition. Do not be fooled by intervening words, such as *do you think* or *did he say.* Just draw a line through such expressions; they do not affect the case of the pronoun.

c. *Select the correct pronoun.* Select *who* or *whoever* if the pronoun is used as a subject or as a predicate nominative; select *whom* or *whomever* if the pronoun is used as a direct object or as an object of a preposition.

d. *Check your answer.* Substitute *he, she,* or *they* for *who* or *whoever* and substitute *him, her,* or *them* for *whom* or *whomever.* Then read the clause in normal order, beginning with the subject.

▶ Note. Use the same procedure for analyzing interrogative sentences. See the second example below.

Mrs. Grice is one [(who, ~~whom~~) really knows interior decorating.]

[(Who, ~~Whom~~) ~~did he say~~ would be elected?]

Spurgeon is a preacher [(~~who~~, whom) we can read with great profit.]

The students [(~~who~~, whom) the Lord gives help to] are those who acknowledge Him.

11.16 For incomplete clauses beginning with *than* or *as,* use the pronoun that you would use if the clause were completed.

Mom can cook as well as (they, them). (problem)

Mom can cook as well *as they* [can]. (solution)

The drought affected the farmers more than (we, us).
(problem)

The drought affected the farmers more *than* $\lceil$ *it* ^{s.}

$$\underset{\text{v.}}{\textit{affected}}\ \rceil\ \underset{\text{d.o.}}{\textit{us.}}\quad\text{(solution)}$$

12 Correct Use of Modifiers

Comparison

12.1 **There are three degrees of comparison:** *positive, comparative,* **and** *superlative.*

12.2 **The** *positive* **degree is used when no comparison is expressed.**
This mattress is *firm.*
Bob is a *skillful* driver.
A diamond is a *valuable* gem.

12.3 **The** *comparative* **degree is used when only two items are being compared.**
This mattress is *firmer* than most.
Bob is a *more skillful* driver than his cousin.
A diamond is *more valuable* than a sapphire.

12.4 **The** *superlative* **degree is used when three or more items are being compared.**
This mattress is the *firmest* that I have ever tested.
Bob is the *most skillful* of all drivers in the field.
A diamond is perhaps the *most valuable* of all gems.

Formation of Comparative and Superlative Degrees

12.5 **Most one-syllable modifiers form the comparative and superlative degrees by adding** *-er* **and** *-est* **to the positive.**

Positive	Comparative	Superlative
close	clos*er*	clos*est*
hard	hard*er*	hard*est*
late	lat*er*	lat*est*
long	long*er*	long*est*
straight	straight*er*	straight*est*

▶ Note. All of the words listed above may be used as adjectives or as adverbs.

Gram. 12.6

12.6 **Most two-syllable modifiers form the comparative and superlative degrees by using the words *more* and *most* before the positive.**

Positive	Comparative	Superlative
active	*more* active	*most* active
careful	*more* careful	*most* careful
gladly	*more* gladly	*most* gladly
honest	*most* honest	*most* honest
quickly	*more* quickly	*most* quickly

12.7 **Modifiers of three or more syllables regularly form the comparative and superlative degrees by using the words *more* and *most* before the positive.**

Positive	Comparative	Superlative
trivial	*more* trivial	*most* trivial
dutifully	*more* dutifully	*most* dutifully
satisfactorily	*more* satisfactorily	*most* satisfactorily

12.8 **The comparative and superlative degrees of a few modifiers are formed *irregularly*.**

Positive	Comparative	Superlative
bad, badly, ill	worse	worst
far	farther, further	farthest, furthest
good, well	better	best
little	less	least
many, much	more	most

12.9 **Use the words *less* and *least* before an adjective or adverb in order to indicate inferiority in a comparison.**

Positive	Comparative	Superlative
familiar	*less* familiar	*least* familiar
helpful	*less* helpful	*least* helpful
rapidly	*less* rapidly	*least* rapidly

Usage

12.10 **Use the *comparative* degree when comparing only *two* persons or things. Use the *superlative* when comparing *three or more* persons or things.**

Of the two blenders, this one works *better* (not *best*).
Of the three platoons, ours was the *most* (not *more*) efficient.

12.11 **Avoid the *double comparison*.** Do not use *-er* and *more* together or *-est* and *most* together. Only one form is needed.

> The Nile is *more longer* than the Mississippi River. (incorrect)
>
> The Nile is *longer* than the Mississippi River. (correct)
>
> St. Augustine grass spreads *more rapidlier* than zoysia grass. (incorrect)
>
> St. Augustine grass spreads *more rapidly* than zoysia grass. (correct)

Gram.
12.14

12.12 **When comparing a person with a group of which that person is a member, use *other* or *else* with the comparative.**

> Jan types faster than any student in her class. (incorrect—Jan is a member of her class. She cannot type faster than herself.)
>
> Jan types faster than any *other* student in her class. (correct)
>
> Steve jumps higher than anyone on his basketball team. (incorrect—Steve is a member of his team. He cannot jump higher than himself.)
>
> Steve jumps higher than anyone *else* on his basketball team. (correct)

12.13 **Do not omit necessary words in a comparison.**

> Your essay is the best. (Best of what?)
>
> Your essay is the best I have read so far. (correct)
>
> **or** Your essay is excellent. (correct)
>
> He helps me more than Brian. (not clear)
>
> He helps me more than he helps Brian. (clear)
>
> **or** He helps me more than Brian does. (clear)

▶ Note. Incomplete constructions like the ones above are often used if there is no danger of misunderstanding.

> I work longer than he. (clear and correct)

12.14 **Avoid illogical comparisons.**

> Bill's garage is smaller than his neighbor. (illogical)
>
> Bill's garage is smaller than his neighbor's garage. (correct)
>
> **or** Bill's garage is smaller than that of his neighbor. (correct)

**Gram.
12.15**

12.15 **Avoid the *double negative*.** The following words are called negatives: *no, not* (or *n't*), *none, never, no one, nothing, hardly, scarcely,* and *but* (meaning *only*). Do not use two negative words where one is sufficient.

> We have*n't scarcely* enough time to memorize our lines. (incorrect)
> We have *scarcely* enough time to memorize our lines. (correct)
> It will *not* require *but* a few days to complete. (incorrect)
> It will require *but* a few days to complete. (correct)
> We do*n't* want *no* failures in this class. (incorrect)
> We do *not* want any failures in this class. (correct)
> **or** We want *no* failures in this class. (correct)

Distinguishing Adjectives from Adverbs

12.16 **Use *adjectives* to modify *nouns* or *pronouns*. Use *adverbs* to modify *verbs, adjectives,* or *adverbs*.**

> Dave is a *faithful* member. (adjective)

> Dave attends church *faithfully*. (adverb)

▶ Note. Although most adverbs end in -*ly*, remember that some adjectives also end in -*ly*.

> cautiously, loudly, hurriedly, carefully (adverbs)
> manly, scraggly, costly, friendly (adjectives)

12.17 **Use a predicate adjective, not an adverb, after a linking verb. Use an adverb after an action verb.** (Remember that some verbs may be linking or action depending on their use: *taste, feel, smell, sound, look,* etc.)

> Their horses looked *swift*. (The adjective *swift* follows the linking verb *looked* and modifies the subject *horses*.)
> She looked *swiftly* around the room. (The adverb *swiftly* modifies the action verb *looked*.)
> The corn tasted *fresh* (not *freshly*).
> The car stopped *suddenly* (not *sudden*) in the middle of the block.
> We need to learn how to work *carefully* (not *careful*).

Part 2

Composing the Sentence

The best style of writing, as well as the most forcible, is the plainest.

Horace Greeley

A sentence should read as if its author, had he held a plow instead of a pen, could have drawn a furrow deep and straight to the end.

Henry David Thoreau

The sentence is a basic unit of thought. No composition can succeed unless it is made up of correct, clear, and effective sentences.

Correctness

13 Sentence Fragment

13.1 **A sentence is a group of words that expresses a complete thought and can stand alone. Every grammatical sentence must have a subject (expressed or understood) and a predicate.** (But see note under 2.2.)

Sent.
13.1

> I don't believe in the goodness of disagreeable people. —*O. Dewey*

13.2 **A *fragment* is a separated sentence part that does not express a complete thought.** *Dependent clauses, verbal phrases,* and *appositive phrases* are common types of fragments. These elements must not be punctuated as sentences.

> Nehemiah sought God's will for four months. *Before he knew exactly what God wanted him to do.* (dependent clause fragment)
> Taylor stayed up late. *Working on an overdue assignment.* (participial phrase fragment)
> They all went to the airport. *To bid goodbye to their friend.* (infinitive phrase fragment)
> The detective discovered the thieves' hideout. *An old abandoned house on the edge of town.* (appositive phrase fragment)

13.3 **A fragment can often be corrected by simply rejoining it to the sentence from which it has been separated.** Notice the way the examples from 13.2 have been corrected.

> Nehemiah sought God's will for four months *before he knew exactly what God wanted him to do.* (corrected)
> Taylor stayed up late, *working on an overdue assignment.* (corrected)
> They all went to the airport *to bid goodbye to their friend.* (corrected)

The detective discovered the thieves' hideout, *an old abandoned house on the edge of town.* (corrected)

▶ Note. Sometimes words may need to be added or deleted and the fragment made into a separate sentence.

One of my friends, who won a contest by playing a variety of instruments. (fragment—The independent part of this group of words has no predicate.)

One of my friends won a contest by playing a variety of instruments. (corrected—The subject of the dependent clause has been removed.)

One of my friends, who won a contest by playing a variety of instruments, has decided to become a conductor. (corrected—A predicate has been added to fill out the independent clause.)

Sent. 14.1

I recently conversed with a prominent senator. *Who thinks that we should bargain from a position of military strength.* (dependent clause fragment)

I recently conversed with a prominent senator. He thinks that we should bargain from a position of military strength. (corrected—The relative pronoun *who* has been replaced with the personal pronoun *he.* Now the group of words can stand alone as a complete sentence.)

14   Run-on Sentence

14.1   **A run-on sentence is two or more sentences written incorrectly as one sentence.** Sentences cannot be correctly written with *only a comma* between the sentences or with *no punctuation* between.

Nothing is all dark, there cannot be a picture without its bright spots. (run-on—only a comma between sentences. This error is often called a *comma splice.*)

Nothing is all dark there cannot be a picture without its bright spots. (run-on—no punctuation between sentences. This error is often called a *fused sentence.*)

Nothing is all dark. There cannot be a picture without its bright spots. (corrected)

14.2   **Run-on sentences may be corrected in the following ways:**

a. If the sentences contain *separate and distinct ideas,* use a *period and a capital letter.*

There are very few who will admit a mistake, such obstinacy is a barrier to all improvement. (run-on)
There are very few who will admit a mistake. Such obstinacy is a barrier to all improvement. (corrected)

b. If the ideas in the sentences are *so closely related as to form one thought* and are *equally important,* use a *comma and coordinating conjunction (and, but, or, nor, for, yet).*

Take time to deliberate, lose no time in executing your resolutions. (run-on)
Take time to deliberate, **but** lose no time in executing your resolutions. (corrected)

c. If the ideas in the sentences are *so closely related as to form one thought* and are *equally important,* you may use a *semicolon* instead of the comma and coordinating conjunction. (See 42.14.)

God will prune His people but not hew them down, the right hand of His mercy knows what the left hand of His severity is doing. (run-on)
God will prune His people but not hew them down; the right hand of His mercy knows what the left hand of His severity is doing. (corrected)

d. If the ideas in the sentences are *so closely related as to form one thought* but are *not equally important,* you should *subordinate* the less important sentence; that is, make the less important sentence into a dependent (subordinate) clause. (See section 17.)

A man's temper gets the best of him, it reveals the worst of him. (run-on)
When a man's temper gets the best of him, it reveals the worst of him. (corrected)

Clarity

15 Unity

15.1 *Unity* means oneness—oneness of thought and of purpose. In order for a sentence to have unity (1) its statements must be closely related, (2) the relationship of its statements must be clear, and (3) the statements must compose only *one* thought.

15.2 **Do not put unrelated ideas into the same sentence.** If the ideas are not closely related, make them separate sentences. If the ideas are not related at all, eliminate one of them.

Sent. 15.4

> Alexander Graham Bell invented the telephone, and his invention was the result of many years of scientific study. (The ideas are not closely related.)
> Alexander Graham Bell invented the telephone. His invention was the result of many years of scientific study. (correct)

15.3 **Make sure the relationship between ideas is immediately clear. (See 16.1.)**

> We were going to school, and we saw a possum. (relationship not clear)
> As we were going to school, we saw a possum. (relationship of time, now clear)
> They wanted to maintain good health, and they started an exercise program. (relationship not clear)
> To maintain good health, they started an exercise program. (relationship of purpose, now clear)

15.4 **The length of a sentence does not necessarily affect its unity. A very long sentence may have unity, whereas a short sentence may not.**

> If we resort for a criterion to the different principles on which different forms of government are established, we may define a republic to be, or at least may bestow that name on, a government which derives all its powers directly or indirectly from the great body of the people, and is administered by persons holding their offices during pleasure, for a limited period, or during good behavior. —*James Madison* (Although this sentence contains sixty-eight words, it has unity because its ideas exhibit a oneness of thought and purpose.)

Dressed in a blue suit, he voted against the bill. (This sentence of only ten words lacks unity because its ideas are unrelated.)

15.5 **Do not introduce so many details that the central thought of the sentence is obscured.** If the details are relevant and necessary, put them into other sentences.

Early in the morning of May 1, long before sunrise, Admiral Dewey, with his fleet of eight warships, consisting of the *Olympia,* which was the flagship, the *Boston,* the *Petrel,* the *Concord,* the *Philadelphia,* the *Baltimore,* the *Raleigh,* and the revenue cutter *McCulloch,* silently entered the harbor of Manila, and was not detected by the Spaniards until he was well past the forts guarding the entrance. (This sentence contains details which obscure the central thought.)

Long before sunrise on the morning of May 1, Admiral Dewey silently entered the harbor of Manila with his fleet of eight warships. Not until he was well past the forts guarding the entrance did the Spanish detect him. (better)

Sent.
15.5

16 Coordination

16.1 **Avoid excessive coordination.** Excessive coordination results from using too many compound sentences—stringing independent clauses together with *and*'s, *so*'s, *and so*'s, and *and then*'s. The problem with coordination is that it often cannot indicate the exact relationship between ideas, nor can it indicate their relative importance. The problem is usually solved through subordination (17) or division.

a. Subordination. Change a compound sentence into a complex sentence (7.4) by making one of the independent clauses into a dependent clause. Usually subordinate those ideas that indicate time, place, manner, cause, purpose, result, condition, concession, or degree.

We were in Alsace-Lorraine, *and* we saw the Rhine River.

When we were in Alsace-Lorraine, we saw the Rhine River. (improved with adverb clause)

They wanted to save money, *so* they bought an economy car.
Because they wanted to save money, they bought an economy car. (improved with adverb clause)
Roger pulled a tendon, *and so* he could not finish the race.
Because Roger pulled a tendon, he could not finish the race. (improved with adverb clause)
Mr. Smith is the county commissioner, *and* he is our neighbor.
Mr. Smith, *who is the county commissioner,* is our neighbor. (improved with adjective clause)

▶ Note. Whenever it will not affect the clarity and effectiveness of a sentence, an independent clause should be reduced to a phrase instead of to a dependent clause. Some of the examples above could be further reduced. (See section 24.)

b. Division. Divide some compound sentences into two or more separate sentences. (See 15.2.)

16.2 **Avoid false coordination.** Do not use a coordinating conjunction (*and, but,* or *or*) to join an adjective clause (6.8) to an independent clause. (See also 22.7.)

Mr. Kryler is a wealthy man, *and* who has always used his wealth to help others. (incorrect)
Mr. Kryler is a wealthy man who has always used his wealth to help others. (correct)

17 Subordination

One of the most valuable things you can do to improve your writing is to learn the principle of subordination. Subordination reduces repetition, aids coherence, and makes the important ideas stand out.

Careful use of subordination will eliminate a stringy style of writing (16) and a choppy style. A choppy style results from using only short, simple sentences. Although short, simple sentences are very effective at times, you must remember that simple sentences indicate main ideas. If you use only simple sentences, you give the false impression that every idea is equally important.

17.1 **The following list will help you know which ideas should be subordinated.**

   a. **Ideas expressing time, place, manner, cause, purpose, result, condition, concession, or degree.**

   b. **Details stating size, color, cost, etc.**

   c. **Predications containing pronouns and the verb "be."**

17.2 **Use subordination to combine the related ideas of two or more simple sentences or of two or more independent clauses.**

Sent.
17.1

   a. **Form a complex sentence that contains an adjective clause (6.8).**

> Erik Hansen was elected class president. He is friendly to everyone.
> Erik Hansen, *who is friendly to everyone,* was elected class president.

   b. **Form a complex sentence that contains an adverb clause (6.11).**

> Ross was late, and he received a demerit.
> *Because Ross was late,* he received a demerit.

▶ Note. Dependent clauses should be reduced to phrases if the reduction will not affect the clarity and effectiveness of the sentence. (See section 24.)

17.3 **Avoid upside-down subordination, which occurs when the main idea is placed in the dependent clause, and the subordinate idea is placed in the independent clause.**

> When everyone panicked, the earthquake struck. (upside-down subordination)
> When the earthquake struck, everyone panicked. (correct)
> Although Tom could not find his lost book, he had searched for several weeks. (upside-down subordination)
> Although Tom had searched for several weeks, he could not find his lost book. (correct)

17.4 **Avoid illogical subordination.** Make sure that clauses serve their proper functions in a sentence.

   a. **Do not use an adverb clause in the place of a noun clause or other substantive.**

Because he was the best qualified was the reason he
got the job. (illogical—adverb clause used as the
subject)
That he was the best qualified was the reason he got
the job. (correct)

or He got the job *because he was the best qualified.*
(adverb clause used correctly)

The reason the train derailed was *because the tracks
were defective.* (illogical—adverb clause used as a
predicate nominative)
The reason the train derailed was *that the tracks were
defective.* (correct—noun clause used as the predicate nominative)

or The train derailed *because the tracks were defective.*
(adverb clause used correctly)

**b. Do not use an independent clause in the place of a
noun clause.**

He wanted to improve himself was the reason he
returned to school. (illogical—independent clause
used as the subject)
That he wanted to improve himself was the reason he
returned to school. (correct—noun clause used as
the subject)

or He returned to school *because he wanted to improve
himself.* (adverb clause used correctly)

Her strong point is *she is an expert in English literature.* (illogical—independent clause used as the
predicate nominative)
Her strong point is *that she is an expert in English
literature.* (correct—noun clause used as the predicate nominative)

17.5 **Avoid excessive subordination.** Ordinarily one does not
write a series of dependent clauses trailing one after another like the familiar example "This is the rat *that* ate the
malt *that* lay in the house *that* Jack built."

Someone has checked out the book *that* Cody needs
for the report *which,* unfortunately, he is scheduled
to give in history class *which* meets first hour
tomorrow. (clumsy)
Someone has checked out the book that Cody needs
for his report. Unfortunately, he is scheduled to
give the report in history class first hour tomorrow.
(improved)

95

18   Misplaced Modifiers

18.1   **Place modifiers near the words they modify.** Notice in the following examples how the meaning changes according to the placement of the modifiers.

Only he liked Sarah.

He *only* liked Sarah.

He liked *only* Sarah.

The missionary *from New York* showed some pictures of heathen tribes.

The missionary showed some pictures *from New York* of heathen tribes.

The missionary showed some pictures of heathen tribes *from New York.*

Sent. 18.1

18.2   **Adjective phrases and adjective clauses, in most instances, should come immediately after the words they modify.**

The car was stopped alongside the road *with one headlight.* (misplaced phrase)

The car *with one headlight* was stopped alongside the road. (corrected)

The house is still owned by our family *that grandfather built.* (misplaced phrase)

The house *that grandfather built* is still owned by our family. (corrected)

18.3   **An adverb phrase or clause that modifies a *verb* may be placed *before* or *after* the verb it modifies.**

When you leave, please close the door. (modifier before the verb—correct)

Please close the door *when you leave.* (modifier after the verb—correct)

18.4   **An adverb phrase or clause that modifies an *adjective* or an *adverb* is usually placed after the word it modifies.**

Kris was anxious *about her new job.* (modifies the adjective *anxious*)

My sister can sing better *than I can.* (modifies the adverb *better*)

18.5   **Place adverb modifiers as close as possible to the words they modify.**

The pastor told how his wife had fallen *from the pulpit.* (misplaced)

From the pulpit, the pastor told how his wife had fallen. (correct)

or The pastor told *from the pulpit* how his wife had fallen. (correct)

18.6 **Avoid "squinting" modifiers.** A "squinting" modifier is one that is placed between two words that it might modify, causing confusion.

The coach said *in Houston* we would have a doubleheader. (modifier between two verbs that it might modify—confusing)

In Houston, the coach said we would have a doubleheader. (clear)

The coach said we would have a doubleheader *in Houston.* (clear)

Sent.
18.7

18.7 **Avoid awkward split constructions.**

a. Avoid awkward division of the parts of a verb phrase (3.4).

She *had* since early last week *been feeling* bad. (awkward)

She *had been feeling* bad since early last week. (better)

▶ Note. The caution here is only against an *awkward* division. In many sentences, adverbs fall naturally and properly within a verb phrase.

One *must* quickly *kick* the extra point in football.

Nate *is* seriously *considering* going to the mission field.

b. Avoid unnecessary and awkward splitting of infinitives. (A split infinitive occurs when a modifier is placed between the infinitive [4.4] and its introductory word *to.*)

They asked him *to* as soon as possible *move* his car. (awkward)

They asked him *to move* his car as soon as possible. (better)

▶ Note. To avoid ambiguity or artificiality it is sometimes necessary and proper to split an infinitive.

He failed fully *to explain* the subject within the time limit. (ambiguous and artificial)

> He failed *to explain* the subject fully within the time
> limit. (ambiguous)
> He failed *to* fully *explain* the subject within the time
> limit. (emphatic and clear)

19   Dangling Modifiers

A dangling modifier is a phrase or an elliptical clause that does
not sensibly modify any other words in the sentence.

19.1   **Avoid a dangling participial phrase.** Participial phrases
may come after the words they modify, or they may be
placed at the beginning of the sentence. If a participial
phrase is placed at the beginning of the sentence, it must
modify the subject of that sentence. Sometimes a dangling
phrase at the beginning of a sentence is merely misplaced
and may be moved to a position after the word it modifies.
At other times the independent clause must be reworded.

> *Hanging on a nail in the closet,* he found his tie.
> (misplaced)
> He found his tie *hanging on a nail in the closet.*
> (corrected)
> *Flying over the city,* the skyscrapers could be clearly
> seen. (dangling)
> *Flying over the city,* we could clearly see the skyscrap-
> ers. (corrected)

► Note. A few participles, which express a general action,
may stand independently, not modifying any word in the
sentence. Such expressions are so general and idiomatic
that no confusion results. The following are some examples: *concerning, considering, providing, regarding,
speaking, talking.*

> *Generally speaking,* cats do not like dogs.
> *Talking about basketball,* where is Wilt Callahan now?

(See also the nominative absolute [3.71], a proper construction which should not be confused with the dangling participle.)

19.2   **Avoid a dangling gerund phrase.**

> By *using a good carnauba wax,* your car will really
> shine. (dangling—Who is using the wax?)
> By *using a good carnauba wax,* you can make your car
> really shine. (improved)

19.3 Avoid a dangling infinitive phrase. *To run a four-minute mile,* excellent condition is required. (dangling—Who is doing the running?) *To run a four-minute mile,* one must be in excellent condition. (improved)

19.4 Avoid a dangling elliptical clause. An elliptical clause is an adverb clause in which the subject (and sometimes the verb) is understood. A dangling clause results if the understood subject of the elliptical clause is not the same as that of the independent clause. One can usually correct the error by supplying the missing words in the adverb clause. Sometimes the independent clause will have to be reworded.

> *When one month old,* my grandmother died. (dangling)
>
> *When I was one month old,* my grandmother died. (corrected)
>
> His leg developed a cramp *while running the marathon.* (dangling)
>
> His leg developed a cramp *while he was running the marathon.* (corrected)
>
> *If fully cooked,* remove the turkey from the oven. (dangling)
>
> *If the turkey is fully cooked,* remove it from the oven. (corrected)
>
> *While emptying the trash at the campground,* a large opossum startled me. (dangling)
>
> While emptying the trash at the campground, *I was startled by a large opossum.* (corrected)

Sent. 20.1

20 Pronoun Reference

The antecedent to which a pronoun refers must be clear and unmistakable.

20.1 Avoid *ambiguous reference.* *Ambiguous* means "having two or more possible meanings." Ambiguity occurs when two antecedents are possible for the same pronoun. You may correct ambiguous reference by (1) repeating the antecedent or (2) rewording the sentence.

> I removed the plastic lids from the cans and threw *them* away. (ambiguous)
>
> I removed the plastic lids from the cans and threw *the cans* away. (clear)

Bill told Kyle that *he* really did not know much about botany. (ambiguous)

Bill said, "Kyle, I really do not know much about botany." (clear)

20.2 **Avoid *implied reference*.** Implied reference means that the antecedent is not actually stated but must be inferred from other words in the sentence. Implied reference occurs when pronouns are used to refer vaguely to verbs, verbals, adjectives, or even nouns that merely suggest the idea of an antecedent. You can often correct this fault by substituting a noun for the unclear pronoun.

Sent. 20.2

We would like to have honest political leaders, but many of our leaders do not seem to know what *it* is. (vague—refers to the adjective *honest* which merely implies the antecedent *honesty*)

We would like to have honest political leaders, but many of our leaders do not seem to know what *honesty* is. (clear—noun substituted for pronoun)

She enjoys stamps and believes *it* to be an exciting hobby. (unclear—refers vaguely to the noun *stamps*)

She enjoys stamps and believes *stamp collecting* to be an exciting hobby. (clear—noun equivalent substituted for pronoun.

20.3 **Avoid *broad reference*.** Broad reference occurs when the pronouns *it, this, that, which* are used to refer vaguely to a clause rather than to some definite noun or pronoun. Correct this fault by (1) supplying a definite antecedent, or (2) rewording the sentence to get rid of the pronoun.

He persistently refused counsel from ungodly students, *which* greatly aided his spiritual progress. (vague—refers to entire clause)

He persistently refused counsel from ungodly students, a *practice* which greatly aided his spiritual progress. (clear—definite antecedent supplied)

His persistent refusal of counsel from ungodly students greatly aided his spiritual progress. (clear—sentence reworded)

20.4 **Avoid the indefinite use of *it, you, they*.**

a. *It* should usually have a definite antecedent.

In this book *it* says that walking is an excellent exercise. (indefinite)

This book says that walking is an excellent exercise. (clear)

▶ Note. In the following idiomatic expressions the use of *it* without an antecedent is correct: *it is raining, it is early, it is warm, it seems,* etc.

b. Do not use *you* unless you are speaking specifically to the reader. If you are referring to people in general, use general words, such as *one, anyone, person, people.*

In communist-controlled countries, *you* live in constant fear. (incorrect)

In communist-controlled countries, the *people* live in constant fear. (correct)

Sent. 21.1

c. Do not use *they* unless it has a definite plural antecedent.

They say that eating pork causes cancer. (indefinite)

Some *people* say that eating pork causes cancer. (clear)

21   Clear and Logical Construction

21.1   Do not omit words that are necessary for clarity.

a. Do not omit a necessary verb.

They thought they *could do* what no one ever *had* before. (The main verb *do* cannot serve for both helping verbs.)

They thought they *could do* what no one *had* ever *done* before. (improved)

I *have* not and probably never *will visit* Europe. (The main verb *visit* cannot serve for both helping verbs.)

I *have* not *visited* and probably never *will visit* Europe. (improved)

b. Do not omit necessary articles (*a, an,* or *the*).

Our neighbor has *a* black and white dog. (not clear—our neighbor owns two different dogs)

Our neighbor has *a* black and *a* white dog. (clear—two dogs)

They built *a* field house and administration building. (not clear)

They built *a* field house and *an* administration building. (clear)

c. Do not omit necessary prepositions and conjunctions.

We have great confidence and respect *for* our President. (not clear)

We have great confidence *in* and respect *for* our President. (clear)

Do not imagine things will automatically correct themselves. (The omission of the conjunction *that* may cause a misreading.)

Do not imagine *that* things will automatically correct themselves. (clear)

**Sent.
21.2**

d. Do not omit words necessary to complete an alternate comparison.

Your suggestion was *as* good, if not better, *than* mine. (The first part of the comparison is not complete. The sentence reads ". . . was *as* good . . . *than* mine.")

Your suggestion was *as* good *as*, if not better *than,* mine.

or Your suggestion was *as* good *as* mine, if not better.

Ed is *one of the tallest* if not the tallest man in college basketball. (incomplete)

Ed is *one of the tallest men* in college basketball, if not the tallest. (correct)

▶ Note. For other incomplete or illogical comparisons see 12.12–12.14.

21.2 **Do not write *non sequiturs*.** The expression *non sequitur* is a Latin phrase that means "it does not follow." Within a sentence a *non sequitur* is a statement that has no logical connection with the rest of the sentence.

Born in Milan, Ohio, in 1847, Thomas Edison became a famous inventor. (It does not logically follow that if one is born in Milan, Ohio, he will become a famous inventor.)

A handsome young man and well liked by all his friends, Greg Brown was fatally injured in an automobile accident today. (It does not follow that if one is handsome and well liked, he will have a fatal accident.)

▶ Note. Correct a *non sequitur* by putting it with information to which it is logically related or by removing it altogether.

22 Parallelism

22.1 **Ideas that are logically parallel should be structurally parallel; that is, they should be stated in the same grammatical form.** Balance noun with noun, adjective with adjective, prepositional phrase with prepositional phrase, infinitive phrase with infinitive phrase, gerund phrase with gerund phrase, dependent clause with dependent clause, independent clause with independent clause, and so on.

22.2 **Look for conjunctions on which parallel items balance:** *and, but, or, either—or, neither—nor, both—and, not only—but also,* **etc.** Make the items they join structurally parallel.

Sent. 22.3

> *That you are a sinner* **and** *your need of the Savior* are two important truths you must face. (not parallel— The first item is a noun clause and the second is a noun with modifiers.)
>
> *That you are a sinner* **and** *that you need the Savior* are two important truths you must face. (parallel—Both elements are noun clauses.)
>
> This ticket permits you to sit **either** *on the main floor* **or** *you may sit in the balcony.* (not parallel—The first element is a prepositional phrase and the second is an independent clause.)
>
> This ticket permits you to sit **either** *on the main floor* **or** *in the balcony.* (parallel—Both elements are prepositional phrases.)

▶ Note. All the items in a series should be parallel even though conjunctions do not appear between each item.
Jon likes *fishing, swimming,* and *to hike.* (not parallel)
Jon likes *fishing, swimming,* and *hiking.* (parallel)

22.3 **A parallelism diagram helps you see whether or not items are parallel.**

Not Parallel		**Parallel**	
Jon likes ‖	*fishing* (gerund)	Jon likes ‖	*fishing* (gerund)
	swimming (gerund)		*swimming* (gerund)
and ‖	*to hike* (infinitive)	and ‖	*hiking* (gerund)

103

22.4 **When checking for parallelism, look at the first word or phrase in each item.** If each item begins with the same kind of word or phrase, you can be sure that they are parallel even if the other parts of each item differ.

All the examples below are parallel, even though the items may not be the same length. The first word or phrase in each item is what determines parallelism, not the length of the items.

Children are *to honor* their parents and *to obey* them whether or not they understand why they are asked to do something.

Jon *fishes* for pleasure, *swims* to stay in condition, and *hikes* to get away from civilization for a while.

Sent. 22.4

22.5 **Each member of a correlative conjunction should be placed *immediately before* a parallel element.**

By flying nonstop over the Atlantic Ocean, Lindbergh **not only** won *a $25,000 prize* **but also** *the respect and admiration of the world.* (faulty—The first member of the correlative conjunction is out of place.)

By flying nonstop over the Atlantic Ocean, Lindbergh won **not only** *a $25,000 prize* **but also** *the respect and admiration of the world.* (correct)

You can **either** hang the painting *here by the window* **or** *there over the piano.* (faulty—The first member of the correlative conjunction is out of place.)

You can hang the painting **either** *here by the window* **or** *there over the piano.* (correct)

22.6 **Repeat any key word necessary to make the parallelism clear.**

Mr. Bean is excellent *in welding* and *supervising* the men in his shop. (not clear—Was he excellent in welding the men?)

Mr. Bean is excellent *in welding* and *in supervising* the men in his shop. (clear)

Bobby likes to read books which describe auto races **and** picture the action in his mind. (confusing—*Describe* and *picture* seem to be parallel.)

Bobby likes *to read books which describe auto races* **and** *to picture the action in his mind.* (clear)

22.7 Do not use the expressions *and who, and whom,* or *and which* unless a parallel *who, whom,* or *which* clause has preceded it in the sentence. (The same holds true for *but who, but whom,* or *but which.*) See also 16.2.

> Mr. Helmser is a man of great political power *but who* uses his power in the best interests of the people he serves. (not parallel—The conjunction *but* joins a dependent clause to an independent clause.)

> Mr. Helmser is a man *who* has great political power *but who* uses his power in the best interests of the people he serves. (parallel—The conjunction *but* joihs two dependent clauses.)

Sent. 23.1

> Our country faces serious problems, *and which* cannot be easily solved. (not parallel—The *and* joins a dependent clause to an independent clause.)

> Our country faces serious problems, *which* cannot be easily solved. (correct—Since the items were not parallel, the *and* was removed from the sentence.)

22.8 Absolute parallelism is not always possible or desirable.

> He greatly enjoys *golf* and *fishing.* (acceptable— Though these expressions are not parallel in grammatical form, they are parallel in use [noun].)

> The commencement speaker spoke *slowly* and *with dignity.* (acceptable—Though these expressions are not parallel in grammatical form, they are parallel in use [adverb]. Also, would it be desirable to say " . . . spoke *slowly* and *dignifiedly"?*)

23 Point of View

As an aid to coherence, you should avoid unnecessary shifts in point of view.

23.1 Avoid unnecessary shifts in *subject.*

> From Caribou Ridge *we* looked down, and before us lay a beautiful *valley.* (awkward)

> From Caribou Ridge *we* looked down and saw a beautiful valley. (improved)

> *I* am studying chemistry, although laboratory *work* does not especially appeal to me. (awkward)

> *I* am studying chemistry, although *I* do not especially like laboratory work. (improved)

105

23.2 **Avoid unnecessary shifts in *voice* (10.31–10.35).** (A shift in voice nearly always causes also a shift in subject.)

Because Maria *wanted* to learn how to sew, a course in home economics *was taken* by her. (awkward— *Wanted* is in active voice; *was taken* is in passive voice.)

Because Maria *wanted* to learn how to sew, she *took* a course in home economics. (correct—Both verbs are in active voice.)

23.3 **Avoid unnecessary shifts in *tense* (10.18–10.30).**

Philip *pulls* over a chair and *sat* down. (not consistent—*Pulls* is present tense; *sat* is past tense.)

Philip *pulled* over a chair and *sat* down. (consistent— Both verbs are in the past tense.)

Before he *leaves* the room, he *checked* the lights. (not consistent—*Leaves* is present tense; *checked* is past tense.)

Before he *leaves* the room, he *checks* the lights. (consistent—Both verbs are in the present tense.)

Before he *left* the room, he *checked* the lights. (consistent—Both verbs are in the past tense.)

▶ Note. Of course a shift in tense is necessary whenever there is a change in time.

He *wrote* a manual, which *is* still *used* today.

23.4 **Avoid unnecessary shifts in *mood* (10.39–10.44).**

If he *were* in difficulty and *was* unable to overcome it, would you not help him? (shift from subjunctive to indicative)

If he *were* in difficulty and *were* unable to overcome it, would you not help him? (correct)

23.5 **Avoid unnecessary shifts in *person* (3.28).**

If *one* really studies hard and learns how to work, *you* can succeed in America. (shift from third person to second person)

If *one* really studies hard and learns how to work, *he* can succeed in America. (correct)

We volunteered to go on the mission, realizing that *one* might never return. (shift from first person to third person)

We volunteered to go on the mission, realizing that *we* might never return. (correct)

23.6 **Avoid unnecessary shifts in *number*.**
It is rewarding for *women* to be *a nurse*. (shift from plural to singular)
It is rewarding for *women* to be *nurses*. (consistent)
A *cat* is supposedly one of the most enjoyable pets to own, but *they* bring with *them* certain disadvantages. (shift from singular to plural)
A *cat* is supposedly one of the most enjoyable pets to own, but *he* brings with *him* certain disadvantages. (consistent)

23.7 **Avoid unnecessary shifts from *indirect* to *direct discourse* (42.31).**

> Sent.
> 24.1

Tim wondered *whether he would make the team* and *will he get to play much*. (shift from indirect to direct discourse)
Tim wondered *whether he would make the team* and *whether he would get to play much*. (correct—indirect discourse)
Tim wondered, "*Will I make the team? Will I get to play much?*" (correct—direct discourse)

23.8 **Avoid unintentional shifts in style or tone within a sentence or within a larger piece of writing.** Do not shift from formal to informal or from informal to formal.
The process of election affords a moral certainty, that the office of President will never fall to the lot of any man who *doesn't have his act together*. (inappropriate shift from formal to informal style)
The process of election affords a moral certainty, that the office of President will never fall to the lot of any man who *is not in an eminent degree endowed with the requisite qualifications*. —*Alexander Hamilton* (appropriate—formal style used throughout)

Effectiveness

4 Conciseness

24.1 **Conciseness means using only as many words as are necessary to express an idea correctly, clearly, and effectively.**
In *Modern American Usage* Wilson Follett says, "To the trained writer it is second nature to go through his

copy for the removal of every syllable he can do without. Those that skip this stage may know the A and B of composition, but they have yet to arrive at its C."

In sections 16 and 17 you learned the value of the complex sentence for showing the exact relationship between ideas and for indicating their relative importance. But writing made up mostly of dependent clauses is ponderous and wordy. You must learn how to reduce some clauses to phrases. Which clauses should be reduced to phrases? Usually those containing details of time, place, manner, cause, purpose, appearance, and so forth. The main idea should be placed in the independent clause.

Sent. 24.2

24.2 When editing your copy to reduce clauses to phrases, try to eliminate the following expressions, which often cause wordiness: (1) pronouns (personal or relative) and the verb *be* (especially *is, are, was,* and *were*) and (2) *and*'s, *so*'s, *and so*'s, and *and then*'s (between independent clauses). If these words are not necessary for clarity and effectiveness, eliminate them. Observe how this was done in the examples under 24.3–24.6.

24.3 Reduce some clauses to *prepositional phrases* (5.3).
> ~~When we were~~ in *Alsace-Lorraine,* we saw the Rhine River.
> *In Alsace-Lorraine,* we saw the Rhine River. (concise—detail of *place* reduced to prepositional phrase)

24.4 Reduce some clauses to *appositive phrases* (3.24).
> Winston Churchill, ~~who was~~ *prime minister of Great Britain,* led his countrymen to victory in World War II.
> Winston Churchill, *prime minister of Great Britain,* led his countrymen to victory in World War II. (concise—detail of *description* reduced to appositive phrase)

24.5 Reduce some clauses to *participial phrases* (5.7).
> *Tutankhamen's tomb* ~~was~~ *discovered in 1922,* ~~and it~~ still contained most of its treasures.
> Tutankhamen's tomb, *discovered in 1922,* still contained most of its treasures. (concise—detail of *time* reduced to participial phrase)

108

24.6   Reduce some clauses to *infinitive phrases* (5.9).
~~We wanted~~ *to save money,* ~~so~~ we bought an economy
car.
To save money, we bought an economy car. (concise—detail of *purpose* reduced to infinitive
phrase)
▶ Note. For other ways to reduce wordiness, see
section 34.

Emphasis

The most important ideas should receive the most emphasis.
You may achieve emphasis through subordination (section 17),
through conciseness (section 24), and through choice of words
(part 3, especially section 29). You may also achieve emphasis
in the following ways:

**Sent.
25.2**

**25.1   Achieve emphasis by placing the important words at
the beginning or the end of a sentence (or independent clause).** The end of the sentence is probably the
most emphatic position. Words other than the subject
receive emphasis when placed at the beginning of the
sentence. The subject receives emphasis if it is placed
near the end of the sentence. Of course, whenever
possible, details and explanatory phrases should be
placed within the sentence (or independent clause).
Language was the immediate gift of God, *as well as
the faculty of speech.* (unemphatic—parenthetical
phrase has taken the important end position)
Language, *as well as the faculty of speech,* was the
immediate gift of God. —*Noah Webster* (emphatic)
Of course, the Industrial Revolution had far-reaching
effects on society. (nonemphatic—parenthetical
phrase has taken the important beginning position)
The Industrial Revolution, *of course,* had far-
reaching effects on society. (emphatic)

**25.2   Achieve emphasis by making some loose sentences
into periodic sentences.** A *loose* sentence completes its
main thought near the beginning, and adds the details at
the end. A *periodic* sentence withholds the completion
of its main thought until the end or near the end, and

places the details at the beginning. You can readily see that the periodic sentence is effective for building suspense.

Try to achieve a judicious mixture of loose and periodic sentences. Overuse of the periodic sentence will make your writing seem unnatural; overuse of the loose sentence produces monotony.

Observe the difference in effect produced in the following sentence, written first as loose, then as periodic.

> *Different opinions will be formed* as long as the reason of man continues fallible, and he is at liberty to exercise it. (loose)

> As long as the reason of man continues fallible, and he is at liberty to exercise it, *different opinions will be formed.* —*James Madison* (periodic)

Sent. 25.3

The following are examples of loose and periodic sentences from the writings of William Elbert Munsey.

> *Punishment is suffering* inflicted by competent authority upon an evildoer as a satisfaction to justice. (loose)

> It [Hell] *may be a dark and frightful sphere,* isolated from all worlds, cursed of God, erratic and lawless, rolling beyond the confines of creation, with no sun or star to light up its darkness and chase away its infernal vapors, with rivers and oceans of liquid fire, continents of incinerated rock and scattered scoriae, and rent with awful chasms. (loose)

> Tell the young wife, widowed by this terrible war, as she rushes with disheveled tresses amid the promiscuous ditches of the battlefield, crammed with mutilated dead, that her husband will never rise, and *her heart is saddened for life.* (periodic)

> Though your bones may lie bleaching in the bottom of the sea, or fossilized be deeply imbedded in rock; though your dust may be scattered over continents, transmuted into animals or plants, diffused in the air, diffused in the water, or mingled with clay, *God's power is able to raise you from the dead, and is pledged to do it.* (periodic)

25.3 **Achieve emphasis by occasionally using balanced sentences.** Balanced sentences contain two or more parts stated in the same or similar grammatical construction.

The parts usually express a comparison or contrast.

He spake, and it was done; he commanded, and it stood fast. *—Psa. 33:9*

The Sabbath was made for man, and not man for the Sabbath. *—Mk. 2:27*

I do not live to eat; I eat to live. *—Quintilian*

The tongue of the just is as choice silver; the heart of the wicked is little worth. *—Prov. 10:20*

The desire of the righteous is only good, but the expectation of the wicked is wrath. *—Prov. 11:23*

25.4 **Achieve emphasis by occasionally placing words out of their normal order.**

Great is Diana of the Ephesians.

Himself he cannot save.

Silver and gold have I none.

Seldom can they pass without revision.

By the door stood an old walking cane.

Sent. 26.5

25.5 **Achieve emphasis by using the active voice. (See 10.38.)**

26 Variety

26.1 **Vary the grammatical form of sentences.** Make some simple, some compound, some complex. Follow the advice given in sections 16, 17, and 24.

26.2 **Vary the rhetorical form of sentences.** Do not use all declarative sentences. Occasionally use an imperative, interrogative, or exclamatory sentence.

26.3 **Vary the use of suspense.** Use both loose and periodic sentences (25.2).

26.4 **Vary the length of sentences.**

Just after my matriculation in college, I got hold of a volume of sermons by the man William E. Munsey. I had never read anything like these sermons. They stimulated my imagination. They stirred my soul. They did something to me. When I get to Heaven, I am going to thank Dr. Munsey . . . for what he did for me when he wrote and preached those great sermons. *—Bob Jones, Sr.*

26.5 **Vary the beginnings of sentences.** Most of the time you will follow the normal order of English sentences and write the subject first and then the verb. However, if every sentence you write begins with the subject, your style becomes monotonous. To improve this situation, you can move certain modifiers, which usually occur later in the sentence, to the beginning. All sentences cannot and should not be done this way, but if you vary the beginning of some of your sentences, you can greatly improve your writing style.

a. Begin the sentence with an *adverb*.

> *Cautiously,* the policeman edged toward the open door.

b. Begin the sentence with an *adjective*.

> *Short* and *stocky,* Chad was at a disadvantage in basketball games.

c. Begin the sentence with a *participle*.

> *Howling* and *protesting,* Eddie was dragged into the dentist's office.

d. Begin the sentence with a *prepositional phrase*.

> *In Death Valley,* summer temperatures reach 125 °F.

e. Begin the sentence with a *participial phrase*.

> *Sauntering along the trail,* we were unaware of the danger ahead.

f. Begin the sentence with an *infinitive phrase*.

> *To show our appreciation,* we gave her a gift certificate from her favorite store.

g. Begin the sentence with an *adverb clause*.

> *When Uncle Guye returned from Germany,* he showed many interesting slides.

Part 3

Choosing the Right Word

How forcible are right words!

Job 6:25

The knowledge of words is the gate of scholarship.

John Wilson

27 The Dictionary

A dictionary is virtually indispensable for competent speaking, writing, and studying. For this reason, it is important to be aware of the various kinds of dictionaries available. Select a good, reliable dictionary, become familiar with it, and refer to it frequently.

Kinds of Dictionaries

There are specialized dictionaries and general dictionaries. A *specialized dictionary* deals with a particular aspect of language: synonyms and antonyms, pronunciation, slang, idiom, usage, etymology, and so forth. A *general dictionary*—the type that will be explained in this section—gives a wide range of information about words, including most of the things that are separately treated in the specialized dictionaries. Of course, most general dictionaries cannot treat these things in as much detail as the specialized dictionaries.

General dictionaries fall into two broad categories.

Word 27.1

27.1 Unabridged dictionaries. An unabridged dictionary is one that has not been cut down from a larger work. It contains many rare and archaic words as well as most words in common use. An unabridged dictionary contains from 300,000 to 600,000 entries. Because of their bulk and expense, they are normally found only in libraries or other study centers. The following are well-known unabridged dictionaries:

> *The Random House Dictionary of the English Language,* Unabridged
> *The Random House Dictionary of the English Language,* Second Edition Unabridged
> *Webster's New International Dictionary of the English Language,* Second Edition Unabridged
> *Webster's Third New International Dictionary of the English Language,* Unabridged

27.2 College or desk dictionaries. College dictionaries are good all-purpose works, ideal for high school, college, or adult use. They contain about 150,000 carefully selected words. Everyone should have ready access to one of these dictionaries. The following are some well-known college dictionaries:

> *The American Heritage Dictionary*
> *Oxford American Dictionary*

The Random House College Dictionary
Webster's New Collegiate Dictionary (now titled
Merriam Webster's Collegiate Dictionary)

Selecting a Dictionary

Although the dictionaries listed above are comparable in size, price, and general contents, each of them has certain features that the others do not have. Before selecting a dictionary, examine it, keeping in mind the following questions.

27.3 Which special features are important to you? *The Random House College Dictionary* has a list of English given names. *The American Heritage Dictionary* has hundreds of usage notes that reflect the opinions of a distinguished Usage Panel. Are any of these features especially important to you?

27.4 How are the entries listed alphabetically? Some dictionaries conveniently list all entries in a single listing, but others list abbreviations, biographical names, geographical names, and foreign words and phrases in separate sections. Which arrangement do you prefer?

27.5 How are the definitions arranged within each entry? Is the etymology (history of the word) given first, and then the definitions listed in chronological order from oldest to most recent? Or is the etymology given last, and the central and most current meanings given first? Compare the following entries.

> **nice** (nīs) *adj.* **nic′er, nic′est** [ME., strange, lazy, foolish < OFr. *nice, nisce,* stupid, foolish < L. *nescius,* ignorant, not knowing < *nescire,* to be ignorant < *ne-,* not (see NO¹) + *scire,* to know: see SCIENCE] **1.** difficult to please; fastidious; refined **2.** delicate; precise; discriminative; subtle [a *nice* distinction] **3.** calling for great care, accuracy, tact, etc., as in handling or discrimination [a *nice* problem] **4.** *a*) able to make fine or delicate distinctions; delicately skillful; finely discriminating *b*) minutely accurate, as an instrument **5.** having high standards of conduct; scrupulous **6.** *a generalized term of approval meaning variously: a*) agreeable; pleasant; delightful *b*) attractive; pretty *c*) courteous and considerate *d*) conforming to approved social standards; respectable *e*) in good taste *f*) good; excellent **7.** [Obs.] *a*) ignorant; foolish *b*) wanton *c*) coy; shy —*adv.* well, pleasingly, attractively, etc.: variously regarded as substandard, dialectal, or colloquial —*SYN.* see DAINTY —**nice and** [Colloq.] altogether, in a pleasing way [likes his tea *nice and* hot] —**nice′ly** *adv.* —**nice′ness** *n.*

Word
27.5

nice (nīs) *adj.* **nicer, nicest. 1.** Pleasing to the senses; attractive; appealing: *a nice dress.* **2.** Kind; considerate; well-mannered: *a nice person.* **3.** Morally upright; virtuous: *a nice girl, careful of her reputation.* **4.** Showing refinement or delicacy; proper; seemly: *a nice way of putting it.* **5.** Difficult to please; fastidious; exacting: *"Good company requires only birth, education, and manners, and with regard to education is not very nice."* (Jane Austen). **6. a.** Showing or requiring sensitive critical discernment; subtle: *a nice distinction.* **b.** Done with precision and skill; deft: *a nice bit of craftsmanship.* **7.** *Obsolete.* **a.** Wanton; profligate. **b.** Affectedly modest; coy. **c.** Silly. [Middle English, foolish, wanton, shy, from Old French, silly, from Latin *nescius,* ignorant, from *nescīre,* to be ignorant : *ne-,* not (see **ne** in Appendix*) + *scīre,* to know (see **skei-** in Appendix*).] —**nice′ness** *n.*

© 1980 by Houghton Mifflin Company. Reprinted by permission from *The American Heritage Dictionary of the English Language.*

27.6 **Does the dictionary give clear guidance concerning proper usage of words?** If there is a question about the correctness or appropriateness of a particular construction, the users of a dictionary want definite advice about what to do. Unfortunately, some dictionary makers do not want to give definite advice. They think that nothing is **right** or **wrong** in the use of language and simply try to **describe** without judgment how people **are using** the language. They refuse to **prescribe** the correct usage. Therefore, some dictionaries are no help as guides to **correct** usage and are actually destructive of standards. At this time, the following dictionaries fit clearly into this category:

Word 27.6

> *Webster's Third New International Dictionary of the English Language* (Note: The second edition was excellent.)
>
> *Webster's New Collegiate Dictionary* (now titled *Merriam Webster's Collegiate Dictionary*)
>
> *The Random House Dictionary of the English Language,* Second Edition Unabridged (Note: The first edition was acceptable.)

Learning the General Content of Your Dictionary

Select a good dictionary and become familiar with its contents and arrangement.

27.7 **Examine the table of contents.**

27.8 **Find out if the words are listed in a single alphabet.** You may discover that some of the following kinds of entries are listed separately in an appendix: abbreviations, prefixes and suffixes, foreign words and phrases, biographical names, geographical names.

27.9 Study the explanatory notes at the front of your dictionary. These notes explain how to use your particular dictionary. Much of the information given under 27.13–27.30 illustrates the kind of information given in the explanatory notes of most dictionaries.

Using the Dictionary

27.10 Find the word.

a. **Locate the fourth of the dictionary where the word appears.** The dictionary can be divided into four nearly equal parts: a–d, e–l, m–r, s–z. If you can remember these sections, you should be able to open to the fourth of the dictionary where the word is located.

b. **Use the guide words to locate the page on which the word appears.** Guide words are in bold type at the top of each page. The word at the left of the page is the first entry word to appear on that page; the word at the right of the page is the last entry to appear on that page. If the word you are looking for comes alphabetically between the two guide words, it will be on that page.

Word
27.12

c. **Find the word in its alphabetical order on the page.** All entries are listed letter by letter in strict alphabetical order, including compound words and phrases. Compound words and phrases, whether hyphenated or open, are considered as if they were written solid.

27.11 Find the definition.

a. **Look for the part of speech label.** If you know the part of speech of the word as used in your sentence, you will not need to look through all the definitions. Look only at the definitions under the relevant part of speech.

b. **Skim all the definitions under the relevant part of speech.**

c. **Find the definition that fits the context of your sentence.**

27.12 Check for a restrictive label or a usage note. If there is a restrictive label or usage note given for the definition you have selected, consider what the label or note is telling you and use good judgment in employing the word. If there is no restrictive label or usage note, the expression is considered standard English. Of course, here we are assuming that you are using a dictionary that gives clear guidance concerning correct usage. (See under 27.6.)

  a. **Avoid nonstandard and substandard words and usages.**

  b. **Avoid vulgar words.**

  c. **Avoid slang in nonfiction writing and in most speech.**

  d. **Use words with geographical or field labels only when suitable to the audience.**

  e. **Avoid archaic, obsolete, or rare words unless there is some special purpose for using them.**

  f. **Avoid informal or colloquial words in formal writing and speaking.** Words labeled informal or colloquial are not to be considered incorrect if used in informal writing or conversation. Such expressions are acceptable in most friendly letters, some business letters, familiar essays, informal speeches, and nonserious books and periodicals.

Word 27.13

The Kinds of Information Given for Entries

27.13 **The entry word.** The *entry word* is the word or phrase to be defined. It is printed in boldface type and set slightly to the left of the information column. All entries—including abbreviations, prefixes and suffixes, phrases, and compounds—are listed in strict alphabetical order. The phrases and compounds are alphabetized as if they were written solid with no spaces between the words.

27.14 **Variant spellings.** Some words have more than one spelling. The first spelling listed is usually the preferred spelling. If the variant form is almost as acceptable as the first spelling, the two forms are separated by a comma or by the word *or*. If the first spelling is definitely preferred, the word *also* will precede the variant spelling.

> **e·soph·a·gus** (i sof′ ə gəs, ē sof′-) *n., pl.* **-gi** (-jī′). *Anat., Zool.* a tube connecting the mouth or pharynx with the stomach gullet. Also, **oesophagus.** [< NL *oesophágus* < Gk *oisophágos* gullet, lit., channel for eating (*oiso-,* akin to *oísein,* fut. inf. of *phérein* to carry + *-phagos* -PHAGE); r. ME *ysophagus* < ML]

> Reprinted by permission from *The Random House College Dictionary,* Revised Edition. Copyright © 1980, 1979, 1975 by Random House, Inc.

27.15 Capitalization. Proper names and proper adjectives are entered with a capital letter. If a word is a proper noun in one or more senses and a common noun in one or more senses, the dictionary will indicate the capitalization for each sense.

> **an·ti·christ** (an′ti krīst′; *see* ANTI-) *n.* [ME. *anticrist* < OFr. *antecrist* < LL. *antichristus* < Gr. *antichristos* < *anti-*, against + *Christos,* Christ] **1.** an opponent of or disbeliever in Christ **2.** [A-] *Bible* the great antagonist of Christ, expected to spread universal evil before the end of the world but finally to be conquered at Christ's second coming: I John 2:18 **3.** a false Christ

27.16 Pronunciation. The pronunciation is usually printed within parentheses immediately after the entry word. The pronunciation is a special respelling of the word that indicates how the word is pronounced. Different dictionaries use different systems of indicating pronunciation. Study the pronunciation key for your dictionary so that you will be able to recognize the pronunciation symbols and use them effectively. The complete pronunciation key is usually near the front of the dictionary with the most common symbols repeated at the foot of each pair of facing pages throughout the dictionary.

Many dictionaries use the same symbols for vowel and consonant sounds, syllabication, and accent. These symbols include *letters* that represent basic sounds and *diacritical marks* that distinguish the sounds of letters of the same form. Some basic diacritical marks are the breve, the macron, and the dieresis.

a. Symbols for vowel sounds.

(1) The breve (˘) indicates a short vowel sound as in cŭp.

(2) The macron (¯) indicates a long vowel sound as in fāte.

(3) The dieresis (¨) indicates a broad vowel sound as in cälm.

(4) The schwa (ə) is used for any unaccented vowel and generally has an "uh" sound as in around (ə·round′).

119

Although the vowel represented by a schwa tends to have an "uh" sound, the sound actually varies according to the vowel being represented and according to adjoining sounds. The use of the schwa does not mean that the original vowel sound is completely obscured: precise speakers pronounce these unaccented vowels so that their original sounds are still recognizable.

The following chart illustrates how common vowel sounds are indicated in many modern dictionaries.

Key Word	Common Symbols	Respelling
pat	ă or a	păt or pat
pet	ĕ or e	pĕt or pet
pit	ĭ or i	pĭt or pit
pot	ŏ or o	pŏt or pot
cut	ŭ or u	kŭt or kut
took	o͞o or oo	to͝ok or took
pay	ā	pā
bee	ē	bē
pie	ī	pī
toe	ō	tō
boot	o͞o	bo͞ot
father	ä	fä′thər
about, item		ə-bout′, i′təm
edible, gallop	ə	ĕd′ə-bəl, găl′əp
focus		fō′kəs

b. **Symbols for consonant sounds.** Most consonant sounds are indicated by the consonant itself; for example, *k* always represents *k, d* always represents *d,* etc. But some consonants have different sounds and must be indicated in some other way. The following chart shows some consonants that must be indicated with other symbols.

Key Word	Common Symbols	Respelling
cat	k	kăt
cereal	s	sîr′ē-əl
phosphorus	f	fŏs′fər-əs
gem, judge	j	jĕm, jŭj
nation, sure	sh	nā′shən, sho͝or
vision, usual	zh	vĭzh′ən, yo͞o′ zho͞o-əl

Word 27.16

c. Syllabication and accent. The respelling of the entry word is divided into syllables by leaving spaces between syllables or by putting dashes between the syllables. Syllables that should be pronounced more strongly than the others are indicated by the stress marks (accent marks). Dictionaries differ in their methods of indicating the syllable to be stressed. Most dictionaries use a bold mark ($'$) *after* a syllable to indicate primary stress, and a light mark ($'$) *after* a syllable to indicate secondary stress. A syllable that has no stress mark is unstressed.

> **in·com·mu·ni·ca·ble** (in′ kə·myoo′ni·kə·bəl) *adj.* **1.** Incapable of being communicated. **2.** *Obs.* Incommunicative. —**in′com·mu′ni·ca·bil′i·ty** *n.*
>
> From *Funk & Wagnalls Standard College Dictionary* by Funk and Wagnalls. Copyright © 1977 by Harper & Row, Publishers, Inc. Reprinted by permission of HarperCollins Publishers, Inc.

27.17 Parts of speech labels. The traditional parts of speech are used to label words. The following abbreviations are commonly used: *n.* (noun), *v.* or *vb.* (verb), *pron.* (pronoun), *adj.* (adjective), *adv.* (adverb), *prep.* (preposition), *conj.* (conjunction), and *interj.* (interjection).

In addition, the labels *v.t.* or *trans.* are used to indicate a transitive verb, and *v.i.* or *intr.* to indicate an intransitive verb. Also the label *pl.n.* is used to indicate nouns used only in the plural.

Word 27.18

27.18 Inflected forms. An inflection is a change in the form of the entry word to indicate different grammatical relationships. Many verbs, adjectives, adverbs, and nouns have inflectional forms listed near the beginning of the entry.

a. Principal parts of verbs. Some dictionaries list the principal parts of all verbs, regular and irregular. Others list the principal parts of irregular verbs and of any other verb that may present difficulty of spelling. The forms are listed in the following order: *past tense, past participle* (if different from the past tense), and *present participle.* The *American Heritage Dictionary* also lists the third person singular present tense.

> **drive** (drīv) *v.* **drove** (drōv) or *archaic* **drave** (drāv), **driven** (drĭv′ən), **driving, drives.** —*tr.* **1.** To push, propel, or press onward forcibly; urge forward.
>
> © 1980 by Houghton Mifflin Company. Reprinted by permission from *The American Heritage Dictionary of the English Language.*

b. Comparison of adjectives and adverbs. The comparative and superlative forms of adjectives and adverbs are given if irregular (good, *better, best;* ill, *worse, worst,* etc.) and often if they are formed by adding *-er* and *-est.*

> **lone·ly** (lōn′lē) *adj.* ·**li·er,** ·**li·est** **1.** Unfrequented by human beings; deserted; desolate. **2.** Sad from lack of companionship or sympathy; lonesome.
>
> From *Funk & Wagnalls Standard College Dictionary* by Funk and Wagnalls. Copyright © 1977 by Harper & Row, Publishers, Inc. Reprinted by permission of HarperCollins Publishers, Inc.

In most dictionaries the *-er, -est* forms are not shown if there is no modification of spelling when the suffix is added.

> **long**[1] (lông, long) *adj.* **1.** Characterized by or denoting extent, dimension, or measurement relatively great in proportion to breadth or width; not short.
>
> From *Funk & Wagnalls Standard College Dictionary* by Funk and Wagnalls. Copyright © 1977 by Harper & Row, Publishers, Inc. Reprinted by permission of HarperCollins Publishers, Inc.

A few dictionaries list all *-er* and *-est* forms, whether or not there is a modification of spelling. Check the introductory matter in your dictionary.

Word 27.18

> **nar·row** (năr′ō) *adj.* **-rower, -rowest. 1.** Of small or limited width, especially in comparison with length. **2.** Limited in area or scope; lacking space or room; cramped.
>
> © 1980 by Houghton Mifflin Company. Reprinted by permission from *The American Heritage Dictionary of the English Language.*

Comparative and superlative forms are not given when formed by adding *more* and *most* before the word.

c. Plurals of nouns. The plural spelling is given for any word that does not form its plural by simply adding *-s* or *-es* to the singular. The plural spelling is also given for those nouns that present a special problem.

> **mouth·ful** (mouth′fool′), *n., pl.* **-fuls. 1.** as much as a mouth can hold. **2.** as much as is taken into the mouth at one time. **3.** a small quantity.
>
> Reprinted by permission from *The Random House College Dictionary,* Revised Edition. Copyright © 1980, 1979, 1975 by Random House, Inc.

Notes are given for words that are always plural in form to explain whether a plural verb or a singular verb should be used with them.

☆**civ·ics** (siv′iks) *n. pl.* [*with sing. v.*] the branch of political science that deals with civic affairs and the duties and rights of citizenship

27.19 **Definitions.** Definitions are given in a definite order. They may be listed with the central and most current meaning first, or they may be listed in historical order or in order of frequency of use.

In entries with more than one definition, the definitions are numbered in separate sequences beginning with 1 for each part of speech. Some dictionaries number the entries consecutively without regard to part of speech, but they still indicate the part of speech.

If a numbered definition has two or more meanings that are closely related, the meanings are indicated by lower-case letters, **a, b, c,** etc.

Words that are spelled identically but are of different origins and thus have distinctly unrelated meanings are listed as separate main entries and are followed by a super-script number.

Word 27.20

grab[1] (grab) *v.* **grabbed, grab·bing** *v.t.* **1.** To grasp or seize suddenly or forcibly. **2.** To take possession of by force or by dishonest means. **3.** *Informal* To get hurriedly, in what little time is available: Let's *grab* a bite before the show. — *v.i.* **4.** To make a sudden grasp. — **Syn.** See GRASP. — *n.* **1.** The act of grabbing. **2.** That which is grabbed. **3.** A dishonest or unlawful acquisition. **4.** A mechanical apparatus used to grasp and lift heavy objects. [Cf. MDu. *grabben* to grip] — **grab′ber** *n.*

grab[2] (grab) *n.* A coasting vessel of the East Indies, having two or three masts and triangular sails. [< Arabic *ghurāb*]

27.20 **Restrictive labels.** Good dictionaries consistently attach warning labels to words that have limitations of usage. These labels help one determine whether a word is correct and appropriate to use and under what circumstances. Four kinds of labels are commonly used.

a. Field labels: *Philosophy, Technology, Chemistry, Architecture, Grammar, Sports,* etc.

b. Geographical labels: *Regional, Dialect, Southwestern U.S., New England, British, Scottish, Canadian,* etc.

c. Time labels: *Obsolete, Archaic, Rare*

d. Usage labels: *Nonstandard, Substandard, Informal, Colloquial, Slang, Vulgar,* etc.

> **skunk** (skungk), *n., pl.* **skunks,** *(esp. collectively)* **skunk,** *v.* —*n.* **1.** a small, black, North American mammal, *Mephitis mephitis,* of the weasel family, having a longitudinal, white, V-shaped stripe on the back, and ejecting a fetid odor when alarmed or attacked. **2.** *Informal.* a thoroughly contemptible person. —*v.t.* **3.** *U.S. Slang.* to defeat thoroughly in a game. [< Algonquian; cf. Abnaki *segankw, segonkw*]
>
> Reprinted by permission from *The Random House College Dictionary,* Revised Edition. Copyright © 1980, 1979, 1975 by Random House, Inc.

27.21 Scientific names for plants and animals. All plants and animals have been classified in accordance with the international codes of zoological and botanical nomenclature. These names are set in italics within the definition.

> **grape·fruit** (-frōōt′) *n.* [so named because it grows in clusters] **1.** a large, round, edible citrus fruit with a pale-yellow rind, juicy pulp, and a somewhat sour taste **2.** the semitropical evergreen tree (*Citrus paradisi*) of the rue family, that bears grapefruit
>
> Reprinted with permission of Macmillan General Reference, a Division of Simon & Schuster Inc., from *Webster's New World Dictionary,* Second College Edition. Copyright © 1970, 1972, 1974, 1976, 1978, 1979, 1980, 1982, 1984, 1986 by Simon & Schuster Inc.

27.22 Cross references. These references lead you to further information that will help you better understand the entry word. The words being referred to are set in SMALL CAPITALS or in **boldface type** and are often accompanied by words like *see, compare* (cf.), *same as, variant of,* etc.

> **liv·er·leaf** (liv′ər-lēf′) *n.* A plant, the **hepatica** *(see).*
>
> © 1980 by Houghton Mifflin Company. Reprinted by permission from *The American Heritage Dictionary of the English Language.*

27.23 Sample contexts. A sample context is a sentence or a part of a sentence given to clarify a definition, to help distinguish similar meanings, and to illustrate the level of usage.

> **es·sen·tial** (ə sen′shəl), *adj.* **1.** absolutely necessary; in-dispensable: *Discipline is essential in an army.* **2.** pertaining to or constituting the essence of a thing. **3.** noting or containing an essence of a plant, drug, etc. **4.** being such by its very nature or in the highest sense; natural; spontaneous: *essential happiness.* —*n.* **5.** a basic, indispensable, or necessary element; chief point. [ME *essenciāl* < ML *essencial(is)* for LL *essentiālis.* See ESSENCE, -AL¹] —**es·sen′tial·ly,** *adv.*
>
> Reprinted by permission from *The Random House College Dictionary,* Revised Edition. Copyright © 1980, 1979, 1975 by Random House, Inc.

27.24 Illustrations. These are photographs or drawings given to clarify a definition.

27.25 Idioms. An idiom is an expression whose meaning cannot be derived from the individual words in the expression. For example: "We must keep a tight rein on our finances." Since idioms are listed under the key word in the expression, you will probably find *keep a tight rein on* under the word *rein.*

> **rein** (rān) *n.* **1.** *Usually plural.* A long, narrow leather strap attached to the bit of a bridle and used by a rider or driver to control a horse or other animal. See **harness. 2.** Any means of restraint, check, or guidance. —**draw in the reins. 1.** To exert pressure on the reins. **2.** To slow or stop. —**give (free) rein to.** To release from restraints. —**keep a (tight) rein on.** To exercise close control over. —*v.* **reined, reining, reins.** —*tr.* **1.** To check or hold back. **2.** To guide or control. **3.** To equip with reins. —*intr.* To control a horse or other animal with reins. Often used with *in* or *up.* [Middle English *re(i)ne,* from Old French *re(s)ne,* from Vulgar Latin *retina* (unattested), from Latin *retinēre,* to RETAIN.]
>
> © 1980 by Houghton Mifflin Company. Reprinted by permission from *The American Heritage Dictionary of the English Language.*

27.26 Etymologies. An etymology gives the origin and history of a word. The information is enclosed within brackets at the beginning or at the end of the entry.

> **liv·id** (lĭv′ĭd) *adj.* **1.** Having discoloration of the skin, as from a bruise. **2.** Ashen or pallid, as with anger, rage, or illness. **3.** Extremely angry; furious. [French *livide,* from Latin *līvidus,* from *līvēre,* to be bluish. See **slī-** in Appendix.*] —**li·vid′i·ty, liv′id·ness** *n.* —**liv′id·ly** *adv.*
>
> © 1980 by Houghton Mifflin Company. Reprinted by permission from *The American Heritage Dictionary of the English Language.*

Word 27.27

27.27 Run-on entries. Run-on entries are words formed from the entry word by the addition of a suffix. The meaning remains basically the same, but the grammatical functions are different. The meaning can be easily understood from the meaning of the entry word plus the meaning of the suffix. For example, under the word *quiet,* you will find the run-ons *quietly* adv. and *quietness* n. Because the suffix *-ly* means "in a specified manner," *quietly* means "in a quiet manner." Because the suffix *-ness* means "a state or condition of being," *quietness* means "in a state or condition of being quiet." If you do not know the meaning of a suffix, you can look it up in its alphabetical place in the dictionary.

> **log·i·cal** (loj′i kəl), *adj.* **1.** according to or agreeing with the principles of logic. **2.** reasoning in accordance with the principles of logic. **3.** reasonable; reasonably to be expected: *the logical consequence of his actions.* **4.** of or pertaining to logic. [< ML *logicāl(is)*] —**log·i·cal·i·ty** (loj′i kal′i tē). **log′i·cal·ness,** *n.* —**log′i·cal·ly,** *adv.*
>
> Reprinted by permission from *The Random House College Dictionary,* Revised Edition. Copyright © 1980, 1979, 1975 by Random House, Inc.

27.28 **Synonyms.** Synonyms (words similar in meaning) are often distinguished in a paragraph at the end of an entry. These words provide important distinctions that are valuable for the precise use of words.

> **in·ten·si·fy** (-fī′) *vt.* **-fied′, -fy′ing** **1.** to make intense or more intense; increase; strengthen **2.** *Photog.* to make (a film, etc.) more dense or opaque by treating with an intensifier —*vi.* to become intense or increase in intensity —**in·ten′si·fi·ca′tion** *n.*
> **SYN.**—**intensify** implies an increasing in the degree of force, vehemence, vividness, etc. *[his absence only intensified her longing]*; **aggravate** implies a making more serious, unbearable, etc. and connotes something that is unpleasant or troublesome in itself *[your insolence only aggravates the offense]*; to **heighten** is to make greater, stronger, more vivid, etc. so as to raise above the ordinary or commonplace *[music served to heighten the effect]*; **enhance** implies the addition of something so as to make more attractive or desirable *[she used cosmetics to enhance her beauty]*

27.29 **Usage notes.** In addition to usage labels, many dictionaries have usage notes at the end of some entries. These notes are very helpful in explaining the current status of words and in illustrating their proper use.

Word 27.28

> **a·ble** (ā′bəl) *adj.* **abler, ablest. 1.** Having sufficient ability or resources. **2.** Especially capable or talented. [Middle English, from Old French, from Latin *habilis,* manageable, apt, expert, from *habēre,* to hold, handle. See **ghabh-** in Appendix.*]
> *Usage: Able* is regularly followed by an infinitive in the active voice *(able to hear),* but not in the passive. Thus, *he could be heard* (not *was able to be heard).*

27.30 **Encyclopedic information.** Most dictionaries give brief biographical, geographical, Biblical, and mythological information. Some dictionaries list encyclopedic entries with all other entries in a single alphabet. Others list such information in separate sections at the back of the dictionary.

> **Lom·bard** (lom′bərd, -bärd, lum′-) *n.* **1.** One of a Germanic tribe that established a kingdom in northern Italy in the sixth century: also called *Langobard, Longobard.* **2.** A native or inhabitant of Lombardy. [< OF < Ital. *Lombardo* < LL *Longobardus,* ? < OHG *lang* long + *bart* beard] — **Lom·bar′dic** *adj.*
> **Lom·bard** (lom′bärd, -bərd, lum′-), Peter, 1100?–60?, Italian theologian. Also called **Peter the Lombard, Pe·trus Lom·bar·dus** (pe′trəs lom-bär′dəs).

28 Appropriateness

28.1 **There are three levels of usage:** *standard formal, standard informal* **(colloquial), and** *substandard* **(nonstandard).** The level you choose depends upon your purpose for writing.

28.2 *Standard formal* **English is the most correct, most highly polished form of written English.** Your nonfictional writing should, as a rule, incorporate formal usage. Here are some examples of formal usage:

> I shall accept his invitation.
> The apartments have not yet been completed.
> Mr. Potter shall return momentarily.
> Those illustrations are indeed fascinating.

▶ Note. Contractions are not used in formal writing.

28.3 *Standard informal* **(or colloquial) English is the language of everyday speech.** It is used to give writing or speaking a friendly, familiar tone. Here are some examples of informal usage:

> I'm going to accept his invitation.
> They haven't finished building those apartments yet.
> Mr. Potter's coming back real soon.
> Those pictures are terrific.

28.4 *Substandard* **(or nonstandard) English is the language of the uneducated.** It is filled with grammatical errors and slang (28.7). You should avoid substandard usage in your conversation, and the only time you should use it in writing is to depict the conversation of uneducated characters in a work of fiction. Here are some examples of substandard usage:

> I'm gonna accept his invite.
> Them apartments ain't done yet.
> That Potter dude'll be back in a sec.
> Them pictures is real cool.

Word
28.4

127

28.5 **Use a good dictionary (see 27.6) to insure that the words you are using are acceptable in standard formal usage.** Words without a usage label or usage note are considered standard. Notice from this entry that *mad* meaning "insane" has no label or note and therefore may be considered standard formal English. When *mad* is used to mean "angry," however, it is labeled *Informal* and would be out of place in formal writing.

> **mad** (mad) *adj.* **mad·der, mad·dest 1.** Suffering from or manifesting severe mental disorder; insane; lunatic; psychotic. **2.** *Chiefly U.S. Informal* Feeling or showing anger; angry. **3.** Going beyond the bounds of reason. decorum.
>
> From *Funk & Wagnalls Standard College Dictionary* by Funk and Wagnalls. Copyright © 1977 by Harper & Row, Publishers, Inc. Reprinted by permission of HarperCollins Publishers, Inc.

28.6 **Choose a level of usage that is appropriate to your purpose in writing.** Standard formal English is used in the most formal and serious contexts: official declarations, petitions, business letters, letters of condolence, serious essays and books, and any learned writing. Standard informal English is used to create a friendly, conversational tone and is appropriate for friendly letters, familiar essays, humorous writings, and other informal contexts. Make sure the style is appropriate to the occasion: using informal language in a formal context makes your writing seem folksy and undignified; whereas using formal language in an informal context can make your writing sound pompous and stuffy.

Word
28.6

28.7 **Avoid *slang* in standard usage.** *Slang* is a language that consists of coined (made-up) words and standard words used to mean something other than their standard definitions. Slang can be witty and can create an especially vivid mental image. Slang should not be used in standard English for several reasons: (1) it is often crude; (2) it usually becomes trite (see section 33) through overuse; (3) its meaning is not always understood by all readers; and (4) most slang expressions quickly disappear from the language. Occasionally a particularly useful slang term will become a permanent part of the language (for example, *mob* started out as slang but is now standard). But until a slang word does become standard, it should be omitted from your writing. The following are some examples of slang:

kill time (to waste time or shirk one's duties)
He saw a shrink. (He saw a psychiatrist.)
Get lost! (Go away!)
cool (first-rate, excellent)
cop-out (a failure to commit oneself)
Get real! (Be serious.)

28.8 Avoid *illiteracies* in writing or speaking. *Illiteracies* include grammatical errors, misspellings, mispronunciations, and other substandard usages.

don't want no (do not want any)
I ain't going nowheres tonight. (I am not going anywhere tonight.)
Irregardless of what he said, that law has done been repealed. (Regardless of what he said, that law has already been repealed.)

28.9 Use **General American diction in most writing.** Do not use forms that are used only in certain sections of the country (*dialectal* forms); your vocabulary and syntax should be intelligible to any reader in any section of the country.

Word
28.10

| Dialectal: | The *emmets* ruined our picnic. |
| General American: | The *ants* ruined our picnic. |

| Dialectal: | What do you have in that *poke?* |
| General American: | What do you have in that *bag?* |

| Dialectal: | After dinner we sat on the *gallery.* |
| General American: | After dinner we sat on the *porch.* |

28.10 Exercise good judgment in using foreign words and phrases. Remember that you are writing in English. Your purpose is to communicate, not to confuse the reader or impress him with your knowledge. A few foreign expressions have gained wide acceptance in English usage, but they should still be used sparingly. Prefer the English equivalent.

Poor: Mark Twain was Samuel Clemens's *nom de plume.* (It would be better to save the reader some trouble and simply say "Mark Twain was Samuel Clemens's pen name.")

129

Acceptable: The military leaders staged a *coup d'etat.*
(This is a brief and effective way of saying
"The military leaders staged a sudden and
forcible overthrow of the existing government.")

28.11 Avoid words that are no longer commonly used.

a. Obsolete words and meanings. These have completely passed out of current usage.

Obsolete words: *ort* (for *morsel of food*), *egal* (for
equal), *eftersoons* (for *soon after*),
yestereen (for *last night*)

Obsolete meanings: *girl* (to mean a child of either sex),
town (to mean a small garden),
deer (to mean any small animal)

b. Archaic words. These are outdated forms used only
.rarely in modern English. They occur most often in
Biblical language.

thou (for *you*), *hast* (for *have*), *mayest* (for *may*),
thine (for *yours*)

c. Poetic words. These words are still occasionally used
in poetry but should not be used in prose.

oft (for *often*), *'tween* (for *between*), *'twill* (for *it will*)

Word
28.11

29 Exactness and Vividness

29.1 Avoid improprieties in writing or speaking. Improprieties are standard words used incorrectly.

They were *mighty* proud of their trophy. (adjective
used as adverb—should be *especially* proud)

He *authored* a book. (noun used as a verb—should
be *wrote*)

The mayor met with some members of the city *counsel.* (wrong word—should be *council*)

Improprieties often occur when a word is confused with
another word similar to it. Following is a list of words
which are often confused. (See also section 35, the Glossary of Diction.)

advice, advise
altar, alter

alumnus, alumna
alumni, alumnae
capital, capitol
cite, site
compliment, complement
dyeing, dying
emigrate, immigrate
hoard, horde
illusion, allusion
imminent, eminent
loose, lose
principal, principle
role, roll

29.2 **Make skillful use of *connotations.*** The *denotation* of a
word is its strict dictionary definition. The *connotation* of
a word goes beyond its strict meaning to the feelings and
images that the word suggests. For example, the denota-
tive meaning of *democracy* is "a government in which the
people hold the ruling power." But *democracy* also connotes America, the heritage of freedom, the Declaration of
Independence, the Bill of Rights—all the things suggested
by the word *democracy.* Skillfully using the connotations
of words can cause your writing to have a powerful effect
upon your readers. However, make sure that your word
does not carry with it a connotation which you do not
desire.

Word
29.3

    Mr. Parks is a *timid* man.
    Mr. Parks is a *pusillanimous* man.

Both words show that Mr. Parks is shy and nonaggressive.
But the second word connotes that he is shy because he is a
coward. Therefore, the first word is neutral; whereas the
second word has a definite negative connotation. When
choosing a word, you must consider both the denotation
and the connotation of the word.

29.3 **Choose exact and vivid *verbs* and *nouns* to make your
writing interesting and forceful.**

    **a. Choose verbs with action and color to create mental
    pictures in the reader's mind.** Notice the following
    sentence: The stream *flowed.* The verb *flowed* is a
    general word that does not show any specific action.

Observe how the mental pictures change when exact verbs are substituted for the word *flowed.*

The stream *gushed.*
The stream *swirled.*
The stream *splashed.*
The stream *gurgled.*
The stream *meandered.*
The stream *trickled.*

b. Wherever possible, use exact and vivid verbs instead of verb-adverb combinations.

The dog *lay carelessly* on the floor. (verb-adverb combination)
The dog *sprawled* on the floor. (exact and vivid verb)
He *ran quickly* from the room. (verb-adverb combination)
He *dashed* from the room. (exact and vivid verb)

c. Learn to select specific nouns rather than general nouns. In the following examples, notice the progression from general to specific.

game, fowl, quail, bobwhite
lumber, hardwood, tropical hardwood, mahogany
food, meat, beef, sirloin

d. Learn to look up synonyms for nouns. Use a dictionary of synonyms to determine the noun that will express your meaning exactly. Do not write *hurricane* if you mean *waterspout, haze* if you mean *smog, obstacle* if you mean *snag,* or *dream* if you mean *nightmare.*

29.4 Use exact and vivid modifiers to enhance the verbs and nouns you have chosen. Adjectives and adverbs, no matter how vivid, can never make up for poorly chosen verbs and nouns; but they are often necessary for preciseness in description and for subtle shades of meaning.

a. Carefully select the exact adjective needed to express your idea. The following words are synonyms, but notice the slight differences in meaning.

witty—amusingly clever in perception and expression
facetious—clumsy or inappropriate in attempted humor
jocular—sustaining a jolly mood to keep others amused

Word
29.4

b. Make good use of participles. They make especially colorful adjectives.

The sound of the *crackling* fire and the smell of the *bubbling* stew lifted the spirits of the cold and weary hunters.

c. Be sparing in the use of adjectives.

We listened with delight to the *sweet, pleasant, agreeable* tones of the harp. (poor)

We listened with delight to the *dulcet* tones of the harp. (better)

d. Use the most *vivid* adverbs you can find. Adverbs that end in *-ly* are usually the most vivid.

foolishly, benignly, menacingly, agilely, fastidiously, jealously

e. Carefully select the *exact* adverb needed to express your idea. For example, the word *slowly* is a general word. Notice the following synonyms that will express the same idea more exactly:

leisurely, deliberately, gradually, reluctantly, hesitantly, sluggishly

Word
30.1

f. The adverbs *very* and *really* are greatly overused. As often as possible, substitute such synonyms as *decidedly, extremely, exceedingly, incomparably, indeed, actually, especially, particularly, notably, strikingly.*

30 Figurative Language

30.1 **Use *figures of speech* to make your writing vivid.** Figures of speech make your writing more vivid and concrete because they create a specific image in the reader's mind. The following are four commonly used figures of speech.

a. Simile—a comparison using the words *like* or *as.* The simile is used to bring an object into sharp focus in the reader's mind by comparing the object to something with which the reader is familiar.

The old prizefighter looked *like* a mass of granite.

His word was in my heart *as* a burning fire shut up in my bones.

133

And custom lie upon thee with a weight
Heavy *as* frost, and deep almost *as* life. —*Burns*

b. **Metaphor**—an implied comparison, one that does not
use *like* or *as*. The metaphor is stronger and more direct
than the simile.

The old prizefighter was a mass of granite.

Jeremiah said that the Word of God was a fire shut up
in his bones.

I am a little world made cunningly. —*Donne*

All the world's a stage,
And all the men and women merely players.

—*Shakespeare*

c. **Hyperbole**—A statement which conveys its meaning
through strong exaggeration.

Were the whole realm of nature mine, that were a
present far too small. —*Watts*

I, for one, don't expect till I die to be so good a man
as I am at this minute, for just now I'm fifty thousand feet high—a tower with all the trumpets
shouting. —*G. K. Chesterton*

d. **Personification**—giving human characteristics to
inanimate objects.

Death, thou shalt die! —*Donne*

The wind stood up and gave a shout.
He whistled on his fingers and
Kicked the withered leaves about
And thumped the branches with his hand.

—*James Stephens*

30.2 Be cautious in your use of *figures of speech.*

a. **Make sure that the image is clear.** A careless writer
will produce images that are vague and hard to understand. For example, "Her eyes were like prisms at the
bottom of a crystal bowl" brings to mind no particular
image.

b. **Do not overuse figures of speech.** It is not necessary
to compare everything to something else. Note how
ridiculous this sounds:

**Word
30.2**

As the fire danced like a thousand tiny sprites, we sat huddled like Eskimos and tried to shield off the wind, which whooped like an angry warrior.

c. Avoid mixed metaphors. A mixed metaphor starts out comparing an object to one thing and ends up comparing it to something else. The result is a fuzzy, distorted comparison which is more ludicrous than poetic:

His pen was a sword which he dipped into the inkwell of truth. [Swords are not dipped in inkwells.]

Another example of a mixed metaphor comes from Shakespeare's *Hamlet.* In his famous soliloquy, Hamlet says, "to take arms against a sea of troubles," which mixes a soldier image ("to take arms") with a sea image ("a sea of troubles"). The image is not consistent because soldiers do not ordinarily draw their swords against the waves of the sea.

d. Avoid trite figures of speech. "Eyes like stars," "wise as an owl," "white as snow"—these rob your writing of freshness and vitality. If you cannot think of an original comparison, perhaps it would be best not to use a figure of speech at all. Otherwise, you run the risk of boring your reader.

Word 31.1

31 Idioms

An idiom is an expression which is peculiar to a language and which cannot be easily explained or analyzed. For example, we can use "Good evening" as a greeting, but not "Good night." We can say "He is hard of hearing," but not "He is hard of seeing."

Often the meaning of an idiomatic expression cannot be derived from the individual words in the expression. The phrase "to catch one's eye" does not actually mean "to catch one's eye," but rather "to capture one's attention."

Idioms make up a large part of our language and add color and vigor to our writing, but we must be careful to use idioms accurately and appropriately.

31.1   Use correct idiomatic English. Native speakers ordinarily have little trouble using idioms correctly, especially if they grow up around those who use the language properly.

135

Perhaps the most common mistake is the use of the wrong preposition after certain verbs, adjectives, and nouns (for example, "The powder *adhered with* the surface" instead of "The powder *adhered to* the surface.") The following is a list of commonly misused idioms.

accuse *of* (not *with*)	essential *to* (not *for*)
adept *in* (not *at*)	independent *of* (not *from*)
averse *to* (not *at*)	listen *to* (not *at*)
avail oneself *of* (not *to* or *with*)	plan *to* work (not *on* working)
charge *with* (not *for*) a crime	prefer one *to* (not *over*) another
comply *with* (not *to*)	prohibit *from doing* (not *to do*)
desirous *of* (not *to*)	
different *from* (not *than* or *to*)	sensible *of* (not *for*)
dissent *from* (not *with*)	superior *to* (not *than*)
enamored *of* (not *about*)	unequal *to* (not *for*)
	vie *with* (not *against*)

31.2   Use effective and appropriate idioms.

Word
31.2

a. Avoid wordy idiomatic expressions if a more concise expression can be used without sacrificing effectiveness (for example, "suddenly" may be used instead of "all of a sudden" and "tolerate" instead of "put up with").

b. Avoid idiomatic expressions that smack of triteness, (for example, "put one's foot in one's mouth" and "raining cats and dogs"). (See section 33.)

c. Avoid idioms that are not appropriate to your purpose for writing. Some idioms are colloquial, dialectal, slang, or illiterate. Check a dictionary to determine the level of usage of a particular expression. (See 27.25.)

32   Jargon and Gobbledygook

32.1   Do not use *jargon* in your writing. Technical terms are necessary when one is writing in fields such as science, business, and government. The precise use of technical terms can help communicate an idea quickly and effectively. Even in writing intended for a general audience, experts may occasionally use technical terms (along with a brief definition) and still convey their thoughts clearly. But some experts—and would-be experts—do not seem as interested in communicating their ideas as they are in impressing the readers with their own knowledge. Sometimes it seems that they use obscure terminology to appear scholarly when actually they themselves do not understand what they are writing about. These are the people who produce *jargon,* an unintelligible and ungraceful style of writing. The following are typical examples of jargon. Notice how simple ideas have been needlessly complicated.

> routine, limited-duration, reinforced, protective-reaction air strikes (translation: bombing missions)
> combat emplacement excavator (translation: shovel)
> pupil stations (translation: desks)
> viable role models (translation: heroes)
> human interment space (translation: cemetery)

The following is an example of jargon from a well-known English journal. Having evidently rejected the reasonable explanation that God created man and gave him language, the writer uses jargon to lend a scholarly air to his silly assumption that language originated by evolution.

Word 32.2

> "Early humans, competing for daytime niches without the advantage of a sensitive olfactory system, required faster information, adapted to their needs, about their environment. The human language system is a response to that requirement."

The best way to avoid jargon is to keep your writing simple. Do not use a high-sounding word when a simpler word would do the job. If you find you must use technical terms, be careful to use them correctly; and define any term which you think might not be familiar to your readers.

32.2 **Avoid the use of *gobbledygook*.** The word *gobbledygook* was coined by Congressman Maury Maverick to describe the language of officialdom. Gobbledygook is a style of writing so pompous and wordy that the meaning is almost completely obscured. To find an example of gobbledygook you need look no further than a government tax form or a directive from a large organization. Here are some examples of gobbledygook:

Gobbledygook: All transactions effected pursuant to this instrument shall be effected for the account and risk and in the name of the undersigned; and the undersigned hereby agrees to indemnify and hold you harmless from, and to pay you promptly on demand, any and all losses arising there from or any debit balance due thereon.

Plain English: You'll be responsible for anything you owe on your account.

—From "War on Gobbledygook—Report from the Front," *U.S. News & World Report,* September 15, 1980.

The following example of gobbledygook was taken from a government directive concerning blackout procedures during World War II; it was "translated" into plain English by Franklin D. Roosevelt:

Gobbledygook: Such preparations shall be made as will completely obscure all Federal and non-Federal buildings occupied by the Federal Government during an air raid for any period of time from visibility by reason of internal or external illumination. Such obscuration may be obtained either by black-out construction or by termination of the illumination.

Plain English: Tell them that in buildings where they have to keep the work going to put something over the windows; and, in buildings where they can let the work stop for a while, turn out the lights.

33 Triteness

Avoid *trite expressions*. *Trite expressions* are those which are dull or stale because of overuse. Such expressions rob your writing of freshness and vitality. Using trite expressions will make your reader think that you do not have the originality to express your ideas in an interesting way or that you are not sincerely interested in your topic. The following are examples of trite phrases:

add insult to injury
after all has been said
and done
age before beauty
almighty dollar
as luck would have it
better late than never
breakneck speed
burning the midnight oil
busy as a bee
cut a long story short
dead as a doornail
depths of despair
diamond in the rough
easier said than done
fate worse than death
few and far between

food for thought
goes without saying
great minds think alike
in this day and age
it dawned upon me
leave no stone unturned
long arm of the law
method in his madness
no place like home
poor but honest
ripe old age
sadder but wiser
skeleton in the closet
slow as molasses
wee small hours
word to the wise

34 Wordiness

34.1 Eliminate *wordiness* from your writing. A good rule for writing is to say what you mean in as few words as possible without sacrificing clarity or expressiveness. By omitting needless words, you make your writing crisper, leaner, more energetic, more forceful. Notice how much a sentence can be improved by removing the excess baggage:

> Wordy: I place in nomination for the office of President the name of Dwight D. Eisenhower.
>
> Better: I nominate Dwight D. Eisenhower for President.

> Wordy: We ran in the direction of the beach.
> Better: We ran toward the beach.

34.2 Check sentences beginning with *there, it,* or *this* for wordiness. Sometimes there is no way to avoid beginning a sentence with *there, it,* or *this;* frequently, however, the sentence can be rewritten to make it more concise. (See also 2.19, 3.72.)

> Wordy: There are three states which will be affected by the new law.
>
> Better: Three states will be affected by the new law.

> Wordy: It is doubtful whether he really saw a UFO.
> Better: I doubt whether he really saw a UFO.

> Wordy: This is a country that is rich and prosperous.
> Better: This country is rich and prosperous.

34.3 Avoid the following wordy expressions:

Wordy	Better
a certain length of time	a certain time
at this point in time	now
before long	soon
call your attention to the fact that	remind you (notify you)
come in contact with	meet
destroyed by fire	burned
during the time that	while
early on	early
he is a man who . . .	he . . .
I would appreciate it if	please
in a hasty manner	hastily
in spite of the fact that	although (though)
in the direction of	toward
in the month of . . .	in . . .
of an indefinite nature	indefinite
one of the things . . .	one thing . . .
prior to	before
subsequent to	after
there is no doubt but that	no doubt (doubtless)
used for lighting purposes	used for lighting
with the exception of	except

Word 34.3

34.4 Eliminate *redundancies* from your writing. *Redundancy,* a specific kind of wordiness, is the needless repetition of words or ideas. Here are some examples of redundancies, together with shortened, more effective versions:

Redundant	Better
blue in color	blue
close proximity	proximity
equally as well	equally well
fellow colleagues	colleagues
final outcome	outcome
large in size	large
new beginners	beginners
7:00 A.M. in the morning	7:00 A.M.
successfully foiled	foiled
true facts	facts

35 A Glossary of Diction

35.1 **a, an** See **3.44.**

35.2 **accept, except** *Except,* as a preposition, means "excluding." *Accept* is a verb and means "to receive" or "to agree to."

> No one knew the answer *except* Mark.
> Can you *accept* criticism graciously?

35.3 **ad, ed, exam, lab, math, phone** Avoid such abbreviated forms in formal writing. Use the full form of the word: *advertisement, education, examination, laboratory, mathematics, telephone.*

35.4 **adverse, averse** *Adverse* means "unfavorable, harmful"; *averse* means "unwilling, opposed to."

> The parade had to be canceled because of *adverse* weather conditions.
> The senator was *averse* to any increased federal spending.

35.5 **affect, effect** *Affect* means "to influence." *Effect* means "to accomplish." (*Effect* as a noun means "the result of some action.")

> What we read does *affect* us.
> The war *effected* great changes in Europe.
> What *effects* did the drug have on laboratory animals?

Word
35.9

35.6 **aggravate** *Aggravate* means "to make worse." *Aggravate* is informal when used to mean "irritate, make angry."

> Informal: Their constant bickering really *aggravated* me.
> Formal: The humid climate *aggravated* his allergy.

35.7 **ain't** This is a substandard form.

> Incorrect: I *ain't* leaving yet.
> Correct: I *am not* leaving yet.

35.8 **All right, alright** *All right* is the correct form; there is no such word as *alright.*

> Incorrect: Do you feel *alright?*
> Correct: Do you feel *all right?*

35.9 **all the farther, all the faster** Do not use *all the farther* or *all the faster* for *as far as* or *as fast as.*

> Incorrect: They rode *all the farther* they could before nightfall.
> Correct: They rode *as far as* they could before nightfall.

35.10 a lot, lots When used to mean *many* or *a great amount,* these expressions are informal.
> Informal: We saw *lots of* meteors last night.
> Formal: We saw *many* meteors last night.

35.11 allude, elude *Allude* means "to refer to"; *elude* means "to escape from, avoid."
> The speaker occasionally *alluded* to the symbolism in Bunyan's *Pilgrim's Progress.*
> The escaped prisoner *eluded* the police for three years.

35.12 allusion, illusion An *allusion* is an indirect reference; an *illusion* is a belief or image that is false or imaginary.
> Milton's poetry is filled with *allusions* to the Greek and Latin classics.
> Intelligent people realize that UFO's are merely *illusions.*

35.13 almost, most In formal writing, do not use *most* as a substitute for *almost.*
> Informal: *Most* all the tickets to the game have been sold.
> Formal: *Almost* all the tickets to the game have been sold.

Word 35.10

35.14 among, between Use *between* when referring to two people or things; use *among* in referring to more than two.
> We hung a hammock *between* two trees.
> He feels at ease even *among* strangers.

▶ Note. *Between* may be used in referring to more than two people or things if they are considered *two at a time.*
> What is the difference in cost *between* a Chevette, a Thunderbird, and a Rolls-Royce?

35.15 amount, number *Amount* is used with a mass of something which cannot be counted; *number* is used with countable items.
> A large *amount* of milk is needed for the recipe.
> A large *number* of eggs are needed for the recipe.

35.16 amounts up to Omit the preposition *up.*
> Incorrect: His daily sales amounted up to $750.00.
> Correct: His daily sales amounted to $750.00.

35.17 and so, and then See **16.1.**

35.18 anxious, eager *Anxious* means "to be filled with concern, to look forward to with dread"; *eager* means "to look forward to with keen desire."

> He is *anxious* about going to the dentist tomorrow.
> She is *eagerly* awaiting the spring concert.

35.19 anywhere, everywhere, nowhere, somewhere Do not add *s* to the ends of these words.

> Incorrect: We could not find Billy's glove *anywheres*.
> Correct: We could not find Billy's glove *anywhere*.

35.20 aren't I This is an ungrammatical construction.

> Incorrect: *Aren't I* capable?
> Correct: *Am I not* capable?

35.21 as, because *As* is usually an imprecise substitute for *because*.

> Doubtful: *As* I don't like baseball, I am not going to Friday's game.
> Correct: *Because* I don't like baseball, I am not going to Friday's game.

35.22 as, that, whether *As* should not be used as a substitute for *that* or *whether*.

> Incorrect: I am not sure *as* I know the answer to your question.
> Correct: I am not sure *that* I know the answer to your question.
> Correct: I am not sure *whether* I know the answer to your question.

Word
35.25

35.23 awful, awfully These words should not be used as intensive modifiers to mean "extremely, very."

> Informal: John seems *awfully* tired.
> Formal: John seems *extremely* tired.

35.24 bad, badly Do not use *bad* for *badly*. *Bad* should be used only as an adjective; *badly* should be used only as an adverb.

> Incorrect: The soldier was wounded *bad*.
> Correct: The soldier was wounded *badly*.

35.25 being as, being that Do not use *being as* or *being that* for *because* or *since*.

> Incorrect: *Being that* Goliath was a giant, he assumed he would be the victor.
> Correct: *Since* Goliath was a giant, he assumed he would be the victor.

35.26 **beside, besides** *Beside* means "by the side of"; *besides* means "in addition to."

> He leadeth me *beside* the still waters.
>
> Do you have any money *besides* that in your checking account?

35.27 **better, had better** Do not use *better* for *had better.*

> Incorrect: You *better* see the principal.
>
> Correct: You *had better* see the principal.

between, among See **35.14.**

35.28 **between you and I** This expression is an illiterate form of *between you and me.*

> Incorrect: The new student will sit *between you and I* in chapel.
>
> Correct: The new student will sit *between you and me* in chapel.

35.29 **bring, take** *Bring* indicates movement toward you. *Take* indicates movement away from you.

> *Bring* a dessert when you come.
>
> *Take* all your things when you leave.

35.30 **bunch** A colloquial term when used to mean "a small group of people." Seek a more precise word in formal writing.

> Informal: A *bunch* of tourists came into the drugstore to buy souvenirs.
>
> Formal: A *group* of tourists came into the drugstore to buy souvenirs.

35.31 **can, may** *Can* refers to *ability. May* refers to *permission.*

> *Can* you play the piano?
>
> *May* I sit down?

35.32 **center around** An illogical expression. *Center at, center in,* or *center on* are preferable.

> Incorrect: The lawyer's arguments *centered around* the prosecution's lack of evidence.
>
> Correct: The lawyer's arguments *centered on* the prosecution's lack of evidence.

35.33 **cite, site** Do not confuse these two words. *Cite* is a verb which means "to quote, state, or mention formally." *Site* is a noun which means "the location of a building; the place, scene, or point of something."

> The tenants *cited* a list of complaints to the landlord.
>
> We visited the *site* of the new administration building.

Word
35.26

144

35.34 complected *Complected* is a nonstandard form for *complexioned.*

Nonstandard: Alicia is a *light-complected* girl.

Standard: Alicia is a *light-complexioned* girl.

35.35 compose, comprise *Comprise* means "to contain or include"; *compose* means "to make up, form the substance of."

Incorrect: The Old Testament is *comprised* of thirty-nine books.

Correct: The Old Testament *comprises* thirty-nine books.

Correct: The Old Testament is *composed* of thirty-nine books.

35.36 continual, continuous *Continual* means "happening again and again at certain intervals." *Continuous* means "constant, unbroken."

A faucet which drips *continually* can be extremely irritating.

The *continuous* roar of the machinery made normal conversation impossible.

35.37 didn't go to Do not use *didn't go to* for *didn't mean to* or *didn't intend to.*

Incorrect: He *didn't go to* hurt you.

Correct: He *did not mean to* hurt you.

35.38 different from, different than Use *different from* before a simple noun or pronoun.

Incorrect: Your answers are *different than* mine.

Correct: Your answers are *different from* mine.

▶ Note. *Different than* is becoming acceptable when a clause follows the expression, but it is usually possible and preferable to reword the sentence to avoid the construction.

Doubtful: Please inform us if your address is *different than* it was in the past.

Better: Please inform us if your address has changed.

35.39 disinterested, uninterested *Uninterested* means "not interested"; *disinterested* means "neutral, impartial."

He seemed *uninterested* in my story.

A *disinterested* arbiter will be brought in to settle the labor dispute.

Word
35.39

35.40 **double subject** Do not use a double subject.
Incorrect: My *father he* can beat me at tennis.
Correct: My *father* can beat me at tennis.

35.41 **double negative** See **12.15.**
eager, anxious See **35.18.**
effect, affect See **35.5.**

35.42 **elicit, illicit** *Elicit* is a verb meaning "to draw forth, to bring out"; *illicit* is an adjective meaning "illegal, unlawful."
His derogatory comments *elicited* a hostile reaction from the crowd.
The candidate was indicted for accepting *illicit* campaign funds.

elude, allude See **35.11.**

35.43 **emigrate, immigrate** *Emigrate* means "to go out from a country"; *immigrate* means "to move into a country."
Many Jews *emigrated* from Nazi Germany in the 1930s.
Mr. Schulberg *immigrated* to the United States in 1935.

35.44 **eminent, imminent** *Eminent* means "conspicuous, prominent, famous"; *imminent* means "about to happen; ready to take place."
Dr. Towers is an *eminent* Shakespearean scholar.
The lowering clouds showed that a rainstorm was *imminent.*

35.45 **enthused** An incorrect verb form not appropriate to writing or speech; *enthusiastic* is the correct form.

35.46 **equally as** The phrase *equally as* is redundant; drop the *as.*
Incorrect: His clothes were quite expensive, and his shoes were *equally as* costly.
Correct: His clothes were quite expensive, and his shoes were *equally* costly.

35.47 **et cetera** This Latin phrase meaning "and others" should be kept out of formal writing except for occasional use in footnotes. If you use *et cetera,* do not use *and* before the phrase. *And et cetera* (or *and etc.*) is a redundancy.
Poor: Several items—paper plátes, napkins, silverware, *etc.*—are needed for the picnic.
Better: Items such as paper plates, napkins, and silverware are needed for the picnic.

**Word
35.40**

everywheres See **35.19.**
except, accept See **35.2.**

35.48 **expect** *Expect* means "to look forward to"; it should not be used as a substitute for "suppose, suspect."

> Incorrect: I *expect* that you will want spaghetti for supper tonight.
> Correct: I suppose that you will want spaghetti for supper tonight.

35.49 **fewer, less** Use *fewer* with items that can be counted; use *less* with a quantity of a substance.

> *Fewer* people are living in rural areas now than in the past.
> This recipe requires *less* sugar than the other one.

35.50 **fix** This verb technically means "to fasten, to make secure." When used to mean "to repair," *fix* is informal.

> Informal: His efforts to *fix* the air conditioner were unsuccessful.
> Formal: His efforts to *repair* the air conditioner were unsuccessful.

35.51 **flaunt, flout** *Flaunt* means "to show off proudly; make a great display of." *Flout* means "to scorn, reject."

> She *flaunted* her new mink coat.
> No man can *flout* the laws of God and expect to find peace.

**Word
35.54**

35.52 **formally, formerly** *Formally* means "done in a formal manner"; *formerly* means "at a former time; at a time in the past."

> The treaty was *formally* signed on October 8.
> Mr. Brewster was *formerly* an agent for the FBI.

35.53 **funny** This word means "humorous"; it is informal when used to mean "strange, odd, peculiar."

> Informal: It's *funny* that the tornado didn't damage any houses.
> Formal: It is *odd* that the tornado damaged no houses.

35.54 **good, well** Always use the word *good* as an adjective. *Well* is an adverb when it modifies a verb; *well* is an adjective when it refers to a person's health.

> This morning's devotional was especially *good.*
> (adjective)
> Koufax pitched *well* in the last two innings. (adverb)
> After a long illness, Mr. Jansen is finally *well.*
> (adjective)

35.55 had of Omit the preposition *of.*
Incorrect: If I *had of* done my best, I would not feel bad.
Correct: If I *had* done my best, I would not feel bad.

35.56 had ought Do not use *had ought* for *ought.*
Incorrect: All of us *had ought* to do right, regardless of the consequences.
Correct: All of us *ought* to do right, regardless of the consequences.

35.57 hanged, hung *Hanged* refers to people; *hung* refers to objects. A man is *hanged,* but a picture is *hung.*
The condemned criminals were *hanged* at sunrise.
The museum's newly acquired Rembrandt was *hung* next to the Vermeer.

35.58 have, of *Of* is a preposition and should not be used for the helping verb *have.*
Incorrect: You *should of* listened to dad's advice.
Correct: You *should have* listened to dad's advice.

35.59 heighth An incorrect form of *height.*
Incorrect: The *heighth* of the building is 1,402 feet.
Correct: The *height* of the building is 1,402 feet.

> **Word 35.55**

35.60 hopefully This word means "full of hope" or "in a hopeful manner," but it is being used more and more to mean "I hope."
Poor: *Hopefully* it will snow tomorrow. (Will it snow in a hopeful manner?)
Better: *I hope* it snows tomorrow.

illicit, elicit See **35.42.**
illusion, allusion See **35.12.**
immigrate, emigrate See **35.43.**
imminent, eminent See **35.44.**

35.61 imply, infer *Imply* means "to suggest." *Infer* means "to draw a conclusion from evidence."
In his statement to the press, he *implied* that he would run again.
From her facial expression, I *inferred* that she approved.

35.62 in, into Use *in* for location within; use *into* for motion from outside to inside.
Make sure you are *in* bed by ten o'clock.
Come *into* the house and get warm.

35.63 inside of, outside of Omit the preposition *of*.
Incorrect: The unbelievers were left *outside of* the ark.
Correct: The unbelievers were left *outside* the ark.

35.64 irregardless This is an illiterate form for *regardless*.
Incorrect: The game will begin at 3:00 *irregardless* of weather conditions.
Correct: The game will begin at 3:00 *regardless* of weather conditions.

irritate, aggravate See **35.6.**

35.65 kind of, sort of These expressions are informal when used as adverbs meaning "rather, somewhat."
Informal: The weather is *kind of* warm for this time of year.
Formal: The weather is *somewhat* warm for this time of year.

35.66 kind of a, sort of a The *a* is redundant.
Poor: What *kind of a* mineral is that?
Better: What *kind of* mineral is that?

35.67 lay, lie See **10.16–10.17.**

35.68 learn, teach *Learn* means "to obtain knowledge." *Teach* means "to give instruction."
How did you *learn* to read Greek?
Dr. Wilson *taught* me to read Greek.

less, fewer See **35.49.**

35.69 let, leave *Let* means "to allow." *Leave* means "to go away from" or "to cause to remain."
Let the ladies be served first.
Leave the lawn mower in the shed.

35.70 like, as, as if Do not use the preposition *like* for the conjunctions *as* or *as if*. *Like* introduces a prepositional phrase; *as* or *as if* introduces a full clause containing a written (not an implied) subject and verb.
Correct: A wombat looks somewhat *like* a beaver. (preposition)

Incorrect: It looks *like* we will arrive early.
Correct: It looks *as if* we will arrive early.

Incorrect: You should recite the poem exactly *like* it is written.
Correct: You should recite the poem exactly *as* it is written.

Word
35.70

35.71 **loose, lose** *Loose* is an adjective meaning "not tight, not fastened, free"; *lose* is a verb meaning "to fail to keep or maintain."

One of my molars seems quite *loose*.

Did you *lose* your report card?

35.72 **mad** Although *mad* is used informally to mean "angry, upset," the word technically means "insane."

Informal: Are you *mad* at me for breaking the vase?

Formal: Suppressed guilt drove the man *mad*.

may, can See **35.31.**

35.73 **media, phenomena** These are plural forms and should be used with plural verbs. The singular forms are *medium* and *phenomenon.*

Incorrect: The media *is* going to cover the President's inauguration.

Correct: The media *are* going to cover the President's inauguration.

most, almost See **35.13.**

Word
35.71

35.74 **myself** When this pronoun is used incorrectly for the pronouns *I* or *me*, it is an affectation. *Myself* is correct when used reflexively or intensively. (See also 3.33.)

Incorrect: Mr. Smithers presented the trophies to Tom and *myself.*

Correct: Mr. Smithers presented the trophies to Tom and *me.*

Correct: I *myself* shook hands with the President. (intensive)

Correct: I treated *myself* to an ice cream cone. (reflexive)

35.75 **nauseated, nauseous** *Nauseated* means "feeling nausea"; *nauseous* means "causing nausea." Therefore, if you say "He is nauseous," you are literally saying "He makes people sick."

35.76 **nice** This word has many meanings: "precise, pleasant, good-natured, pretty." It is a vague word that should be replaced in your writing with something more specific.

Vague: Mrs. Gilman is a *nice* lady.

Better: Mrs. Gilman is a *courteous* lady.

nowheres See **35.19.**

number, amount See **35.15.**

of, have See **35.58.**

outside of, inside of See **35.63.**

35.77 **party, person** The use of *party* for *person* is acceptable in legal documents but is informal in ordinary writing.

> Informal: Mr. Thomas talked with the *party* who had found his lost ring.
> Formal: Mr. Thomas talked with the *person* who had found his lost ring.

phenomena, media See **35.73.**

35.78 **pore, pour** *Pore* as a verb means "to concentrate on, to study intently" and is always used with the preposition *over.* The verb *pour* means "to cause to flow."

> He *pored* over his notes shortly before getting up to speak.
> She *poured* the cinnamon tea into the cups.

35.79 **pretty** Overused as an adverb to mean "moderately, somewhat, fairly."

> Poor: It is *pretty* cold outside.
> Better: It is *fairly* cold outside.

35.80 **raise, rise** See **10.14–10.15.**

35.81 **real, really** *Real* is an adjective; *really* is an adverb.

> Incorrect: The soup is *real* hot.
> Correct: The soup is *really* hot.

35.82 **reason is because** A redundancy; use *reason is that* instead.

> Poor: The *reason* he gave for being late *was because* his car broke down.
> Better: The *reason* he gave for being late *was that* his car broke down.
> or He said that he was late *because* his car broke down.

35.83 **seldom ever** An illogical construction; use *hardly ever, seldom if ever,* or just *seldom.*

> Incorrect: It *seldom ever* snows in Florida.
> Correct: It *seldom* snows in Florida.

Word
35.83

35.84 **sensual, sensuous** *Sensuous* is a neutral word which merely means "pertaining to, or perceived by, the senses"; *sensual* means "pertaining to physical desires, especially sexual desires."

>Living next door to a baker affords great *sensuous* pleasures.
>Salome's *sensual* dance led to John the Baptist's death.

35.85 **set, sit** See **10.12–10.13**.
site, cite See **35.33**.

35.86 **so** *So* is a vague conjunction which should be avoided between independent clauses.

>Poor: It rained, *so* the game was canceled.
>Better: Because of the rain, the game was canceled.

So should not be used by itself as an intensifying adverb; it should be followed by a clause beginning with *that*.

>Poor: This water is *so* clear.
>Better: This water is *so* clear *that* I can easily see the bottom of the stream.

Word 35.84

35.87 **some, somewhat** Do not use the adjective *some* for the adverb *somewhat*.

>Incorrect: Their baseball team is *some* better than ours.
>Correct: Their baseball team is *somewhat* better than ours.

somewheres See **35.19**.
sort of, kind of See **35.65**.
sort of a, kind of a See **35.66**.

35.88 **sure, surely** *Sure* is an adjective; *surely* is an adverb.

>Incorrect: You were *sure* fortunate to find such a bargain.
>Correct: You were *surely* fortunate to find such a bargain.

35.89 **swell** *Swell* is slang when used as a general term of approval. Use words such as *good* or *excellent* instead.

>Incorrect: Apple pie and ice cream makes a *swell* dessert.
>Correct: Apple pie and ice cream makes an *excellent* dessert.

take, bring See **35.29**.
teach, learn See **35.68**.

35.90 terrible, terribly These words should not be used as intensive modifiers to mean "extremely, very."
    Incorrect: He is asking a *terribly* high price for that old Studebaker.
    Correct: He is asking an *extremely* high price for that old Studebaker.

35.91 that, which, who Use *who* or *whom* to refer to persons; use *which* to refer to things; use *that* to refer to persons or things.
    The man *who* reads is the man who succeeds.
    The Treaty of Utrecht, *which* was signed in 1712, ended the War of Spanish Succession.
    A man *that* hath friends must show himself friendly.
    The treaty *that* ended World War I was the Treaty of Versailles.

35.92 the See **3.45.**

35.93 them, those Do not use *them* as an adjective or as a demonstrative pronoun; use *those* instead.
    Incorrect: *Them* weeds are a nuisance.
    Correct: *Those* weeds are a nuisance.

35.94 this, that, these, those Use *this* and *that* to modify *singular* nouns; use *these* and *those* to modify *plural* nouns (this kind, these kinds, that sort, those sorts, this type, those types).
    This type of battery lasts longer than *those* types.

35.95 took sick Do not use *took sick* for *became ill.*
    Incorrect: The cold rain caused him to *take sick.*
    Correct: The cold rain caused him to *become ill.*

35.96 tortuous, torturous *Tortuous* means "crooked, twisting, winding"; *torturous* means "pertaining to torture or pain."
    He drove the jeep over the *tortuous* mountain trail.
    The survivors of the crash endured *torturous* heat while waiting to be rescued.

35.97 toward, towards American English commonly uses *toward; towards* is the preferred form in Britain.

35.98 transpire *Transpire* means "to come to light, become known." It is colloquial when used to mean "happen, occur, come to pass."
    Informal: Melanie records everything which *transpires* during our class meetings.
    Formal: Melanie records everything which *occurs* during our class meetings.

Word
35.98

35.99   **try and** Do not use *and* after the words *try* and *sure*. Use *to* after them instead.

       Incorrect: Try *and* finish your assignment by 8:30.

       Correct: Try *to* finish your assignment by 8:30.

35.100 **type** This word is a noun, not an adjective; it should not come immediately before a noun in such expressions as "What *type* car is that?" Use *type of* instead.

35.101 **used to could** Do not use *used to could* for *used to be able to.*

       Incorrect: Hank *used to could* eat a dozen eggs for breakfast.

       Correct: Hank *used to be able to* eat a dozen eggs for breakfast.

35.102 **wait on, wait for** *Wait on* is formal when used to mean "serve, attend to," but it is informal when used in place of "wait for."

       Informal: We *waited on* him for six hours.

       Formal: We *waited for* him for six hours.

       Formal: The salesman *waited on* his customers courteously.

Word 35.99

35.103 **want in, want on, want out, want through** These expressions are incorrect.

       Incorrect: He *wants on* the bus.

       Correct: He *wants to get on* the bus.

35.104 **way, ways** Do not add *s* to *way* when referring to distance.

       Incorrect: This Honda car can travel a long *ways* on a gallon of gas.

       Correct: This Honda car can travel a long *way* on a gallon of gas.

well, good See **35.54.**

35.105 **where, that** Do not use *where* for *that.*

       Incorrect: I read in the paper *where* price controls are being lifted.

       Correct: I read in the paper *that* price controls are being lifted.

35.106 where . . . at, where . . . to The *at* and the *to* are redundant.

> Incorrect: *Where* was Uncle Richard stationed *at* in Korea?
>
> Correct: *Where* was Uncle Richard stationed in Korea?

> Incorrect: *Where* are you going *to?*
>
> Correct: *Where* are you going?

35.107 when, where Do not use *when* or *where* to introduce definitions.

> Incorrect: A somnambulist is *where* someone walks in his sleep.
>
> Correct: A somnambulist is *one who* walks in his sleep.

> Incorrect: Mayonnaise is *when* a sauce is made of vegetable oil, egg yolks, and vinegar.
>
> Correct: Mayonnaise is a sauce made of vegetable oil, egg yolks, and vinegar.

who, which, that See **35.91.**

35.108 widow woman The word *woman* is redundant.

> Redundant: Mrs. Parker is a *widow woman.*
>
> Better: Mrs. Parker is a *widow.*

35.109 -wise Used by writers of jargon to turn nouns into adverbs. Avoid such ungraceful terms as *taxwise, policywise, profitwise,* and *productionwise.*

> Poor: *Territorywise,* Britain made great gains in the nineteenth century.
>
> Better: Britain gained much territory during the nineteenth century.

35.110 without, unless Do not use *without* for *unless.*

> Incorrect: You cannot get your bowling shoes *without* you first pay the deposit.
>
> Correct: You cannot get your bowling shoes *unless* you first pay the deposit.

Word
35.110

Part 4

Mechanics for Writers

*The smallest word has some unguarded
  spot,
And danger lurks in i without a dot.*
Oliver Wendell Holmes

*Punctuation marks are the traffic signs
and signals placed along the reader's
road. They tell him when to slow down
and when to stop, and sometimes they
warn him of the nature of the road
ahead.*
Theodore M. Bernstein

36 Manuscript Form

Follow standard practice in writing or typing compositions.

Materials

36.1 **Paper.** Use 8½ by 11-inch paper. If you write, use white, wide-ruled paper; if you type, use white paper of 20 pound weight. Use only one side of the paper.

36.2 **Ink.** Use blue or black ink.

Arrangement

36.3 **Name, date, and subject.** Follow your school's policy for placing your name, the date, and the subject.

36.4 **Title.** Center the title on the page. Do not underline the title or put quotation marks around it, unless it is itself the title of a book or a quotation. Use no period after the title, but use a question mark or exclamation point if the title calls for it. Place the title on the first line of ruled paper or two inches from the top of typing paper. In typewritten copy, triple-space between the title and the first line of copy; in handwritten copy, skip one line.

36.5 **Margins.** Leave a margin of about one inch at the top, bottom, and sides of the paper. On the first page, leave two inches at the top. If the paper is to be put into a folder, leave one and one-half inches at the left.

36.6 **Indention.** Indent the first line of each paragraph .8 inch (8 spaces) from the margin in typewritten copy and about an inch from the margin in handwritten copy.

Mech.
36.1

A long quotation (usually called a block quotation) should be inset .4 inches (4 spaces) from the left margin and should not be enclosed in quotation marks. Wherever the quotation is indented in the original source, it should be indented .4 inch (4 spaces) in the block quotation—a total of .8 inch (8 spaces) from the left margin. If the first line of the block quotation is not indented in the original source, it should begin flush.

Indent the first line of each footnote .8 inch (8 spaces) from the left margin and extend each succeeding line of the footnote to the left margin.

36.7   **Spacing.** Double-space between the lines of text in type-written copy. Single-space block quotations and footnotes (double-space between footnotes).

36.8   **Pagination.** Use arabic numerals to number every page in the body of the paper. In handwritten copy, center the number on the top line; in typewritten copy, center the number one inch from the top edge of the paper. Do not use a period or parentheses with the number.

> ▶ Note. On every page with a major heading (for example, the first page of the paper and the first page of the bibliography), place the number at the bottom of the page. In handwritten copy, center it on the bottom line; in typewritten copy, center it one inch above the bottom edge of the page. Leave a minimum of one blank line between the last line of text and the page number.

Appearance

36.9   **General appearance.** If writing, write legibly. Form each letter distinctly so that it will not be confused with a similar letter. Dot your *i*'s (use real dots, not little circles) and cross your *t*'s. Be sure the capital letters stand out clearly from the lower-case letters. If you find an error when proofreading the final handwritten or typed copy, you may draw one or two neat lines through the entire word and rewrite the word in ink. If you have three or more corrections of that kind on a page, you need to rewrite or retype the entire page.

> ▶ Note. For detailed information about how to **type** papers, see pages 271–281.

37 Abbreviations

37.1   **Abbreviations should be kept out of the text of formal writing, except for those that have become customary. (See 37.3–37.10.)**

37.2   **Abbreviations are used freely in footnotes and in highly technical matter.**

37.3   **Use the following abbreviations before a name:**
        Dr.   Mr.   Mrs.   M.   Mml.   Mlle.

37.4 **Use the abbreviation *Dr.* before a name, but otherwise spell out the word *doctor.***
Dr. Forrester is our family doctor.

37.5 **Use abbreviations for scholastic degrees after a name.**
B.S.   M.A.   Ph.D.   M.D.
Notice that a comma precedes the abbreviation.
Eric Gerard, M.D.   Prentiss Claypoole, Ph.D.

37.6 **Use the abbreviations *Jr., Sr.* (*Junior, Senior*) after a full name. Notice that a comma precedes the abbreviation.**
Carlos Whipple, Jr.   Mrs. Wilmot Carson, Sr.

37.7 **The titles *Reverend* and *Honorable* may be abbreviated if used with the full name.**
Rev. Aldridge (incorrect)
Rev. Hugh Aldridge (correct)
Hon. Mallory (incorrect)
Hon. Lyle Mallory (correct)

▶ Note. The titles *Reverend* and *Honorable* must be written out if preceded by *the.*

the Rev. Hugh Aldridge (incorrect)
the Reverend Hugh Aldridge (correct)
the Hon. Lyle Mallory (incorrect)
the Honorable Lyle Mallory (correct)

37.8 **Use the abbreviations *A.M.* (before noon), *P.M.* (after noon), and *M.* (noon) for time designations. Do not use *o'clock* with A.M. or P.M. or with numbers, and do not use *in the morning* with A.M. or *in the evening* with P.M.**
We arrived at 6:00 A.M. (**not** 6:00 *o'clock* A.M. **or** 6:00 A.M. *in the morning*)
We arrived at six o'clock in the morning. (**not** 6 o'clock in the morning)
Noon is written as 12:00 *M.,* and midnight as 12:00 *P.M.*

Mech. 37.4

▶ Note. Time of day is usually spelled out unless the exact time is to be emphasized.

37.9 **Use the abbreviations *A.D.* (in the year of the Lord) and *B.C.* (before Christ) for date designations. A.D. should precede the year number.**
The year 722 B.C. came before the year A.D. 70.

37.10 **The following abbreviations are common in footnotes and in parenthetical references:** (1) i.e., *id est,* that is; (2) e.g., *exempli gratia,* for example; (3) c. or ca., *circa,* about, approximately—used before approximate dates (ca. 1596).

▶ Note. These abbreviations are preferably not italicized.

37.11 **Abbreviations for well-known organizations are acceptable.**

CIA   USMC   OAS   UPI   VFW

▶ Note. It is now general practice to omit periods for abbreviations of organizations.

37.12 **Do not use & or ᛉ for** *and.*

38   Numbers

38.1 **In nonscientific writing spell out all numbers of one or two words.**

twenty   thirty-two
forty-five hundred   five thousand
but 527   5,001

▶ Note. Year numbers and numbers referring to parts of a book are exceptions to this rule.

44 B.C.   A.D. 1066   page 86
chapter 5   unit 12

38.2 **If you are writing several numbers, some of them only one or two words and some more than two, use figures for all.**

Only 45 of the 109 prisoners survived the cruelty of the Viet Cong.

Mech.
38.4

38.3 **Do not begin a sentence with figures.**

105 new cars arrived at the dealership. (incorrect)
One hundred five new cars arrived at the dealership. (correct)
or At the dealership, 105 new cars arrived. (correct)

38.4 **Write out numbers like** *first, fifth, fifty-second,* **and so on.**

first (**not** 1st)
fifth (**not** 5th)
fifty-second (**not** 52nd)

38.5 **Names of numbered streets under one hundred are preferably written out.**
First Avenue   Forty-ninth Street

39 Word Division

39.1 **Do not divide one-syllable words.** (hissed, **not** hiss-ed)

39.2 **Divide only between pronounceable syllables.** (prejudice, **not** pre-judice)

39.3 **Do not divide after a single letter.** (abound, **not** a-bound)

39.4 **Do not carry over a two-letter syllable if it can be avoided.** (money, **not** mon-ey)

39.5 **Divide words with prefixes after the prefix.** (postnatal, **not** postna-tal)

39.6 **Divide words with a double consonant between the consonants.** (recom-mend, net-ted, sag-ging, hit-ting)

▶ Exception. This rule does not apply to words that already end in a double consonant before a suffix is added. (thrill-ing, add-ing, dwell-ing, miss-ing)

39.7 **Divide hyphenated words only at the hyphen.** (self-composed, **not** self-com-posed; president-elect, **not** presi-dent-elect)

40 Correction Symbols

Mech.
38.5

The following symbols may be used to indicate errors that require correction. The numbers after the explanations refer to sections of the handbook.

ab	abbreviations, **37**
agr	agreement, **9**
appr	appropriateness, **28**
awk	awkward construction
ca	wrong case, **11**
cap	use a capital letter, **41**
coh	coherence, **44.5**
comp	faulty comparison, **12**
coord	faulty coordination, **16**
dict	see your dictionary

div	division of words, **39**
dm	dangling modifier, **19**
emph	emphasis, **35, 44.6**
ex	exactness and vividness, **29**
fig	figurative language, **30**
frag	sentence fragment, **13**
gl	glossary of diction, **35**
gr	error in grammar
id	idioms, **31**
il	illegible writing
jarg	jargon and gobbledygook, **32**
lc	use lower case, no capital, **41**
logic	illogial construction, **21**
m	wrong mood, **10.39–10.44**
mm	misplaced modifier, **18**
mod	modifier misused, **12**
ms	manuscript form, **36**
nc	not clear, **21** (also used to indicate general lack of clarity)
num	use of numbers, **38**
p	error in punctuation, **42**
par	error in parallelism, **22**
pass	ineffective use of passive voice, **10.38**
pv	unnecessary shift in point of view, **23**
R	rewrite page or portion indicated
ref	faulty pronoun reference, **20**
rep	unnecessary repetition
ro	run-on sentence, **14**
sp	error in spelling
sub	faulty subordination, **17**
t	error in tense, **10.18–10.30**
trite	triteness, **33**
u	lack of unity, **15, 44.4**
var	lack of variety, 26
vf	wrong verb form, **10.7–10.17**
wdy	wordiness, **24, 34**
ww	wrong word
X	obvious fault

Mech.
40

163

¶	begin a new paragraph
No ¶	no new paragraph
^	omission of necessary words
◡	join the words
#	space between words

41 Capitalization

Proper Names

41.1 **Capitalize** *proper names.*

    a. Capitalize names of *particular persons, places, and things:*

    (1) Words referring to the Deity—God, Father, Son, Holy Spirit, Almighty, Creator, King of Kings, Comforter, Prince of Peace, Lord and Savior (Do not capitalize the word *god* when referring to pagan deities.)

        ▶ Note. Capitalize pronouns that refer to the Deity.

        God always keeps His promises.

    (2) Names of Satan, angels, and human beings—the Devil, Apollyon; Gabriel, Michael; Lori Barker, Eugene Black, Jr., Daniel Graham, Sr. (Notice that the abbreviations *Jr.* and *Sr.* are capitalized following a name.)

    (3) Continents, countries, states, counties, cities— Antarctica, Burma, Arkansas, Hawkins County, Yellville

Mech. 41.1

    (4) Recognized political or geographical regions—the South, the Far West, the Northwest (U.S.); the Far East, the Near East (Do not capitalize *north, east, south, west, northwest,* etc. when they refer to a direction: west of town, driving east on I-10.)

        ▶ Note. Do not capitalize adjectives that merely indicate a portion of a region: southern France, northern Idaho, eastern Mexico

        Do capitalize adjectives that are part of a name referring to a political or a geographical division:

Central America, West Germany, Northern Ireland, Eastern Samoa, South Korea, Western Europe

(5) **Islands, bodies of water, mountains, parks**—Baffin Island, Isle Royale; Old Harbour Bay, Caribbean Sea; Big Horn Mountains, Mount Whitney; Saratoga National Historical Park

(6) **Streets and highways**—Wimpole Street, Grand Concourse Boulevard, Forty-second Street (The second part of a hyphenated number is not capitalized.)

(7) **Special organizations**—the Security Council, Congress, State Department, Library of Congress, New York Philharmonic, Circuit Court of Escambia County

(8) **Calendar items and special events**—Friday, May, Easter, Savannah Arts Festival

▶ Note. Names of the seasons (spring, summer, fall, autumn, winter) are not capitalized unless personified: Then came Autumn in her multicolored garb.

(9) **Historical events and periods**—Hundred Years War, Battle of Bannockburn, Great Depression, Gilded Age

(10) **Nationalities, races, and tribes**—Chinese, Canadian, Hottentot, Pygmy, Timbira

(11) **Religious writings, groups, and terms**—the Bible, Scripture, Authorized Version, Codex Sinaiticus, Pentateuch, the Beatitudes, Baptist, Methodist, Catholic, Apostles' Creed, Original Sin, the Fall, the Crucifixion, the Atonement

Mech. 41.1

(12) **Languages and particular courses**—Hindustani, Japanese, Physics 402, Computer Science 205 (The number after the subject indicates a particular course.)

(13) **Brand names of business products**—Yale lock, Dunlop tires, Curity bandage (Do not capitalize the common noun after the brand name.)

(14) **Monuments, bridges, buildings, documents, planets, ships, and any other particular persons, places, or things**—Death Valley National Monument, Man-

hattan **B**ridge, the **W**hite **H**ouse, **T**reaty of **P**aris, **N**eptune, **U.S.S.** *Lexington*

▶ Note. Do not capitalize *earth, sun,* and *moon* except when used (without the article *the*) in a list with other planets.

The four planets nearest the sun are **M**ercury, **V**enus, **E**arth, and **M**ars.

b. Capitalize common names, such as *avenue, building, bridge, church, park, school, street* **only when part of an official name:** **P**ensacola **C**hristian **C**ollege, a college; **F**ort **N**iagara, a fort; **L**ittle **C**reek **B**aptist **C**hurch, the **B**aptist church

41.2 **Capitalize** *words derived from proper names.*

a. Capitalize *abbreviations of proper names:* **NRA** (National Rifle Association), **FAA** (Federal Aviation Administration), **TVA** (Tennessee Valley Authority), **G**en. (Genesis), **M**al. (Malachi), **M**att. (Matthew), **R**ev. (Revelation), **G**a. (Georgia), **M**ont. (Montana), **F**r. (France), **G**er. (Germany), **U.S.** (United States)

▶ Note. Of the examples listed here, the organizations are the only ones usually abbreviated in general writing; the others may be abbreviated in parenthetical references, footnotes, and bibliographies.

b. Capitalize *proper adjectives:* **S**panish, **G**recian, **J**effersonian, **A**ristotelian, **M**achiavellian, **E**lizabethan, **R**oman, **C**olumbian, **A**ustralian, **S**emitic

c. Sometimes *proper names and their derivatives* **lose their original meanings through frequent usage and are** *no longer capitalized:* frankfurter, italicize, japan (varnish), pasteurize, quixotic

▶ Note. When you are in doubt about a word, refer to your dictionary. Be sure to locate the definition of the word as used in your sentence, because the word may be capitalized for one definition and not capitalized for another.

Pharisaical (capitalized—refers to the Pharisees)

pharisaical (lower-cased—refers to anyone who acts like a Pharisee)

Mech.
41.2

Titles

41.3 **Capitalize** *titles of persons.*

  a. **Capitalize titles when they are used** *before a person's name.*

   President Eisenhower, Secretary of the Treasury Glass, Governor Egan, General Hershey, Mayor Thorp, Queen Gertrude, Dr. Paine

  b. **Titles** *following a name or used alone in place of a name* **are not usually capitalized unless used in direct address.**

   ▶ Exception. *President* is usually capitalized when it refers to the President of the United States of America.

   Dwight D. Eisenhower, President of the United States; the President of the United States; Carter Glass, secretary of the treasury; William A. Egan, governor; Lewis B. Hershey, general; W. A. Thorp, mayor; Gertrude, the queen of Denmark; Robert Paine, our doctor; the senator; the congressman; the pastor; the archbishop of Canterbury; "Good morning, Governor, Senator, Congressman, etc."

  c. **Capitalize** *family-relationship words* **when they are used** *before a person's name* **and when used** *alone in place of the name.*

   We visited Uncle Gene and Aunt Mary in Dallas, Texas.
   What shall we buy Mother for Christmas?
   Yes, Dad, we will be glad to help.
   Her father died at the age of ninety-two.
   Several cousins have come to visit.

   ▶ Note. Do not capitalize family-relationship words when they are preceded by a possessive unless the title is considered *part of the name.*

   my Uncle Jesse, my Aunt Louise (*Uncle* and *Aunt* are considered part of the name.)
   my cousin Frank, his sister Jill (*Cousin* and *sister* are not usually considered part of the name.)

Mech.
41.3

167

41.4 **Capitalize the *titles of works*.**

Capitalize the first and last words and all important words in the titles of *books, magazines, newspapers, poems, stories, plays, musical compositions, paintings, sculpture,* and *other works of art*. (Unimportant words are coordinating conjunctions, prepositions, and the articles *a, an,* and *the.*)

> *Valiant for the Truth* (book)
> *Mechanix Illustrated* (magazine)
> "Stopping by Woods on a Snowy Evening" (poem)
> "Bartleby the Scrivener" (story)
> *The Spanish Tragedy* (play)
> *Pines of Rome* (musical composition)
> *Saint John on Patmos* (painting)
> *The Cheyenne* (sculpture)

▶ Exception. The article *the* is not capitalized before the title of a magazine or a newspaper when the title is written within a sentence.

> the *Atlanta Constitution* (newspaper)
> the *Farm Journal* (magazine)

Miscellaneous

41.5 **Capitalize the *first word of every sentence* (including quoted sentences).**

> The sleep of a labouring man is sweet.
> Vince Lombardi said, "Fatigue makes cowards of us all."

Mech. 41.4

41.6 **Capitalize the pronoun *I* and the interjection *O*.** (The more common interjection *oh* is capitalized only when it stands at the beginning of a sentence. *Oh* is followed by a comma or an exclamation point; *O* is never followed by punctuation.)

> Return, **O** Lord, deliver my soul: **oh,** save me for Thy mercies' sake.

41.7 **Capitalize the *first word in every line of poetry,* whether or not the word begins a sentence.**

> Strong Son of God, immortal Love,
> Whom we, that have not seen Thy face,
> By faith, and faith alone, embrace,
> Believing where we cannot prove;
> —*Tennyson*

42 Punctuation

End Marks

42.1 **Use a *period* to end a *declarative sentence* or an *imperative sentence*.**

An effective way to show your Christianity is to always keep your word. (declarative)
Do not promise more than you can fulfill. (imperative)

42.2 **Use a *period* to end an *indirect question*.**
He asked who had moved the chair.

42.3 **Use a *period* to end a *polite request* disguised as a question.**
Will you please take this to the office.

42.4 **Use a *period* to indicate an *abbreviation*.**
Mr.   Mrs.   Dr.   B.A.   Ph.D.   A.M.   M.   P.M.
A.D.   B.C.

a. It is now general practice to omit periods for abbreviations of organizations.

OTS   FICA   CIA   SAC   UPI   OAS

b. If the abbreviating period ends a declarative sentence, no additional punctuation is needed; but if the abbreviating period ends an interrogative sentence or an exclamatory sentence, a question mark or an exclamation point must also be used.

The airliner arrived at 9:20 P.M.
Wasn't Julius Caesar murdered in 44 B.C.?
How foolish of them to call at 2:00 A.M.!

Mech.
42.7

42.5 **Use a *question mark* to end an *interrogative sentence*.**
Does it please God for one to have other humans as idols?

42.6 **Use an *exclamation point* to end an *exclamatory sentence*.**
How wonderful that Christ should die for all!

42.7 **Use an *exclamation point* to end an *imperative sentence* strongly stated.**
Don't let the cat into the house!

Comma

42.8 Use a *comma and a coordinating conjunction* (*and, but, or, nor, for, yet*) to join two independent clauses. (, and)

The *hope* of the righteous *shall be* gladness, **but** the *expectation* of the wicked *shall perish*. (two independent clauses—one on either side of the conjunction)

A good *man will be* honest **and** *will* therein *be* successful. (one independent clause with a compound verb—no comma needed)

▶ Note. It is always correct to apply rule 42.8; however, if the clauses are very short, the comma is sometimes omitted when there is no possibility of misreading the sentence.

He spoke and everyone listened.

42.9 Use a *single comma* to indicate that a word or words have been omitted, or to avoid a possible misreading. (,)

a. Use single commas to separate three or more *items in a series.*

Fruit, nuts, and *vegetables* are just a few of the crops grown in Florida. (words in a series)

At the reunion people were sitting *in the yard, on the porch,* and *in the house.* (phrases in a series)

He sang, he preached, and *he showed his slides.* (short clauses in a series)

▶ Note. Independent clauses in a series are usually separated by semicolons rather than by commas. The commas are acceptable in this example because the clauses are very short.

(The first comma in each example above is used because the word *and* has been omitted; the second comma in each example is used to avoid a possible misreading.)

Centipede **and** Bermuda **and** zoysia grasses grow well in warm climates. (No commas are needed in this series because no words are omitted between the words in the series.)

Mech.
42.8

b. Use single commas to separate *two or more adjectives preceding a noun.* (Do not put a comma between the last adjective and the noun it modifies.)

Mount Everest is a steep, forbidding mountain. (The single comma is placed after the word *steep* because the word *and* has been omitted.)

▶ Note. If the last adjective is so closely related to the noun it modifies that the two words seem to form one expression, do not use the comma to separate that adjective from the other adjectives.

Blair bought an antique rocking chair. (No comma is used between *antique* and *rocking* because the words *rocking chair* form one expression. You can usually determine whether the comma is needed if you insert *and* between the adjectives. If the *and* sounds awkward, the comma is not needed. You may also reverse the adjectives, and if the adjectives sound awkward in the new position, the comma is not usually needed)

Blair bought an antique *and* rocking chair. (*and* sounds awkward—no comma needed)

Blair bought a rocking antique chair. (adjectives reversed sound awkward—no comma needed)

c. Use a single comma any time *to avoid misreading.*

Before eating my grandfather would always drink a large glass of water. (This sentence would probably be misread.)

Before eating, my grandfather would always drink a large glass of water. (The comma after *eating* prevents the misreading.)

Mech.
42.10

The morning after we arrived safely in London. (confusing without the comma)

The morning after, we arrived safely in London. (corrected)

42.10 Use a *pair of commas* to indicate a *nonessential element* in a sentence. (,—,)

▶ Note. The *pair of commas* is one mark of punctuation composed of two symbols, but these symbols are *not* to be thought of as *two single commas.*

171

Robert E. Lee, *who commanded the Confederate Army,* was a great general. (nonessential—The clause is *not necessary* to identify the word it modifies. The proper noun is sufficient identification.)

The man *who commanded the Confederate Army* was a great general. (essential—The clause is *necessary* to identify the word it modifies.)

Sometimes the nonessential elements come first or last in a sentence. In these cases, only one half of the pair of commas is necessary.

For instance, the katydid's ears are just below its front knee joints.

The plane landed at Chicago-O'Hare International Airport, *the world's busiest airport.*

a. Use commas to set off *nonessential appositives*. An appositive is a noun or noun equivalent placed beside another noun or noun equivalent to identify or to explain it.

Mississippi, *the Magnolia State,* has a wide variety of plant life. (The appositive *the Magnolia State* merely adds explanatory information; it is not needed to identify *Mississippi.* Therefore it is nonessential and requires commas.)

▶ Note. If the appositive is short and closely related to the expression it follows, it is usually an essential appositive and no commas are needed. Essential appositives are often only one word.

his friend Sam	the conjunction *and*
Charles the Bald	the novel *The Horse's Mouth*
His poet Edgar Guest	

b. Use commas to set off nonessential *participial phrases*, nonessential *adjective clauses*, and nonessential *adverb clauses*. A *nonessential element* can be omitted and the remaining words will still mean what they were intended to mean. The nonessential element merely gives additional information about something already identified. An *essential element* cannot be omitted without causing a change in the intended meaning. The essential element identifies what particular person, place, thing, or time is meant.

Harry, *grinning mischievously,* poked his head into the room. (nonessential participial phrase)

The man *playing third base* is an excellent fielder. (essential participial phrase)

Mrs. Butler, *who is an interior designer,* likes bold colors. (nonessential adjective clause)

He dislikes women *who talk constantly.* (essential adjective clause)

They always attend church, *whether it is convenient or not.* (nonessential adverb clause)

No one can have real peace *unless he knows Christ.* (essential adverb clause)

c. Sometimes an element may be interpreted as essential or as nonessential. The writer of the sentence must punctuate the sentence so that it conveys the meaning he intends.

Direct any questions about writing style to our secretary *who is an expert on such matters.* (Here the italicized clause is essential because the writer wants to indicate that we have *more than one* secretary and that questions about writing style should be directed to the one who is an expert in such matters.)

Direct any questions about writing style to our secretary, *who is an expert on such matters.* (Here the clause is nonessential because the writer wants to indicate that we have *only one* secretary and that she is an expert on writing style.)

My uncle *who is a mechanical engineer* works at Fort Rucker. (essential—more than one uncle)

My uncle, *who is a mechanical engineer,* works at Fort Rucker. (nonessential—only one uncle)

Mech. 42.10

d. Use commas to set off words used in *direct address*.

The troops are ready, *General,* for your inspection.

e. Use commas to set off *well, yes, no,* and other interjections at the beginning of a sentence.

Yes, you should always do as you promise.

f. Use commas to set off parenthetical expressions: *in fact, for example, of course, indeed, however, incidentally, nevertheless, on the contrary, in my opinion, at any rate, I think, I suppose,* etc.

On the contrary, his proposal seems very satisfactory.

At any rate, I will be there on time.

▶Note. When these expressions do not cause a distinct break in the flow of the sentence and do not require a pause in reading, the commas may be omitted. (See also the note under rule 42.16.)

The hurricane is *indeed* a bad one.

We *therefore* ask that no one remain in low-lying areas.

42.11 Use a comma to set off *introductory modifying phrases or clauses.* (Do not set off introductory phrases or clauses used as the subject of a sentence.)

In Nazareth, Christ faced scorn and ridicule. (short adverb phrase)

Outside the city of Jerusalem, Christ died for our sins. (long adverb phrase)

Nailed to a cross, Christ bore our punishment for all eternity. (participial phrase)

To have more faith, one must read God's Word. (infinitive phrase)

When the day begins with prayer, it is bound to end well. (adverb clause)

To submit to authority is a first step toward greatness. (no comma—infinitive phrase used as subject)

Praying for God's help each day is a wise practice. (no comma—gerund phrase used as subject)

That the wicked can have no peace is an eternal principle. (no comma—noun clause used as subject)

Mech.
42.11

▶Note 1. Sometimes good writers will omit the comma after very short phrases or clauses if there is no possibility of misreading, but in this book you should follow rule 42.11.

▶Note 2. Do not use a comma after an introductory adverb phrase that comes immediately before the verb it modifies.

In my Father's house are many mansions.

42.12 **Use commas to separate the parts of *dates and addresses* within sentences. Use a comma after the last part if it does not end the sentence. Do not use a comma between the month and the day or between the state and the ZIP code.**

> On Tuesday, October 29, 1929, stockholders sold 16,410,030 shares of stock.
> His new office will be built at 16 Sunnyside Drive, Eugene, Oregon 97404.

42.13 **Use a comma after the *salutation of a friendly letter.* Use a comma after the closing of all letters.**

> Dear Uncle Jerry,   Dear Linda,
> Your loving son,   Very truly yours,

Semicolon

42.14 **Use a *semicolon* between independent clauses *if you do not use a comma and a coordinating conjunction.*** (The coordinating conjunctions are *and, but, or, nor, for, yet.*)

> Punishment brings wisdom; it is the healing art of wickedness. —*Plato*

42.15 **A *semicolon* may be used between independent clauses even *with a coordinating conjunction* (1) if there are *commas within the clauses* or (2) if the *clauses are long.*** This semicolon is often necessary to make clear the major break between independent clauses.

> Ignorance of all things is an evil neither terrible nor excessive, nor yet the greatest of all; but great cleverness and much learning, if they be accompanied by a bad training, are a much greater misfortune. —*Plato*

Mech.
42.16

42.16 **Use a *semicolon* between independent clauses joined by transitional words, such as *accordingly, consequently, for example, for instance, however, namely, nevertheless, that is, then, therefore, thus.*** (These words are not equivalent to coordinating conjunctions.)

▶ Note. These words are followed by a comma if they cause a distinct break in the flow of the sentence, but if the transitional word seems closely connected to the following clause (not requiring a pause when read), the comma may be omitted. The expressions *for example, for instance, that is, however,* and *namely* are always followed by a comma when they function as a connective.

The Bible teaches that God is a Spirit; thus we cannot see Him.

The Bible also teaches that God is a holy Being; that is, He is free from any sinful attributes or dispositions.

42.17 **Use a** *semicolon between items in a series* **if the items themselves contain commas.**

These are the three oldest universities in the United States: Harvard University in Cambridge, Massachusetts; William and Mary College in Williamsburg, Virginia; and Yale University in New Haven, Connecticut.

Colon

42.18 **Use a** *colon* **before listed items, especially when announced by such words as** *as follows* **or** *the following.* **Do not use a colon to introduce a list that is the complement of a verb or the object of a preposition.**

The items that we took to the reunion were: salad, green beans, and tea. (incorrect—colon separates the verb from its complement)

We took these items to the reunion: salad, green beans, and tea. (correct)

On our vacation, we traveled through: Indiana, Ohio, and Pennsylvania. (incorrect—colon separates the preposition from its object)

On our vacation, we traveled through the following states: Indiana, Ohio, and Pennsylvania. (correct)

42.19 **Use a** *colon* **to introduce a statement or quotation that is formally announced.** (A statement or quotation that is not formally announced is regularly set off with a comma.)

William Congreve once made this statement: "Music hath charms to soothe the savage breast." (colon—quotation formally announced)

It was William Congreve who said, "Music hath charms to soothe the savage breast." (comma—quotation not formally introduced)

Mech.
42.17

42.20 **Use a *colon* between independent clauses when the second clause gives a fuller explanation of what is stated in the first clause.**

Summer camp had a tremendous effect on the young people: they came home with a genuine desire to serve the Lord.

42.21 **Use a *colon* between the *chapter and verse* of a Biblical reference.**

Genesis 9:6   Hebrews 7:25   Philippians 2:5–11

42.22 **Use a *colon* between the *hour and the minute* of a time reference.**

9:45 A.M.   12:00 M.   5:00 P.M.

42.23 **Use a *colon* after the *salutation of a business letter*.**

Dear Mr. Grindstone: Dear Sir: Gentlemen:

Dash

42.24 **Use a *dash* after a series of words or phrases that give details about the statement that is to follow.** (In handwriting, make the dash twice as long as the hyphen; in typewriting, use two successive hyphens.)

Rachmaninoff, Puccini, and Ravel—these were the composers he most enjoyed.

▶ Note. This is exactly the opposite of the way a colon is used. Compare this sentence with the one above.

The composers he most enjoyed were these: Rachmaninoff, Puccini, and Ravel.

42.25 **Use a *dash* to indicate a break in faltering speech or an unfinished construction.**

I—I—think that—that—something is lurking in the shadows!

While you are out, could you—oh, never mind.

"But what if—" His voice trailed off, and he said no more. (No end mark is needed after a dash that breaks off a sentence.)

42.26 **Use a pair of *dashes* to indicate parenthetical elements that are *emphatic* or that *contain internal punctuation*.**

When the game was over—what a game!—we celebrated. (dashes for emphasis)

Mech. 42.26

The time had come for Huss to stand before the
council—a council already predisposed against him.
(Dashes for emphasis. The second half of the pair
of dashes is not needed at the end of the sentence.)
Several members of his bowling team—Bill, Dave,
and Hugh—were good enough to be professionals.
(dashes because of internal punctuation)

▶ Note. If the parenthetical element calls for a question
mark or an exclamation point, this additional punctuation should be placed inside the second dash. See the
first example on the previous page.

Parentheses

42.27 Use *parentheses* to enclose *brief confirmatory information.*

The Willets prepared to go to Ghana (formerly Gold
Coast) as missionaries.

John Wooden, former coach at the University of
California at Los Angeles (UCLA), was the most
successful college basketball coach in history.

42.28 Use *parentheses* to enclose *confidential comments to the
reader* and *supplementary or explanatory information
added merely for clarity.*

His idea (do you think it was a good one?) was
adopted by the committee.

Today we studied ultraviolet light (invisible light
which has a wavelength shorter than visible violet
light); tomorrow we will study about infrared light.

A science writer often uses illustrations to clarify his
statements (see fig. 25 as an example).

Mrs. Jones insists on baking chocolate pies for me. (I
seldom discourage her.)

▶ Note 1. *Question marks* and *exclamation points* go
inside the closing parenthesis when they apply to the
parenthetical matter only. *Commas, colons,* and *semicolons* always go outside the closing parenthesis. *Periods*
are placed inside a closing parenthesis only when the
parentheses enclose a sentence that is not part of another
sentence. (See the examples above.)

Mech.
42.27

▶ Note 2. *Commas, dashes,* and *parentheses*—all are used to set off parenthetical elements. Be sparing in the use of dashes and parentheses: do not use dashes or parentheses when commas will serve the purpose. *Commas* are used when the elements are closely connected, logically and grammatically, to the rest of the sentence. *Dashes* and *parentheses* are used when the logical connection is more remote and when the grammatical structure of the sentence is abruptly interrupted by the parenthetical insertion. When you use *dashes,* you *emphasize* the element; when you use *parentheses,* you *minimize* the importance of the element.

Brackets

42.29 **Use brackets to enclose editorial corrections, comments, or explanations in quoted matter.**

"Certain species of these army ants which inhabit tropical America, he [Mr. Belt] considered to be the most intelligent of all the insects of that part of the world."

"In February of that year [1962] John H. Glenn, Jr., became the first American astronaut to orbit the earth."

▶ Note. Brackets enclose insertions which you make in other people's writing; parentheses enclose insertions in your own writing.

42.30 **Use brackets, when necessary, as parentheses within parentheses.**

He referred them to a section on symbolic logic (see Irving M. Copi, *Introduction to Logic* [New York: Macmillan Co., 1953], pp. 219–25.

Mech.
42.31

Quotation Marks

42.31 **Use quotation marks to enclose the *exact words* of a speaker (a direct quotation).** Do not use quotation marks for an indirect quotation, which is a rewording of the person's statement.

The war hero said, "I fear nothing but doing wrong." (direct quotation)
The war hero said that he feared nothing but doing wrong. (indirect quotation)

179

42.32 **Capitalize the** *first word* **of a direct quotation. If the quotation is** *interrupted by other words,* **the second part should not begin with a capital letter unless the second part is the beginning of a new sentence or is a word that would be capitalized anyway.**

"Rather than love, than money, than fame," said Thoreau, "give me truth."

"Though I am always in haste," said Wesley, "I am never in a hurry."

"Dost thou love life?" asked Franklin. "Then do not squander time, for that is the stuff life is made of."

42.33 **The exact words of a speaker should be** *set off* **from the rest of the sentence by using a comma, a question mark, or an exclamation point.** (Observe this usage in the examples above.)

► Note. If the quotation is a grammatical part of the writer's sentence, the quotation should not be set off by commas, nor should it begin with a capital letter.

The Lord told Jonah to "go to Nineveh, that great city, and cry against it."

42.34 *Commas* **and** *periods* **always go** *inside* **the closing quotation marks.**

42.35 *Colons* **and** *semicolons* **always go** *outside* **the closing quotation marks.**

The following students still have to recite the poem "Silver": Amy Turner, Jean Phelps, and Randy Gerrand.

The book of John contains the verse "Jesus wept"; it is the shortest verse in the Bible.

42.36 *Question marks* **and** *exclamation points* **go** *inside* **the closing quotation marks when they apply to the quoted matter only. They go** *outside* **when they refer to the whole sentence.**

After murdering Abel, Cain said, "Am I my brother's keeper?" (The question mark applies to the quoted words only.)

Who said, "Let no corrupt communication proceed out of your mouth"? (The question mark applies to the whole sentence.)

Was it Moses or Joshua who asked, "Who is on the Lord's side?" (A second question mark is not needed after the closing quotation marks.)

Job exclaimed, "How forcible are right words!" (The exclamation point applies to the quoted words only.)

42.37 **In quoting *more than one sentence,* use quotation marks only at the beginning and at the end of the whole quotation.** Do not put quotation marks around each sentence.

Our teacher read us this good quotation by Thomas Arnold: "Real knowledge like everything else of value, is not obtained easily. It must be worked for, studied for, thought for, and, more than all, must be prayed for."

42.38 **If a quoted passage consists of *more than one paragraph,* quotation marks are used at the *beginning of each paragraph* and at the *end of the last paragraph.*** Do not use quotation marks after any paragraph except the last.

▶ Note. A long quotation is usually typed as a block quotation, and the quotation marks are omitted. A block quotation is one that is set off from the text and single-spaced.

42.39 **In writing conversation, begin a new paragraph each time the speaker changes.**

42.40 **Use quotation marks to enclose *titles* of *short stories, short poems, songs, chapters, articles,* and other *parts* of books or magazines.** (Italicize long poems of book length and long musical compositions, such as operas, concertos, and symphonies.)

O. Henry included the short story "The Ransom of Red Chief" in an anthology entitled *Whirligigs.*
Act 2 of *Il Trovatore* features the exciting "Anvil Chorus."

Mech.
42.42

42.41 **Use single quotation marks for an *element within a quotation* that also requires quotation marks.**

"What poem begins with the line 'April is the cruelest month'?" asked the teacher.

Italics

42.42 **Underline (italicize) the titles of *books, magazines, newspapers, plays, works of art,* and the names of *ships, submarines, aircraft,* and *spacecraft.*** (Underlining indicates those words that would be italicized if the sentences were set in type by a typesetter.)

<u>The Prairie</u> (book)   <u>Boy's Life</u> (magazine)

<u>Twelfth Night</u> (play)   <u>Prometheus</u> (sculpture)
<u>Nautilus</u> (submarine)   <u>Mariner X</u> (spacecraft)

▶ Note. The articles *a, an,* and *the* at the beginning of a title are italicized only when they are part of the title.

▶ Exception. The article *the* is not italicized before the title of a magazine or a newspaper even if the article is actually a part of the title.

the <u>Washington Star-News</u>

42.43 **Underline (italicize) *words, letters,* and *numbers* referred to as such.**

The words <u>affect</u> and <u>effect</u> are often used incorrectly.
Your <u>a</u>'s look like <u>u</u>'s and your <u>9</u>'s look like <u>y</u>'s.

42.44 **Underline (italicize) *foreign words* and *phrases* that have not been accepted as English.**

<u>lapsus linguae</u>   <u>experto credite</u>
but   filet mignon   carte blanche

Hyphen

42.45 **Use a hyphen if you must divide a word at the end of a line. (See section 39.)**

42.46 **Use a hyphen in *compound numbers* from *twenty-one* through *ninety-nine.***

forty-five chapters   sixty-one tiles
eighty-eight signatures

42.47 **Use a hyphen in *fractions* used as *adjectives.***

a ***two-thirds*** majority (used as adjective)
one third of the stock (used as noun)

42.48 **Use a hyphen with the prefixes *all-, ex-, self-* and with the suffix *-elect.***

all-powerful   ex-convict
self-reliant   senator-elect

42.49 **Use a hyphen with *prefixes before a proper noun* or *proper adjective.***

Pan-Asiatic   pro-America
anti-Russian   un-Biblical

42.50 **Use a hyphen with most *compound adjectives* used *before a noun.***

cross-country runner   how-to-do-it book
two-inch margin   red-faced man

Apostrophe

42.51 Use an apostrophe to form the *possessive case of nouns.*

a. To form the possessive case of a *singular noun,* first write the *singular spelling* of the word. Then add an *apostrophe and* s. ('s)

woman**'s** shoe   cat**'s** paw   Muir**'s** writings
Hertz**'s** answer   Burns**'s** poems   Richards**'s** novel
Charles**'s** theory

▶Exception. The following may be correctly written by adding the apostrophe only: (1) ancient proper names ending in *-es,* (2) the name *Jesus,* (3) such expressions as *for conscience' sake.*

Socrates**'** pupil   Pericles**'** role
Aristophanes**'** comedies   Moses**'** rod
Jesus**'** birth   for righteousness**'** sake
for conscience**'** sake   for goodness**'** sake

b. To form the possessive case of a *plural noun that does not end in* s, first write the *plural spelling* of the word. Then add an *apostrophe and* s. ('s)

children**'s** books   policemen**'s** protection
women**'s** gloves

▶Note. Do not use an apostrophe to form the *plural* of a noun.

three nails (**not** three nail**'s**)
two hats (**not** two hat**'s**)

c. To form the possessive case of a *plural noun that ends in* s, first write the *plural spelling* of the word. Then add an *apostrophe.* (')

boys**'** socks   lions**'** den   Williamses**'** house

**Mech.
42.51**

d. When forming the possessive case of *compound words* and *words that show joint possession,* make only the last word possessive.

son-in-law**'s** car   someone else**'s** pen
board of directors**'** plan   Jill and Ann**'s** room
Finch and Hatch**'s** Food Store

▶Exception. If the second word is a possessive pronoun, the first word must also be possessive.

Jill**'s** and **my** room (**not, Jill** and **my** room)

e. For words that show *individual possession*, make each word in the group possessive.

Jack**'s** and Joe**'s** ideas
Mrs. Bellis**'s** and Mrs. Howe**'s** girls

42.52 **Use an *apostrophe and* s to form the *possessive case of indefinite pronouns*. (See 3.36.)**

anybody**'s** guess   everyone**'s** cooperation
somebody**'s** job

▶ Note. Possessive pronouns (see 11.3) and the pronoun *whose* do not require apostrophes to show possession.

its stem   **his** article   **your** advice
became **theirs**   **whose** ring

42.53 **Use an apostrophe to show that *letters or numbers* have been *omitted* from a word.** Such *contractions* are used only in informal writing or in conversation.

Tom**'s** = Tom is   it**'s** = it is
you**'re** = you are   **'**79 = 1979

Several words require a slight change in spelling.

won**'t** = will not   shan**'t** = shall not   can**'t** = cannot

42.54 **Use an *apostrophe and* s to form the *plurals* of *letters, numbers, signs,* and *words used as words*.**

*b***'s** and *c***'s**   *4***'s** and *5***'s**
+**'s** and −**'s**   &**'s** and *and***'s**

▶ Note. The plurals of years written as numerals may be formed by adding *s* alone.

1800**s**   1900**s**

Part 5

Compositions

Easy writing makes hard reading.
Ernest Hemingway

*Every man of education should make it
the object of his unceasing concern to
preserve his language pure and entire,
to speak it, so far as is in his power, in
all its beauty and perfection.*
Friedrich Von Schlegel

43 The Writing Process

Is the ability to write well a mysterious gift granted by God to only a few, or can everyone learn how to write well? Professional writers have learned through experience that writing does not come easily for anyone. They know that good writing is mainly the result of careful planning and hard work just as quality work is the result of planning and diligence in other worthwhile professions.

An architect does not naturally know how to build buildings that are functional and efficient and that will stand the stress of time; he must learn the process of putting a building together piece by piece. He must know the strengths and weaknesses of the various raw materials that he selects to go into the building. He must know the purpose of the building and how it is to be used and by whom. Some architects are better than others because they are careful to follow the basic principles that make a building functional. Some even become famous if they can add the artistic element to the functional. Others are only fair because they do not spend enough time thinking and planning before they begin to draw. As a result they put electric switches behind doors, or neglect to put a door where one is needed, causing inconvenience and distress for the users of the building.

Similar principles apply to writing. No one naturally knows how to write well. He must learn how to do it. Not everyone can become a great writer, but everyone can and should learn how to communicate his ideas clearly and effectively. One can do this by following the basic writing process as practiced by most successful writers. This process is basically the same regardless of the length of the composition. In brief, the process consists of (1) focusing on a subject and planning what to say about it, (2) writing a rough draft without interruption, (3) rewriting, and (4) editing.

Comp. 43.1

43.1 **The Writer Plans.** The amateur writer often starts writing too soon. He gets a vague idea about a subject, gathers a few specifics, and starts writing. The professional writer spends most of his time focusing on a subject and gathering and organizing information about his subject. He does not begin to write until he has an abundance of supporting material from which to choose.

One writer said that every finished page in his recently published book was written from approximately fifteen pages of supporting material: lists of descriptive details, examples, reasons, statistics, quotations, incidents. That means that if his book contained two hundred pages, he had three thousand pages of material from which to select.

Effective writing flows from an abundance of specific information about the subject, which has been evaluated, selected, and organized. This first part of the writing process may indeed be the most important of all.

43.2 **The Writer Writes.** After the planning is complete, the writer prepares the first draft. Writing on every other line, he writes the first draft as rapidly as possible. He does not allow anything to interrupt. If at a certain point, he cannot think of just the right word or is not sure of the spelling of a word, he does not stop to look it up; he leaves a blank for the word he cannot think of and circles the word that may be misspelled. If he realizes that he has written a garbled sentence, he does not stop to straighten it out. If he recognizes that his supporting material is insufficient, he does not stop to look for more; he just keeps writing. It is important that he push on to the end of the paper. Certainly he wants his sentences to be grammatically correct and free from mechanical errors. Of course, he wants his words to be exact and correctly spelled, but in the first draft the most important thing is to get his ideas down onto paper. He will then go back and fill in the gaps in his thinking, straighten out twisted sentences, and find those words that will exactly express his meaning.

A writer should overcome the tendency to "perfect" one sentence at a time in the first draft. Most writers do not work that way. Trying to perfect one sentence at a time is like trying to build one wall at a time. A builder does not normally build one wall, paint it, and hang pictures on it before he erects the basic structure of all the others. Neither should a writer attempt to polish each sentence before he knows if or how it will fit into the overall composition. He should write the first draft without interruption no matter how clumsy and inadequate the wording may be.

Comp.
43.3

43.3 **The Writer Rewrites.** Often when the first draft has been completed the inexperienced writer thinks that he is finished, except for proofreading. The professional writer knows that the writing has just begun. He knows that good writing results from rewriting again and again until the piece finally takes the desired shape.

Listen to these statements from some famous authors. Leo Tolstoy: "I can't understand how anyone can write without rewriting everything over and over again." Anthony Trollope: "There is no way of writing well and also of writing easily." James A. Michener: "I have never thought of myself as a good writer. Anyone who wants reassurance of that should read one of my first drafts. But I'm one of the world's great rewriters. I find that three or four readings are required to comb out the clichés, line up pronouns with their antecedents, and insure agreement in number between subjects and verbs. . . . You write the first draft really to see how it's going to come out. My connectives, my clauses, my subsidiary phrases don't come naturally to me and I'm very prone to repetition of words; so I never even write an important letter in the first draft. I can never recall anything of mine that's ever been printed in less than three drafts." Robert E. Sherwood, who worked with Franklin D. Roosevelt on his speeches: "I don't know what was the record number of distinct drafts of a single speech but it must have been well over twelve, and in the final draft there might not be one sentence that had survived from the first draft."

Though many such quotations could be given, from these the student writer should realize that rewriting is normal; it is an essential part of the writer's work.

How then does a writer rewrite? First he looks at the work as a whole. He is not yet concerned about grammar and mechanics; he will check those things later. Right now he wants to know whether he has everything on paper that needs to be there—no more and no less—and whether everything is in the proper order. He asks himself some questions: Does the work have *unity?* (Do all the parts contribute to the single idea of the whole, or has some detail slipped in that is interesting but unrelated?) Does the work have *coherence?* (Are the ideas carefully distinguished from one another? Are the ideas in good order so that the thought flows smoothly from beginning to end? Are additional continuity devices needed?) Does the work have the proper *emphasis?* (Has each part been developed at a length proportionate to its importance in the composition?) In short, is the composition clear, complete, and effective?

The writer will indicate on the first draft what needs to be removed, added, or rearranged. Sometimes he may have to make an outline of what he has written in order to see how to straighten out the arrangement. Then the writer will often find it necessary to write a complete new draft from beginning to end. If such a draft is necessary, he writes it in much the same manner as he did the first: he writes through to the end without interruption. When he completes the second draft, he subjects it to the same scrutiny as the first. He keeps rewriting and rewriting until he is sure that he has included just the right amount of information necessary to develop his subject fully and effectively, and that he has the material in the best order. When that draft is complete, the writer assumes the role of an editor.

43.4 **The Writer Edits.** Now the writer goes back and examines everything in the minutest detail. First he checks each *paragraph* for unity, coherence, and emphasis (section 44.4–44.6). Next he checks each *sentence* for correctness, clarity, and effectiveness (sections 13–26). At the same time, he checks the grammar and mechanics. Then he checks the *phrases* for accurate figures of speech and correct idiom. He eliminates jargon, triteness, and wordiness (sections 30–34). Finally he checks the *words.* He checks to see that he has used vivid verbs and concrete nouns, and that his words are appropriate to his audience (sections 28–29). He also checks for misspelled words. After all corrections have been made, the writer makes his final copy and proofreads it for mechanical accuracy.

Plan, write, rewrite, edit—these are the things that writers do.

44 The Paragraph

A paragraph is a group of sentences developing one topic. A paragraph contains a topic sentence, sentences supporting the topic sentence, and sometimes a summarizing sentence. Good paragraphs are arranged and developed according to a definite plan.

Comp
44

44.1 **Topic sentence. The *topic sentence* is the sentence that states the *main idea* of the paragraph.** The topic sentence is usually the first sentence in the paragraph. For variety, however, it may be placed at the end or within the paragraph. Sometimes the topic sentence is only implied, not written.

44.2 **Summarizing sentence.** A *summarizing* (or clincher) *sentence* is sometimes used at the end of a paragraph, especially if the paragraph is long. This sentence states in different words the topic sentence used earlier in the paragraph.

In the following paragraph, the first sentence is the topic sentence and the last sentence is a summarizing sentence.

> **1** The human instruments which God uses in great triumphs of faith are no pacifists, but great fighters like Paul himself. Little affinity for the great apostle has the whole tribe of considerers of consequences, the whole tribe of the compromisers ancient and modern. The real companions of Paul are the great heroes of the faith. But who are those heroes? Are they not true fighters, one and all? Tertullian fought a mighty battle against Marcion; Athanasius fought against the Arians; Augustine fought against Pelagius; and as for Luther, he fought a brave battle against kings and princes and popes for the liberty of the people of God. Luther was a great fighter; and we love him for it. So was Calvin; so were John Knox and all the rest. It is impossible to be a true soldier of Jesus Christ and not fight.
>
> —From "The Good Fight of Faith" by Dr. J. Gresham Machen in *Valiant for the Truth* edited by David Otis Fuller, copyright © 1961 David Otis Fuller.

44.3 **Development. To develop a paragraph, write sentences containing specific details that will support the idea of the topic sentence.** The following are four common ways of developing paragraphs: giving *examples,* telling *incidents,* giving *reasons,* and using *comparison and contrast.*

Comp.
44.1

DEVELOPMENT BY *EXAMPLES*

2   The English government began to have some suspicion that "Brown Bess" was not all that a gun might be. . . . At the battle of Salamanca, there were three million five hundred thousand cartridges, and six thousand balls fired, and several charges made both by the foot and cavalry, and yet there were only eight thousand men killed and wounded, from which comes the inference that only one shot in four hundred and thirty-seven took effect. During the Caffre war, in a single engagement there were eighty thousand cartridges fired, resulting in the knocking over of twenty-five of the enemy. A square of British infantry, at Waterloo, fired at short range on a body of French cavalry which was charging, and emptied only two or three saddles. In another case, a fire of a square on cavalry, at thirty paces, brought down only three men. The French troops during the Crimean war fired some twenty-five million cartridges, of which not more than one in two thousand took effect.

—From *The Great Inventions* by F. B. Wilkie.

DEVELOPMENT BY AN *INCIDENT*

3   Peter the Great, a half-savage in his manners, never had pleasantry enough to play a joke, though some of his rudeness had a very comical effect. On his second visit to a town in Holland, he and the burgomaster attended Divine service, when an unconscious action of the Czar almost upset the gravity of the congregation. Peter, feeling his head growing cold, turned to the heavily-wigged chief magistrate by his side and transferred the wig, the hair of which flowed down over the great little man's shoulders, to his own head, and sat so till the end of the service, when he returned it to the insulted burgomaster, bowing his thanks. The great man's fury was not appeased till one of Peter's suite assured him that it was no practical joke that his

Comp.
44.3

majesty had played; that his usual custom when at church, if his head was cold, was to seize the nearest wig he could clutch.

—From *Worthington's Stories of Natural History.*

DEVELOPMENT BY *REASONS*

4 Young man, your personal value depends entirely upon your possession of religion. You are worth to yourself what you are capable of enjoying; you are worth to society the happiness you are capable of imparting. To yourself, without religion, you are worth very little. A man whose aims are low, whose motives are selfish, who has in his heart no adoration for the great God, and no love of his Christ, whose will is not subordinate to the Supreme will—gladly and gratefully—who has no faith, no tenable hope of a happy immortality, no strong-armed trust that with his soul it shall be well in all the future, cannot be worth very much to himself. Neither can such a man be worth very much to society, because he has not that to bestow which society most needs for its prosperity and its happiness. A locomotive off the track is worth nothing to its owner or the public so long as it is off the track. The conditions of its legitimate and highest value are not complied with. It cannot be operated satisfactorily to the owner, or usefully to the public, because it is not where it was intended to run by the man who made it.

—Josiah Gilbert Holland

DEVELOPMENT BY *COMPARISON AND CONTRAST*

Use comparison and contrast to show the similarities and differences between two or more subjects (persons, places, things, or ideas). Select significant points of comparison directly related to your purpose, and then develop those points. There are three common methods of presenting points of comparison: (1) *Subject-at-a-time.* In the first portion of the paragraph, you present a complete picture of the first subject; in the second portion of

Comp.
44.3

the paragraph you present a complete picture of the second subject, discussing comparable points. If the discussion is of some length, you may wish to use separate paragraphs for each subject. (2) *Point-by-point.* You take up one point and tell how each subject compares on that point; then you take up the next point and tell how each subject compares on that point, etc. Use this method if you wish to emphasize the individual points of comparison and not the overall picture of each subject. (3) *Likeness-difference.* You give all the similarities of the subjects being compared; then you give the differences, or vice versa.

The first selection below is an example of *subject-at-a-time* development; the second, *point-by-point;* and the third, *likeness-difference.*

5 For full success the two, genius and talent, should coexist in one mind in balanced proportions so that they can play smoothly together in effective combination. Genius is that quality or character of the mind which is inventive, or generates; which gives to the world new ideas in science, art, literature, morals, or religion; which recognizes no set rules or principles, but is a law unto itself, and rejoices in its own originality; which admitting of a direction, never follows the old beaten track, but strikes out for a new course; which has no fears of public opinion, nor leans upon public favor—always leads but never follows; and which admits no truth unless convinced by experiment, reflection, or investigation.

Talent is that power or capacity of mind which reasons rapidly from cause to effect; which sees through a thing at a glance, and comprehends the rules and principles upon which it works; which can take in knowledge without laborious mental study, and needs no labored illustrations to impress a principle or a fact, no matter how abstruse, hidden, complex, or intricate. Differing from genius by following rules and principles, but capable of comprehending the works of genius, talent is the able, comprehensive agent; while genius is the master director.

—Haines and Yaggy

Comp.
44.3

193

6 Thus it is, that in the children of God, repentance and faith exactly answer each other. By repentance, we feel the sin remaining in our hearts, and cleaving to our words and actions: by faith we receive the power of God in Christ, purifying our hearts, and cleansing our hands. By repentance we are still sensible that we deserve punishment for all our tempers, and words, and actions: by faith we are conscious that our Advocate with the Father is continually pleading for us, and thereby continually turning aside all condemnation and punishment from us. By repentance we have an abiding conviction, that there is no help in us: by faith we receive not only mercy, "but grace to help in" *every* "time of need." Repentance disclaims the very possibility of any other help: faith accepts all the help we stand in need of, from Him that hath all power in heaven and earth. Repentance says, "Without Him I can do nothing": Faith says, "I can do all things through Christ strengthening me." Through Him I can not only overcome, but expel, all the enemies of my soul. Through Him I can "love the Lord my God with all my heart, mind, soul, and strength"; yea, and "walk in holiness and righteousness before Him all the days of my life."

—From "The Repentance of Believers" by John Wesley.

7 So Grant and Lee were in complete contrast, representing two diametrically opposed elements in American life. Grant was the modern man emerging; beyond him, ready to come on the stage, was the great age of steel and machinery, of crowded cities and a restless, burgeoning vitality. Lee might have ridden down from the old age of chivalry, lance in hand, silken banner fluttering over his head. Each man was the perfect champion of his cause, drawing both his strengths and his weaknesses from the people he led.

Yet it was not all contrast, after all. Different as they were—in background, in personality, in underlying aspiration—these two great soldiers had much in common. Under everything else, they were marvelous fighters. Furthermore, their fighting qualities were really very much alike.

Each man had, to begin with, the great virtue of utter tenacity and fidelity. Grant fought his way down the Mississippi Valley in spite of acute personal discouragement and profound military handicaps. Lee hung on in the trenches at Petersburg after hope itself had died. In each man there was an indomitable quality . . . the born fighter's refusal to give up as long as he can still remain on his feet and lift his two fists.

Daring and resourcefulness they had, too; the ability to think faster and move faster than the enemy. These were the qualities which gave Lee the dazzling campaigns of Second Manassas and Chancelorsville and won Vicksburg for Grant.

Lastly, and perhaps greatest of all, there was the ability, at the end, to turn quickly from war to peace once the fighting was over. Out of the way these two men behaved at Appomattox came the possibility of a peace of reconciliation. It was a possibility not wholly realized, in the years to come, but which did, in the end, help the two sections to become one nation again. . . . Two great Americans, Grant and Lee—very different, yet under everything very much alike. Their encounter at Appomattox was one of the great moments of American history.

—Bruce Catton, "Grant and Lee: A Study in Contrasts" from *The American Story,* ed. Early Schenck Miers. Copyright United States Capitol Historical Society, all rights reserved.

DEVELOPMENT BY A *COMBINATION OF METHODS*

Up until now we have seen how paragraphs may be developed by one of four methods: incident, examples, reasons, and comparison and contrast. Good writers, however, rarely use just one method to develop paragraphs; they often combine several methods to effectively support their topics.

Comp. 44.3

The following paragraph is developed by a combination of methods. The four sentences before the topic sentence contain *examples* supporting the idea that Johnson's writings had declined in popularity. The first three sentences following the topic sentence give the *reasons* that Johnson, the man, was still popular. The next sentence gives *descriptive details* about Johnson. The last sentence is a clincher sentence.

8 Since his death the popularity of his works—the *Lives of the Poets,* and, perhaps, the *Vanity of Human Wishes,* excepted—has greatly diminished. His *Dictionary* has been altered by editors till it can scarcely be called his. An allusion to his *Rambler* or his *Idler* is not readily apprehended in literary circles. The fame even of *Rasselas* has grown somewhat dim. **But though the celebrity of the writings may have declined, the celebrity of the writer, strange to say, is as great as ever.** Boswell's book [*The Life of Samuel Johnson*] has done for him more than the best of his own books could do. The memory of other authors is kept alive by their works. But the memory of Johnson keeps many of his works alive. The old philosopher is still among us in the brown coat with the metal buttons and the shirt which ought to be at wash, blinking, puffing, rolling his head, drumming with his fingers, tearing his meat like a tiger, and swallowing his tea in oceans. No human being who has been more than seventy years in the grave is so well known to us.

—From *The Life of Samuel Johnson* by Macaulay.

44.4 **Unity. A good paragraph has *unity.*** *Unity* means that every sentence in the paragraph develops the idea stated in the topic sentence. Any sentence that does not support the topic sentence should be removed from the paragraph.

In each of the following paragraphs, the sentence in italics does not support the topic sentence (in bold type) and destroys the unity of the paragraph.

Comp.
44.4

9 **Of all the weapons used by the ancients none were so effective as the bow in the hands of the English archer.** Every reader is familiar with romances in which the English bow plays an essential part, and of battles in which it decided the victory. It was brought into England by the Normans, who had obtained it from some of the Norse tribes. Its regulation height was that of the bowman, and the arrow was half the length of the bow, or about three feet, and thus obtained the name of the "cloth-yard shaft." *Although they also used spears and clubs, most North American Indians fought their wars armed with the bow and arrow.* Some of the tales which are narrated of the skill with which the bow was handled, would prove that even the best of the sharp-shooters of modern time, with their weapons of precision, are in no respect superior to the experts who twanged the bow of yew in the days of Robin Hood, and his "merrie archers." To hit a branch a half an inch in thickness, set upright at a distance of three hundred feet, was considered a feat of no extraordinary character. As to penetrating power, it was not an uncommon feat for an English archer to drive a shaft clean through a breastplate of steel, and through the body of the knight behind it.

—From *The Great Inventions* by F. B. Wilkie.

10 **The style of Bunyan is delightful to every reader, and invaluable as a study to every person who wishes to obtain a wide command over the English language.** The vocabulary is the vocabulary of the common people. *William Wordsworth believed that a good poet would write in the language of the common people.* There is not an expression, if we except a few technical terms of theology, which would puzzle the rudest peasant. We have observed several pages which do not contain a single word of more than two syllables. Yet no writer has said more exactly what he meant to say. For magnificence, for pathos, for vehement exhortation, for subtle disquisition, for every purpose of the poet, the orator, and the divine, this homely dialect, the dialect of working men, is perfectly sufficient.

Comp.
44.4

—Macaulay

44.5 **Coherence.** *Coherence* **means that your details are in such good order and the relationships between the details are so clear that the resulting paragraph is** *easy to understand.* Following are some things you can do to make your paragraph coherent.

a. *Arrange your details* **in a definite order.**

(1) **Chronological (time) order**

(2) **Space order**

(3) **Order of importance**

b. *Use continuity devices* **to help your ideas flow smoothly from one sentence to the next.**

(1) **Pronoun reference**—Use pronouns to refer to a noun in a preceding sentence.

(2) **Repetition**—Repeat key words and phrases.

(3) **Transitional expressions** (The following are frequently used transitional expressions.)

and, but, yet, nor	for instance
therefore	first, second, third, etc.
as a result	in the first place
nevertheless	on the contrary
next	then
finally	here
still	however
meanwhile	moreover
nearby	above
otherwise	whereas
in addition	similarly
below	beyond
in fact	in short
again	also
opposite to	next to
just as	accordingly
furthermore	besides
across from	before me
in other words	thus
likewise	equally important
in the distance	for example
to the left	to the right
to sum up	

CHRONOLOGICAL ORDER

This arrangement is used when the writer must give events in the order they happened. Chronological order is used in explaining the steps in a process and in writing stories and incidents.

11 When I was a boy, I had to study the Latin grammar; but it was dull, and I hated it. My father was anxious to send me to college, and therefore I studied the grammar, till I could bear it no longer; and going to my father, I told him I did not like study, and asked for some other employment. It was opposing his wishes, and he was quick in his answer. "Well, John, if Latin grammar does not suit you, you may try ditching; perhaps that will; my meadow yonder needs a ditch, and you may put by Latin and try that." This seemed a delightful change, and to the meadow I went. But I soon found ditching harder than Latin, and the first forenoon was the longest I ever experienced. That day I ate the bread of Labour, and glad was I when night came on. That night I made some comparison between Latin grammar and ditching, but said not a word about it. I dug next forenoon, and wanted to return to Latin at dinner; but it was humiliating, and I could not do it. At night, toil conquered pride; and though it was one of the severest trials I ever had in my life, I told my father that, if he chose, I would go back to Latin grammar. He was glad of it; and if I have since gained any distinction, it has been owing to the two days' labour in that abominable ditch.

—John Adams

SPACE ORDER

This arrangement is used especially for descriptions. The details of the descriptions may be presented from near to far, from far to near, from top to bottom, from right to left, from center to periphery, and so forth. Regardless of the method you use, details must be presented in a way that

Comp.
44.5

199

makes their location clear. Can you easily determine the location of the details in the following paragraph?

12 I found myself in a lofty antique hall, the roof supported by massive joists of old English oak. It was soberly lighted by a row of Gothic windows at a considerable height from the floor, and which apparently opened upon the roofs of the cloisters. An ancient picture of some reverend dignitary of the Church in his robes hung over the fireplace. Around the hall and in a small gallery were the books, arranged in carved oaken cases. They consisted principally of old polemical writers, and were much more worn by time than by use. In the centre of the library was a solitary table with two or three books on it, an inkstand without ink, and a few pens parched by long disuse. The place seemed fitted for quiet study and profound meditation. It was buried deep among the massive walls of the abbey, and shut up from the tumult of the world.

—Washington Irving

ORDER OF IMPORTANCE

This arrangement is common in paragraphs that are developed by reasons or examples. If the details vary in importance, the writer usually begins with the least important or least dramatic reason or example and progresses to the most important or most dramatic reason or example. Can you determine the order of the details in the following paragraph?

13 Digging coal from the ground is dangerous work. Sometimes the rock in the roof of a tunnel will fall and completely block the passage. Then the men working in the innermost parts of the mine are suffocated before they can be rescued. If a coal mine gets on fire near the entrance, the miners in the far interior will perish if the fire cannot be extinguished quickly. There is a third danger, the most serious of all. Coal has tucked away between its atoms of carbon a very dangerous gas, called firedamp. When the miner cuts out great blocks of coal from the end of the tunnel, sometimes quantities of this gas escape and fill the mine. Not only is it suffocating, if there is too much of it, but also it is very explosive. A spark will cause an explosion which will wreck a mine and sometimes kill hundreds of miners.

—From *America's Treasure* by W. Maxwell Reed, published by Harcourt Brace Jovanovich, Inc.

PRONOUN REFERENCE

Coherence can be maintained by using pronouns to refer to a noun in a preceding sentence, as is done in the following selection.

14 The **Bible** is wonderfully adapted to all. Simple as the language of a child—**it** charms the most fastidious taste. Mournful as the voice of grief—**it** reaches to the highest pitch of exultation. Intelligible to the unlearned peasant—**it** supplies the critic and the sage with food for earnest thought. Silent and secret as the reproofs of conscience—**it** echoes beneath the vaulted dome of the cathedral, and shakes the trembling multitude. The last companion of the dying and destitute—**it** seals the bridal vow, and crowns the majesty of kings. Closed in the heedless grasp of the luxurious and the slothful—**it** unfolds **its** awful record over the yawning grave. Bright and joyous as the morning star to the benighted traveler—**it** rolls like the waters of the deluge over the path of him who willfully mistakes his way.

—Sarah S. Ellis

REPETITION

Coherence can be maintained by repeating key words and phrases to remind the reader of the central idea of the paragraph.

15 Though I speak with the tongues of men and of angels, and have not **charity,** I am become as sounding brass, or a tinkling cymbal. And though I have the gift of prophecy, and understand all mysteries,

Comp.
44.5

and all knowledge; and though I have all faith, so that I could remove mountains, and have not **charity,** I am nothing. And though I bestow all my goods to feed the poor, and though I give my body to be burned, and have not **charity,** it profiteth me nothing. **Charity** suffereth long, and is kind; **charity** envieth not; **charity** vaunteth not itself, is not puffed up, doth not behave itself unseemly, seeketh not her own, is not easily provoked, thinketh no evil; rejoiceth not in iniquity, but rejoiceth in the truth; beareth all things, believeth all things, hopeth all things, endureth all things. **Charity** never faileth: but whether there be prophecies, they shall fail; whether there be tongues, they shall cease; whether there be knowledge, it shall vanish away. For we know in part, and we prophesy in part. But when that which is perfect is come, then that which is in part shall be done away. When I was a child, I spake as a child, I understood as a child, I thought as a child: but when I became a man, I put away childish things. For now we see through a glass, darkly; but then face to face: now I know in part; but then shall I know even as also I am known. And now abideth faith, hope, **charity,** these three; but the greatest of these is **charity.**

—1 Corinthians 13

TRANSITIONAL EXPRESSIONS

Coherence can be maintained by using transitional words and phrases (44.5b). These expressions usually occur near the beginning of a sentence, showing the relationships between sentences.

16 **Moreover,** brethren, I declare unto you the gospel which I preached unto you, which also ye have received, and wherein ye stand; by which also ye are saved, if ye keep in memory what I preached unto you, unless ye have believed in vain. **For** I delivered unto you **first of all** that which I also received, how that Christ died for our sins according to the scriptures; and that He was buried, and that He rose again the third day according to the scrip-

Comp.
44.5

tures: and that he was seen of Cephas, **then** of the twelve: **after that,** He was seen of above five hundred brethren at once: of whom the greater part remain unto this present, but some are fallen asleep. **After that,** He was seen of James; **then** of all the apostles. **And last of all** He was seen of me also, as one born out of due time.

—1 Corinthians 15:1–8

44.6 **Emphasis. A paragraph has proper *emphasis* when the relative importance of its points is made plain by their position and by the amount of space given to them.** The most important point is usually placed at the end or at the beginning of the paragraph. Each point should be developed at a length proportionate to its importance.

44.7 **Writing the paragraph**

a. Write the topic sentence making sure to treat only one aspect of your subject.

b. Make an abundant list of details to support the topic sentence.

c. Eliminate from the list any unrelated ideas.

d. Select the most convincing and most interesting details, keeping your audience in mind. Use as much detail as necessary to make the paragraph clear and effective.

e. Put your details in order (44.5a).

f. Write the first draft. Use every other line. (See 43.2.)

g. Rewrite the paragraph. (See 43.3, the last two paragraphs.)

h. Edit the paragraph. (See 43.4.)

i. Make a final neat copy.

45 The Essay

Comp.
45

This section explains how to write a full-length composition. Section 44 dealt with individual paragraphs, and many of the same principles that apply to writing good paragraphs also apply to writing full-length compositions. Specific kinds of compositions are explained in sections 49–63. Those various kinds of compositions, treated separately there, are often equivalent to minor portions of a full-length composition.

The following are the main steps in writing a composition.

1. Select a subject.
2. Limit the subject.
3. Organize the ideas.
4. Write the first draft.
5. Rewrite the composition.
6. Edit the composition.
7. Write the final draft.

45.1 Select a subject.

a. **Select a subject that is of special interest to you.** It is difficult to interest others in something that you are not interested in.

b. **Select a subject that the general reader will care to hear about.**

c. **Whenever the assignment permits, select a subject about which you can write from personal experience.** This experience may be something you have actually done or something you have observed in the experiences of others.

45.2 Limit the subject.

a. **Select an aspect of your subject that can be adequately treated within the assigned number of pages.** It is better to write "more about less" than to write "less about more." Observe these progressive limitations of a very broad subject.

> School Activities
> Student Organizations
> Departmental Clubs
> Debating Club

b. **Write out your purpose.** Stating your purpose for writing will give your paper direction and will help you to avoid the inclusion of unrelated ideas. The statement of purpose tells what or how you will write about your subject. You may put forth a judgment which you intend to *prove,* or you may simply *explain, describe, demonstrate,* or *explore* your subject.

If you can inject an argumentative element into your statement of purpose, you can more readily determine what your purpose is and at the same time arouse the interest of your readers. An example: "This paper will explain why it was wrong to give away the Panama Canal." Such a statement is much more provocative than "This paper will discuss the Panama Canal Treaty." Saying that the treaty was wrong will arouse those who think it was right, and will cause those who agree with you to read on to see how you prove your point.

The following are two ways one could treat the subject "Our Debating Club":

> "My purpose is to explain the various functions of our debating club."
>
> "My purpose is to show that the debating club does more than any other club to bring city-wide recognition to our school."

Taking plenty of time to state your purpose exactly will save you time overall, will help you to write a better paper, and will make the writing of the paper easier.

c. **Analyze your audience.** Ask yourself the following questions.

(1) Who makes up my audience? (Is this a specific, clearly limited audience or is it a general audience of readers? Consider people you know, such as classmates, friends, relatives, and neighbors, as part of your audience. What is their age, economic status, religion, education, philosophy, vocation, and so forth?)

(2) What do these readers already know about this subject?

(3) What do these readers want to know or need to know about this subject?

Comp.
45.2

(4) What effect do I want to have on these readers?

205

45.3 **Organize the ideas.**

a. Make a list of ideas. Write down any idea related to your purpose that you think you might use. Do not be concerned about the order. Of course you may need to do some research to supplement what you already know about your subject. Make sure that you have an abundance of supporting material. (See 43.1.)

b. Cross out any unnecessary or unrelated ideas. Compare each idea in your list with your statement of purpose. If you find any ideas that do not support your purpose, cross them off your list.

c. Make these points into an outline.

(1) Determine the main headings. Sometimes the main headings come from the list you made. Many times you will have to make up your own headings. Refer to your statement of purpose to help you make your main headings.

(2) Group the remaining ideas under the main headings.

(3) Decide which points will be subheadings and which points will be supporting details. You may have to make up some of the subheadings.

(4) Arrange the main points and subpoints in some clear order (chronological, order of importance, comparison / contrast, and so forth).

(5) Decide what kind of outline to use—topical or sentence. (See 46.1.)

(6) Make the outline according to the proper form. (See 46.2 and 46.3i–k.)

▶Note. A complete formal outline may not always be necessary for some of the shorter compositions, but you should at least jot down your ideas, eliminate unrelated ideas, and put your points in order.

Comp.
45.3

45.4 **Write the first draft. (See 43.2.)** Compositions have three parts: the *introduction,* the *body,* and the *conclusion.* All three parts are important. You cannot neglect any of the three parts and expect to have an effective composition.

a. The introduction

(1) Length. The length of the introduction varies with the length of the composition. A long composition may have a paragraph or two; a short composition may have only one brief paragraph; some short compositions may have only one sentence which is a part of the first paragraph in the body.

(2) Content. The purpose of the introduction is to capture your readers' attention and to lead them into your subject. Begin the introduction with a good attention-getter: startling statistics, a brief story, a quotation or proverb, a statement of an unusual opinion, a reference to a historical or current event, the revelation of a controversy, or a description of a compelling scene. End the introduction by making clear what you intend to discuss and what plan you shall follow. Use your statement of purpose, but rephrase it as a thesis sentence. For example, "The debating club does more than any other club to bring city-wide recognition to our school."

b. The body

(1) Follow your outline.

(2) Maintain the proper emphasis. Give your more important points proportionately more space in your composition.

(3) On your outline, mark off the points that are to be included in each paragraph. Sometimes you may write only one paragraph for each main point, including all the subpoints. Sometimes you may have two or three paragraphs for a main point— perhaps one paragraph for each of the subpoints under a main point.

▶ Note. As you write the first draft, do not be overly concerned about the paragraphing. The most important thing in the first draft is to keep your thoughts flowing and to get all the ideas onto paper. You will go back later and check each paragraph. (See 45.6.)

Comp. 45.4

(4) Develop each paragraph fully. Have a topic sentence for each paragraph and develop the topic sentences by using examples, incidents, reasons, etc. (See 44.3.)

(5) Use all the methods of maintaining unity and coherence taught in 44.4–5. Especially important is the use of transitions. Transitions are necessary to tie the various paragraphs together into a unified whole. In a long composition the transition may be a sentence, a phrase, or a word (usually placed at the beginning of the next paragraph rather than at the end of the preceding paragraph). The following are some common transitional expressions:

Time—*first, second, third, in the first place, next, then, meanwhile, in the meantime, finally*

Space—*here, nearby, above, below, beside, beyond*

Addition—*and, moreover, in addition, similarly, again, besides*

Contrast—*but, yet, nor, on the other hand, nevertheless, on the contrary, however*

Alternative—*otherwise, whereas, else*

Repetition—*in fact, in short, that is, in other words*

Result—*consequently, accordingly, thus, hence, therefore, as a result*

c. The conclusion

(1) Do not just stop after writing the body of your composition. You must round out your composition and leave your reader with a sense of assurance that you are finished.

(2) The conclusion should reemphasize the main idea of your paper by harking back to your thesis sentence and by referring to the attention-getter that you used in your introduction. You may expand the conclusion with a prediction, an apt quotation, an appropriate anecdote, or a suggestion of results and significances.

▶ Note. For a short paper, it is not necessary or desirable to summarize your points.

Comp.
45.4

d. The Title. Give each composition a title. Your title should capture attention, suggest the topic of your paper, and set the tone. Make it as short as possible. Sometimes you can settle on a title before you begin your first draft; sometimes you cannot decide on a good one until you have finished your paper. Professional writers often write a hundred or more titles before they hit upon just the right one.

45.5 **Rewrite the composition.**
Look at the work as a whole. Do not be concerned about grammar, sentence structure, or mechanics at this point.

a. Ask yourself the following questions.

(1) Is the work *complete?* (Is everything on paper that needs to be there—no more and no less?)

(2) Are all the parts in the right *order?*

(3) Does the work have *unity?* (Do all the parts contribute to the single idea of the whole, or has some unrelated detail slipped in?)

(4) Does the overall work have *coherence?* (Does the thought flow smoothly from one paragraph to the next? Are additional continuity devices needed? 44.5b)

(5) Does the work have the proper *emphasis?* (Has each part been developed at a length proportionate to its importance in the composition?)

b. Rewrite until you have satisfied the five questions above. (See 43.3, the last paragraph.)

45.6 **Edit the composition.**

a. Check each *paragraph* for unity, coherence, and emphasis (sections 44.4–44.6).

b. Check the *sentences* for correctness, clarity, and effectiveness (sections 13–26). Also check the grammar and mechanics.

c. Check the *phrases* for accurate figures of speech and correct idiom. Eliminate jargon, triteness, and wordiness (sections 30–34).

Comp. 45.6

    d. Check the *words*. Did you use vivid verbs and concrete nouns? Are your words appropriate to your audience (sections 28–29)? Are there any misspelled words?

45.7   **Write the final draft.**

    a. Write an appropriate title for your paper. The title should indicate your subject and purpose and should attempt to attract the reader's interest.

    b. Write a neat final copy of your composition according to the information given in section 36.

    c. Read your final copy and make neat corrections for any copying errors you may have made.

The following is a good example of a full-length composition.

The Marks of an Educated Man

¶ 1. A question often asked is "What are the marks of an educated man?" It is plain that one may gain no inconsiderable body of learning in some special field of knowledge without at the same time acquiring those habits and traits which are the marks of an educated gentleman. A reasonable amount of learning must of course accompany an education, but, after all, that amount need not be so very great in any one field. An education will make its mark and find its evidences in certain traits, characteristics, and capacities which have to be acquired by patient endeavor, by following good example, and by receiving wise discipline and sound instruction.

¶ 2. These traits or characteristics may be variously described and classified, but among them are five that should always stand out clearly enough to be seen of all men.

¶ 3. The first of these is correctness and precision in the use of the mother tongue. The quite shocking slovenliness and vulgarity of much of the spoken English, as well as not a

Comp. 45.7

210

little of the written English, which one hears and sees proves beyond peradventure that years of attendance upon schools and colleges that are thought to be respectable have produced no impression. When one hears English well spoken, with pure diction, correct pronunciation, and an almost unconscious choice of the right word, he recognizes it at once. How much easier he finds it to imitate English of the other sort!

¶ **4.** A second and indispensable trait of the educated man is refined and gentle manners, which are themselves the expression of fixed habits of thought and action. "Manners makyth the man," wrote William of Wykeham over his gates at Winchester and at Oxford. He pointed to a great truth. When manners are superficial, artificial, and forced, no matter what their form, they are bad manners. When, however, they are the natural expression of fixed habits of thought and action, and when they reveal a refined and cultivated nature, they are good manners. There are certain things that gentlemen do not do, and they do not do them simply because they are bad manners. The gentleman instinctively knows the difference between those things which he may and should do and those things which he may not and should not do.

¶ **5.** A third trait of the educated man is the power and habit of reflection. Human beings for the most part live wholly on the surface of life. They do not look beneath that surface or far beyond the present moment and that part of the future which is quickly to follow it. They do not read those works of prose and poetry which have become classic because they reveal power and habit of reflection and induce that power and habit in others. When one reflects long enough to ask the question *how?*, he is on the way to knowing something about

Comp. 45.7

science. When he reflects long enough to ask the question *why?*, he may, if he persists, even become a philosopher.

¶ **6.** A fourth trait of the educated man is the power of growth. He continues to grow and develop from birth to his dying day. His interests expand, his contacts multiply, his knowledge increases, and his reflection becomes deeper and wider. It would appear to be true that not many human beings, even those who have had a school and college education, continue to grow after they are twenty-four or twenty-five years of age. By that time it is usual to settle down to life on a level of more or less contented intellectual interest and activity. The whole present-day movement for adult education is a systematic and definite attempt to keep human beings growing long after they have left school and college, and, therefore, to help educate them.

¶ **7.** A fifth trait of the educated man is his possession of efficiency, or the power to do. The mere visionary dreamer, however charming or however wise, lacks something which an education requires. The power to do may be exercised in any one of a thousand ways, but when it clearly shows itself, that is evidence that the period of discipline of study and of companionship with parents and teachers has not been in vain.

¶ **8.** Given these five characteristics, one has the outline of an educated man. That outline may be filled in by scholarship, by literary power, by mechanical skills, by professional zeal and capacity, by business competence, or by social and political leadership. So long as the framework or outline is there, the content may be pretty much what you will, assuming, of course, that the fundamental elements of the great tradition which is civilization, and its outstanding records and achievements in human personality, in letters, in science, in the fine arts, and in human institutions, are all present.

—From "The Marks of an Educated Man" by Nicholas Murray Butler in the *Columbia Daily Spectator.*

Topics for Composition

1. Guns	17. Vitamins
2. Cars	18. Swimming strokes
3. Boats	19. Hats or shoes
4. Airplanes	20. Conservation or
5. Engines	pollution
6. Welding	21. Cities or towns
7. Pets	22. Students
8. Clouds	23. Fathers
9. Cooking	24. Salesmen
10. Advertising	25. Customers
11. Literature	26. Waitresses
12. Noises	27. Service station
13. Musical instuments	attendants
14. Propaganda	28. Sports fans
15. Trees	29. News commentators
16. Preserving food	30. Drivers

46 The Outline

An outline is valuable for several purposes: (1) for organizing one's thoughts before writing, (2) for checking the organization of a piece after it has been written, and (3) for understanding a difficult reading assignment.

There may be a few writers with very logical minds and excellent memories who can think through the organization of a work and retain its structure in their mind as they write. But most writers find that making an outline of some kind is absolutely essential to clear and effective writing.

The two most common kinds of outlines are explained here.

46.1 Kinds of outlines

Comp.
46.1

a. Topical outline. In the topical outline every heading is a word or a phrase, not a complete sentence. This kind of outline is often sufficient for short papers. It is especially suited to papers such as exposition of a process or classification, in which logical connections are no problem.

b. Sentence outline. In the sentence outline, every heading consists of a complete sentence. This kind of outline is usually more helpful for longer papers, such as a research paper. It is much better than the topical outline for *any* paper that requires the writer to see the logical relationships of the various parts.

46.2   The form of an outline

a. Outline form illustrated

    I. First main idea
        A. Subheading—supports first main idea
            1. Detail—supports subheading A
            2. Detail—supports subheading A
        B. Subheading—supports first main idea
    II. Second main idea
        A. Subheading—supports second main idea
        B. Subheading—supports second main idea
            1. Detail—supports subheading B
            2. Detail—supports subheading B

b. Outline form explained

(1) Use roman numerals for main ideas.

(2) Use capital letters for subheadings.

(3) Use arabic numerals for supporting details.

(4) Place a period after the numerals and letters that introduce the points in the outline.

(5) Indent each level of the outline.

(6) If there is an *A,* there must also be a *B.* If there is a *1,* there must also be a *2.*

(7) Begin every point in the outline with a capital letter.

(8) In a topical outline, state each point as a word or a phrase, not as a complete sentence.

(9) Do not place periods after any of the points in a topical outline.

(10) In a topical outline, state the points of each division in parallel form. Use the same kind of word or phrase within each division.

c. Parallelism in topical outline illustrated

Stars

Not Parallel	**Parallel**
I. White or yellow stars	I. White or yellow stars
II. Some stars are red.	II. Red stars
III. Blue-white are hottest.	III. Blue-white stars

46.3 How to make an outline

 a. Select a subject. Choose one that is not too broad to be adequately treated within the assigned number of pages. The subject "Diseases" is too broad for a brief composition, but the subject "Nutrition in Disease Prevention" is probably limited enough. The subject "Applied Science" is too broad even for a research paper, but "Refining and Fashioning Metals" is probably manageable.

 b. Write out your purpose. Your statement of purpose tells how you intend to treat your subject. For some compositions the statement of purpose can indicate only that your intention is to explain, narrate, describe, etc. For other compositions you can and should express your attitude toward your subject. Compare the following statements of purpose.

  "My purpose is to explain how metals are refined and fashioned."
  "My purpose is to explain why refining and fashioning of metals is important to the economy."
  "My purpose is to demonstrate that refining and fashioning of metals can be done more efficiently with the aid of computers."

 c. Make a list of ideas that support your subject. List the ideas as they occur to you. Do not be concerned about the order.

Comp.
46.3

 d. Cross out any unnecessary or unrelated ideas. Compare each idea in your list with your statement of purpose. If you find any ideas that do not support your purpose, cross them off your list.

e. Determine the main headings. Sometimes the main headings come from the list you made. Many times you will have to make up your own headings. Refer to your statement of purpose to help you make your main headings.

f. Group the remaining ideas under the main headings.

g. Decide which points will be subheadings and which points will be supporting details. You may have to make up some of the subheadings.

h. Arrange the main points and subpoints in some clear order.

i. If the outline is to be a topical outline, make sure that each point is only a word or phrase and that each point is stated in parallel grammatical form. Check all the points within each division to see that they are stated the same way: all adjectives, all nouns, all the same kind of phrase, etc.

j. If the outline is to be a sentence outline, make all the points into complete sentences. For each point that is still stated as a topic, ask yourself "What do I want to say about this topic?" Then write down a sentence in answer to that question.

k. As one writes from an outline he may make changes—crossing out points, adding some, moving others. If you are to turn in your outline with your composition, make sure to correct your outline so that it reflects the final organization of your paper.

46.4 Example of an outline going through successive stages of completion.

a. Purpose stated, ideas listed and evaluated

Refining and Fashioning Metals

Purpose: To explain how metals are refined and then fashioned into products.

refining by electrowinning ~~history of metallurgy~~

~~mining minerals~~ fashioning by centrifugal casting

distilling to refine metals using water to refine metals

refining by roasting
fashioning by cold rolling
~~properties of metals~~
fashioning by die casting
refining by heat

sand-casting to fashion
  metals
refining by electrochemical
  means

melting to refine metals
~~oxidized metals~~
~~uses of ores~~
fashioning by hot rolling
fashioning by the drawing
  process
fashioning by press
  forging
electrorefining process

b. Ideas grouped under main headings

I. Refining metals
  refining by electrowinning
  distilling to refine metals
  refining by roasting
  refining by heat
  refining by electrochemical means
  using water to refine metals
  melting to refine metals
  electrorefining process

II. Fashioning metals
  fashioning by cold rolling
  fashioning by die casting
  sand-casting to fashion metals
  fashioning by centrifugal casting
  fashioning by hot rolling
  fashioning by the drawing process
  fashioning by press forging

c. Subheadings and supporting details arranged in good order

I. Refining metals
  A. Using water to refine metals
  B. Refining by electrochemical means
    1. Electrorefining process
    2. Refining by electrowinning
  C. Refining by heat
    1. Distilling to refine metals
    2. Refining by roasting
    3. Melting to refine metals

Comp.
46.4

217

II. Fashioning metals
   A. Fashioning by press forging
   B. The rolling process
      1. Fashioning by hot rolling
      2. Fashioning by cold rolling
   C. Fashioning by the drawing process
   D. Fashioning by casting
      1. Sand-casting to fashion metals
      2. Fashioning by die casting
      3. Fashioning by centrifugal casting

d. Points of each division stated in parallel form

Refining and Fashioning Metals

Purpose: To explain how metals are refined and then fashioned into products.

I. Refining metals
   A. By water usage
   B. By electrochemical means
      1. Electrorefining
      2. Electrowinning
   C. By heat application
      1. Distilling
      2. Melting
      3. Roasting

II. Fashioning metals
   A. Forging
   B. Rolling
      1. Cold rolling
      2. Hot rolling
   C. Drawing
   D. Casting
      1. Die-casting
      2. Centrifugal casting
      3. Sand-casting

Comp.
47.1

47   The Paraphrase

47.1   **A paraphrase is a rewording of the meaning of a given passage.** To write a paraphrase is not merely to substitute synonyms for each word in the original, but rather to take into one's mind the ideas of another and to send those same ideas forth in a different form. Since the paraphrase retains all the ideas in the original passage, it may be as long as the original, or longer.

47.2 **Writing paraphrases is especially valuable for the following reasons:**

a. **It helps one to write better articles and research papers.**

b. **It improves one's reading and vocabulary.**

c. **It sharpens one's ability to think.**

d. **It allows one to practice writing, revising, and editing without having to provide the subject matter.**

47.3 **Follow these suggestions when writing a paraphrase.**

a. **Study the original carefully.** Read the selection over and over until you gain a complete understanding of the author's ideas and his purpose for writing. Look up the definitions of any words you do not know.

b. **Use your own words.** Avoid using the author's wording except in those instances when no satisfactory substitute is available. If all available substitutes distort the author's meaning, use the same word as in the original.

c. **Do not omit any ideas.** Omission of significant ideas will distort the author's meaning.

d. **Do not add any ideas.** Seek to reproduce faithfully all the ideas of the author, whether expressed or implied; but do not insert your own opinions or evaluations.

e. **Conserve the tone of the original.** The author's tone may be formal or informal, humorous or serious. Reproduce it as closely as possible.

f. **Revise and edit your paraphrase.**

(1) Read your first draft to see if you have accurately reproduced the thought of the original and have conserved its tone. Make any necessary revisions.

Comp. 47.3

(2) Edit every sentence, phrase, and word. (See 43.4.)

Study the following examples of paraphrase.

Original: One may smile and smile, and be a villain.

—Shakespeare

Paraphrase: A man may affect sincerity and friendliness even while planning evil against another.

Original: Who is a wise man and endued with knowledge among you? let him shew out of a good conversation his works with meekness of wisdom. But if ye have bitter envying and strife in your hearts, glory not, and lie not against the truth. This wisdom descendeth not from above, but is earthly, sensual, devilish. For where envying and strife is, there is confusion and every evil work. But the wisdom that is from above is first pure, then peaceable, gentle, and easy to be intreated, full of mercy and good fruits, without partiality, and without hypocrisy. And the fruit of righteousness is sown in peace of them that make peace. —James 3:13–18

Paraphrase: If a man claims to be wise, let him prove his wisdom by his conduct. True wisdom shows itself in modesty, recognizing the immensity of the universe and the narrow limits of man's capacity, and bowing in reverence to God who made both man and the universe. The mixing up of personal feelings, envy, jealousy, ambition and party spirit, with the attempt to teach others, proves the absence of true wisdom. Such a teacher sets up self above truth: his wisdom ceases to be a gift from God: it is charged with other elements derived from the flesh, the world and the devil. It is materialistic, irreligious, hating God and goodness, and is attended by unrest, disquietude and every kind of evil. On the other hand, the wisdom which comes from God is first of all pure: it has gained the victory over all the lower impulses of our nature: it is at peace with itself, with God and with man: it is gentle, reasonable, compassionate, singleminded, free from dissimulation, abounding in good fruits. It is by the peaceful activity of such lovers of peace that the seed, which will spring up into a harvest of righteousness, is sown in the hearts of men.

—*Joseph B. Mayor*

48 The Précis

48.1 **A précis is a brief summary that restates the essential meaning of a longer piece of writing.**

48.2 **A précis should be no longer than one third the length of the original.** (Generally, the longer the original, the greater the possibility of reduction.)

48.3 **Prepare the précis according to the following steps:**

a. Read the article to discover the overall idea.

(1) Skim the article rapidly, noticing any statements in bold type or italics.

(2) The overall idea is often stated at the beginning or the end of the article.

(3) Write down the overall idea in your own words.

b. Read the article carefully, looking for the main ideas in each paragraph and observing the examples, illustrations, and details that develop the paragraph.

c. Go through the article again, jotting down the main ideas from each paragraph. (Do not include any examples, illustrations, or repetitions.)

(1) The first or last sentence in a paragraph is often the topic sentence, which states the general idea developed in that paragraph.

(2) Key words or phrases (such as *a primary cause* or *another major reason*) can point you to the main ideas.

(3) The last paragraph of a long article may list all the main ideas contained in the preceding paragraphs.

Comp 48.3

(4) Look up all words or phrases that are unfamiliar to you.

(5) Do not add any ideas or opinions of your own.

221

d. Write a summarizing sentence for each paragraph.

(1) Use the ideas that you jotted down.

(2) Write each sentence in your own words without changing the meaning of the original. (Of course some significant words from the original must be used.)

(3) Each summarizing sentence should usually be complex, occasionally simple, but rarely compound. (Try a complex sentence first: put the main idea into the independent clause; put important related ideas into dependent clauses. If the paragraph is not complicated, use a simple sentence with modifying phrases.)

e. Write the précis, putting all the summarizing sentences into one well-written paragraph. (Do not simply write the summarizing sentences one after the other: some rewording will be necessary, and some sentences may need to be combined. Sometimes all the summarizing sentences can be combined into one sentence.)

(1) The wording can be condensed by using appositives, verbals, and series.

(2) Do not change the order of the ideas in the original paragraph.

(3) Do not begin by saying *"This article was about. . . ."* Write as if you are the author of the original article.

f. Rewrite and edit your précis.

(1) Did you include all the main ideas?

(2) Did you omit all examples, illustrations, and repetitions?

(3) Are your ideas in the same order as the original?

(4) Did you write in your own words?

(5) Are your sentences concise and well constructed?

(6) Are there any grammatical or mechanical errors?

Comp.
48.3

Read the original selection which follows. Study the list of ideas, the summarizing sentences, the précis, and finally the revised précis.

Original Selection

¶**1.** Among the Jews of the Dispersion, education must have taken on an important place at an early date, for they were dependent solely upon the perpetuation of their national convictions for their survival. Uprooted from their land, with no military defense of their own, they could keep their national identity only as they maintained themselves as a separate group with their own culture and spiritual life. As far back as the time of Ezra, there was public reading of the law and instruction in its meaning—a kind of adult education that was consistently maintained by the synagogue.

¶**2.** Along with the synagogue developed the school. There never was in Judaism the general compulsory education that prevails in America at the present day; but the Jewish community usually provided some sort of instruction for children that they might learn to read the Torah, to write, and to do some simple arithmetic. . . .

¶**3.** Vocational education was favored by the Jews. The rabbis had a saying, "Whosoever does not teach his son a trade makes him a thief." Usually every Jewish boy learned how to work with his hands and thus to support himself. According to the Gospel records, the Lord Jesus was a carpenter (Mark 6:3). . . . Paul worked at the tentmakers' trade (Acts 18:3). This healthy emphasis on manual training made the Jewish male citizen independent. It balanced his intellectual pursuits with physical skills and it enabled him to find gainful employment. [239 words]

—From *New Testament Survey* by Merrill C. Tenney, copyright © 1961 Wm. B. Eerdmans Publishing Co.

List of Ideas

Comp. 48.3

¶**1.** Jews during dispersion

education important early

education necessary to their survival as
    separate nation

adults instructed in the law in synagogues

¶**2.** schools developed for children
   reading the Torah
   writing
   doing simple arithmetic

¶**3.** fathers strongly encouraged to train their sons in a
   useful trade

Summarizing Sentences

¶**1.** Early in the Dispersion the Jews established synagogues to instruct the adults in the Scriptures because
they knew they must educate their people if they were to
survive as a separate nation.

¶**2.** The Jewish community established schools to instruct
the children how to read the Torah, how to write, and
how to do simple arithmetic.

¶**3.** The rabbis strongly encouraged all the fathers to
teach their sons a useful trade in addition to their other
education.

Précis

Early in the Dispersion the Jews established synagogues to instruct the adults in the Scriptures because
they knew they must educate their people if they were to
survive as a separate nation. Later they established
schools to instruct the children how to read the Torah,
how to write, and how to do simple arithmetic. The
fathers, at the urging of the rabbis, taught their sons a
useful trade in addition to their other education.

Revised Précis

Early in the Dispersion the Jews realized the importance of education to their survival as a separate nation.
Therefore, they established synagogues to instruct the
adults in the Scriptures; started schools to instruct the
children how to read the Torah, how to write, and how
to do simple arithmetic; and strongly encouraged all the
fathers to teach their sons a useful trade in addition to
their other education. [70 words]

Comp.
48.3

9 Exposition of a Process

The exposition of a process explains to your reader how something is made, how something is done, or how something operates. Your primary goal in describing a process should be *clarity*. Your paper should be so clear that a reader without previous experience in the field could either complete the process himself or explain clearly the steps in the process.

Follow these suggestions:

49.1 **Select a process with which you are familiar.** The process should be one that can be treated clearly and completely in the assigned number of pages.

49.2 **Write a brief introduction.** Identify the process you will be explaining.

49.3 **List all equipment or materials needed to carry out the process.** You may list them all at once or as they are needed in the process.

49.4 **Break the process into steps.** Make sure the steps are in clear, logical order.

49.5 **Give complete, accurate instructions.** Assume that your reader knows nothing about the process. Define all technical terms and describe any unfamiliar tools, materials, etc. Perhaps warn your reader what will happen if he is careless or if he omits a particular step.

49.6 **Select good transitional expressions. (See 44.5b.)** Do not overuse the word *then*.

49.7 **Use a diagram or an illustration if necessary.**

49.8 **Write a distinct and separate conclusion.** Do not just end the paper after the last step. For example, the conclusion of a paper which shows how to make something might describe the results of a successfully completed process.

How to Measure Blood Pressure

Reprinted from *Better Homes and Gardens* Magazine

Blood pressure—whether high, low, or normal—is a vital sign valued by all doctors in assessing your physical well-being. Next to your temperature, it is the single most common measure recorded in the doctor's log on your health.

Comp
49.8

The procedure for measuring blood pressure may be familiar to you. A pressure cuff is wrapped around your upper arm, and air is then squeezed into it from a rubber bulb until the cuff begins to feel uncomfortably tight. This pressure device, called a sphygmomanometer, firmly compresses the main artery in your arm until blood flow is blocked.

Your blood pressure goes up and down, like waves of water, in perfect time with the beat of your heart. The crest of the wave corresponds to your *systolic* blood pressure, reached each time your heart pushes five ounces of blood into the big arteries in your body. The trough would be your *diastolic* blood pressure, present when your heart is relaxed and refilling with blood before its next beat.

After your doctor blocks the blood flow with the pressure device, he then places a stethoscope to the artery and listens. At first, with high pressure in the cuff, he hears nothing. As he slowly reduces the pressure, he suddenly begins to hear a series of sharp clicks, each click corresponding to one heartbeat. He notes the pressure at which he begins to hear these clicks; this is your systolic pressure. Then he slowly lowers the pressure in the cuff, noting a gradual change in the quality of the clicks, which become less sharp and gradually change into a sort of rushing or swishing sound. He quickly reads the cuff pressure again and writes the number down: this is your diastolic pressure.

These two pressures, usually expressed in millimeters of mercury, make up your complete blood pressure reading. They are recorded, for example, as "one hundred twenty over eighty" (120/80) or "ninety over sixty" (90/60), with systolic pressure over diastolic pressure.

The normal range of blood pressure varies according to one's age. In children it may easily run as low as 85/55, with an average reading of perhaps 90/60. In adults normal blood pressure ranges from 100/80 to 135/90. Most doctors consider an adult pressure of 135/95 as suspiciously high. But your doctor knows that many everyday things can cause your blood pressure to fluctuate widely from one moment to the next; he takes these into account.

Comp.
49.8

—From Gerald M. Knox, "How to Keep Your Blood Pressure Normal," *Better Homes and Gardens,* February 1968. Copyright © Meredith Corporation, 1968. All rights reserved.

Suggested Topics

How to do something: How to set a table, how to study, how to shop for groceries, how to set up a tent, how to build a personal library, how to start a club, how to clean a house, how to plant a garden, how to decorate a cake, how to perform artificial respiration.

How to make something: How to build a dog house, how to make a meat loaf, how to make a dress, how to make an ant farm, how to make ice cream.

How something works: An automobile engine, a record player, a sewing machine, a refrigerator, the water cycle, a telescope or microscope, an electromagnet, a camera, the metamorphosis of an insect, a telephone.

Classification

Classification is a type of exposition which separates a subject into its parts or types. Everyone classifies things. For example, the American Kennel Club (AKC) divides purebred dogs into six types: sporting dogs, hounds, working dogs, terriers, toy dogs, and nonsporting dogs. Dentists classify teeth as being incisors, canines, bicuspids, or molars. Just about anything can be broken down into several divisions. In your paper you will take a broad subject (cars, airplanes, schools, cereals, bodies of water, minerals, etc.) and break it down into several *distinct divisions*.

Follow these steps when writing your classification:

50.1 **Select a subject with which you are familiar.** If you know very little about your subject, you probably won't know how to break it down into divisions.

50.2 **Make a list of the possible divisions of your subject.** If your subject is "cars," make a list of as many different types of cars as you can think of.

50.3 **Group your list of types into a few main divisions.**

a. **Examine your types.** As you look over your list, you will notice that some of the types have common characteristics. Group these similar items together.

Comp.
50.3

b. **Find a "label" that describes them.** These "labels" are your divisions. For example, you might list fifteen different cars. Of these, some might be labeled "com-

227

pact economy cars"; some might fall under the heading "family sedans"; while those remaining might be classified as "foreign sports cars." Thus, you have broken down your subject into three main divisions, and you have examples of each division.

50.4 **Check your divisions.** Before you write your paper, look at your divisions. Do they represent only *one* type of classification? For example, cats may be classified according to breed, according to color, or perhaps according to size. But breaking the subject "cats" down into "Siamese cats," "gray cats," and "large cats" would not be good because more than one type of classification was used. Stick to one type of classification—for example, cats classified according to breed: domestic shorthairs, Siamese cats, longhair cats, etc. Using one type of classification will insure that your divisions do not overlap. "Students who bring their lunch," "students who buy their lunch," and "students who ride the bus" are not satisfactory divisions since the last grouping would obviously include both students who bring their lunch and students who buy.

50.5 **Write your paper.**

a. Write the introduction. The introduction should include your thesis statement that announces the main divisions of the topic to be discussed.

b. Write the body of the paper.

(1) Deal with each division in a separate paragraph.

(2) Do not make each paragraph simply a catalog of examples. Examples are good, but you must also describe the division, give its characteristics, and perhaps show how it differs from the other divisions.

(3) Use humor where possible to keep the paper interesting.

(4) Use transitional devices to maintain clarity. Besides the usual devices, you may use run-in subheadings (italicized and capitalized), as in the example below.

(5) Use a variety of sentence structure to avoid monotony.

Comp.
50.4

(6) Use diagrams and illustrations where necessary to add interest and clarity.

c. **Write the conclusion.** The conclusion should restate the subject and the divisions in an interesting way. The motorcycle example below is a part of a longer article and does not have a conclusion at the end of the part. If this example were a separate article, a conclusion for it might read like this: "Whether a person wants to be on the road or off, he can certainly find something he likes in the wide variety of motorcycles available today."

Motorcycles

Manufacturers produce motorcycles in a variety of sizes, types, and weights. But there are two main kinds: (1) those designed primarily for use on streets and other paved surfaces, and (2) those intended chiefly for off-the-road riding. The first group consists of street and touring bikes, and also motor scooters. The second group includes trail bikes and such motorcyclelike vehicles as minibikes and minicycles.

Street Bikes are used on roads and highways for short trips and intown riding. They weigh from 135 to 350 pounds (61 to 159 kilograms) and can reach speeds of 50 to 80 miles (80 to 130 kilometers) per hour.

Touring Bikes, used mainly for cross-country travel, can carry heavy loads. Most of these bikes weigh from 350 to 700 pounds (159 to 320 kilograms), but oversized models may weigh 800 pounds (360 kilograms) or more. Touring bikes can travel up to 100 mph (160 kph).

Motor Scooters have the engine mounted over or directly in front of the rear wheel. The driver sits with both feet on a floor board because a motor scooter does not have a bicycle-type frame.

Trail Bikes can travel rough country trails, climb hills, and cross streams. They weigh from 150 to 250 pounds (68 to 110 kilograms) and go as fast as 70 mph (110 kph).

Comp. 50.5

Minibikes and Minicycles may be seen in country areas and on trails. They are not intended for use on paved streets or roads because most models do not meet minimum motor vehicle standards. Minicycles are sturdier than minibikes. They have motorcycle-type engines but weigh less and are more compact than most motorcycles.

Excerpted from *The World Book Encyclopedia.* ©1996 World Book, Inc. By permission of the publisher.

Suggested Topics

Types of books, types of outlines, kinds of machines, classes of levers, types of tissue in the human body, types of lenses or telescopes, types of painting techniques, types of musical instruments, types of plants, the branches of science, types of cowboys, types of barbers, kinds of cereals, friends, brothers, sisters, hats, shoes, restaurants, etc.

51   Extended Definition

If you define *bravery* as "brave spirit or conduct; courage; valor" you are giving a dictionary type of definition. But if you go beyond a simple phrase and discuss the significance of the word *bravery,* or the broad concepts associated with the word, or the characteristics of a brave person, then you are writing an extended definition. Usually the extended definition will be a part of a longer paper. Make sure that your definition maintains the style and tone of the longer paper of which it is a part.

The following suggestions will help you to write fresh and interesting definitions:

51.1   **Tell what the word means by using synonyms.**

51.2   **Tell what the word does *not* mean by using antonyms.** ("Bravery is not foolishness.")

51.3   **Give the derivation and history of the word:** show the origins of the word and how the meaning of the word has changed through the years.

51.4   **Explain the word by using examples and anecdotes.** As an example of bravery you might give an account of a person who risked his life to save others.

51.5   **Quote an authority, and then expand his statement.** ("Ernest Hemingway defined *courage* as 'grace under pressure.' This means that . . .")

51.6   **Explain the word from as many different aspects as possible, telling what it is and what it is not.**

51.7   Usually use more than one of the suggestions above.

The Gospel

The gospel, according to Isaiah, is, "Incline your ear, and come unto me; hear, and your soul shall live." It is ours, then, to give men something worth their hearing; in fact, to instruct them. We are sent to evangelize or to preach the gospel to every creature; and that is not done unless we teach them the great truths of revelation. The gospel is good news. To listen to some preachers you would imagine that the gospel was a pinch of sacred snuff to make them wake up, or a bottle of ardent spirits to excite their brains. It is nothing of the kind; it is news, there is information in it, there is instruction in it concerning matters which men need to know and statements in it calculated to bless those who hear it. It is not a magical incantation or a charm whose force consists in a collection of sounds; it is a revelation of facts and truths which require knowledge and belief. The gospel is a reasonable system, and it appeals to men's understanding; it is a matter for thought and consideration, and it appeals to the conscience and the reflecting powers. Hence, if we do not teach men something, we may shout, "Believe! Believe! Believe!" but what are they to believe? Each exhortation requires a corresponding instruction, or it will mean nothing. "Escape!" From what? This requires for its answer the doctrine of the punishment of sin. "Fly!" But whither? Then must you preach Christ and His wounds; yea, and the clear doctrine of atonement by sacrifice. "Repent!" Of what? Here you must answer such questions as, What is sin? What is the evil of sin? What are the consequences of sin? "Be converted!" What from? What to? The field of instruction is wide if men are to be made to know the truth which saves. "That the soul be without knowledge, it is not good," and it is ours as the Lord's instruments to make men so to know the truth that they may believe it and feel its power. We are not to try and save men in the dark, but in the power of the Holy Ghost we are to seek to turn them from darkness to light.

Comp.
51.7

—From "What Is It to Win a Soul?" by Charles Haddon Spurgeon.

Suggested Topics

Loyalty, love, honesty, courage, service, meekness, ambition, patriotism, liberty, faith, democracy, art, literature, doctrine, evangelism, happiness, genius, hypocrisy, culture.

52 Essay Answer

An essay test goes beyond your knowledge of names, dates, and other isolated facts; it requires you to fit the facts together into a logical framework. Essay tests are challenging because they force you to write a composition in a limited amount of time. You must think quickly. Since the best aid to quick thinking is organization, follow these steps to produce clear, effective essay answers:

52.1 Read all the questions on the test.

a. If you are asked to select one or two questions from a list, decide which question(s) you have the best knowledge of and cross out the others.

b. If you are asked to answer all the questions, decide how much time to devote to each, depending upon their point value. A question that counts for 30 points out of 100 should take up only 30 percent of your time. Do the question that has the highest value first.

52.2 Analyze the question.

a. Read carefully every word in the question.

b. Note the key words in the question and be sure to do exactly what you are asked to do. Here are some common examples:

classify—give the main divisions or classes
compare—give likenesses
contrast—give differences
define—give an extended definition
explain—tell how and why
illustrate—give examples or incidents
summarize—give briefly the main points

52.3 Plan your answer before you begin to write.

a. Think through your answer completely.

Comp.
52.1

b. Make a list of your main ideas. (It is seldom wise to have more than five main topics. Usually three topics are enough for any essay answer.)

▶ Note. Planning is especially important on an essay test because one seldom has time to do much, if any, rewriting.

52.4   **Write the essay answer.**

a. Write a brief introduction.

(1) Make a direct reference to the wording of the question.

(2) Write a thesis sentence that gives your main points.

b. Develop each main idea in a separate paragraph.

(1) Use the main ideas as the topic sentences of the paragraphs.

(2) Support the topic sentences with examples, illustrations, quotations, etc.

(3) Do not pad your answers with repetition, wordiness, or irrelevant details.

c. Write a brief concluding paragraph. Reassert your thesis.

52.5   **Proofread your answer.**

a. It is important to your grade to leave enough time for proofreading.

b. Check grammar, usage, and mechanics.

c. Check for misspelled words and omitted words.

Model Essay Question and Answer:

What emotions dominate Hawthorne's *House of the Seven Gables?* Discuss the characters in the novel which illustrate these emotions.

In *The House of the Seven Gables* Nathaniel Hawthorne treats a number of abstract qualities and emotions. *Although these emotions are as varied as the characters exhibiting them, there seem to be three emotions which dominate the entire novel and which are*

Comp.
52.5

symbolized by one or more of the characters: greed, hatred, and love. Hawthorne develops these characteristics through the lives of his characters throughout the novel and eventually shows their results. Were one emotion to be singled out as the main theme of the novel, it most assuredly would be greed. From the opening chapter Hawthorne points out the greed of Colonel Pyncheon, the Puritan forefather, for the acreage of Matthew Maule. In return Maule's greed for his own land, though totally human, drives Pyncheon to desperate straits and results in Maule's trial and execution as a wizard. Judge Jaffrey Pyncheon is described almost completely in terms of his resemblance to his ancestor. This resemblance, Hawthorne shows, is not only physical, but emotional and spiritual as well. The reader first sees Judge Pyncheon as greedy for fame and popularity. Eventually, however, the Judge is shown to be greedy for the wealth which he could realize from a legal claim to the ancient Pyncheon landholdings. It is this great desire for wealth which leads to his final confrontation with Hepzibah and, consequently, his own death. Sandwiched between these two incidents is the daguerreotypist's tragic story of Alice Pyncheon. Holgrave aptly describes her as the victim of her father's greed. A young, loving maiden, she becomes a somber, even ghostly, symbol of the Pyncheon family and their House, as the innocent victims of another's greed. Greed directly destroys Colonel Pyncheon, Alice, Judge Pyncheon, and, indirectly, the whole family.

Although it does not figure as prominently in the novel as greed, hatred is also an emotion exposed by Hawthorne. It is represented primarily by two characters, Hepzibah and Holgrave. Hepzibah's hatred is directed toward her cousin Jaffrey Pyncheon for his part in the imprisonment of her brother Clifford. She believes the Judge to have been greatly responsible for Clifford's physical and mental demise. Although Hepzibah's well-known scowl is a result of near-sightedness, it is certainly made worse by her hatred for the Judge and his society. The hatred of Holgrave is not actually directed toward one person; rather it is directed toward a period of time—the past. During his discussion with Phoebe, he verbalizes his hatred for ancestors, ancestral homes, ancient ideas and creeds. This emotion no doubt stems from his ambivalence toward society's ignorance in condemning his ancestor, Matthew Maule. His hatred is relieved only by the influence of the beautiful and charming Phoebe. Only through her can he finally cease to hate the past or any enduring situation. Through her he comes to appreciate the goodness and stability of both the past and the present.

Finally, love is expressed in *The House of the Seven Gables* almost entirely by Phoebe Pyncheon. From her entrance as a bouncy, Pollyanna-type bundle of cheer, she develops into a mature woman, capable of mature love. Her love for nature, all society, her heritage, and her kinsmen is seemingly contagious. She and her growing love conquer greed, hate, and their malignant effects on two families and a house over which they have fought. Hawthorne would seem to say that, truly, love does conquer all. It may appear weak and ineffectual at first, but it can expand and ripen into a tool useful for healing many scars.

The effects of greed, hatred, and love encompass all of the action involved in *The House of the Seven Gables.* These three emotions are treated by Hawthorne as basic societal qualities which are present in varying degrees in all situations.

—Darrell Holley

Description

Good writers use description as a basic element in all forms of writing, whether it be narration, explanation, or argument. Sometimes they write purely descriptive paragraphs about persons, places, or things. The purely descriptive paragraph is the kind explained in this unit.

To write good descriptive paragraphs, you cannot merely *tell* your reader that you have seen, heard, or felt something. You must *make the reader see, hear,* or *feel* what you have experienced. You can learn how to write good descriptions by following the suggestions in this unit and by analyzing the model paragraphs supplied from the works of famous authors.

Comp.
53

53.1   **Determine your point of view.** Your point of view is
mental as well as physical. *Physical point of view* is the
position from which you observe your subject. You may
observe the subject from a cliff, a pier, a window, etc.
Mental point of view is your attitude toward your subject.
This mental attitude or impression may be that of like or
dislike, boredom or interest, gloom or cheer, beauty or
ugliness, dullness or brilliance, etc.

Model Paragraphs

1 For reasons of his own, Stephen Smith was stirring a
short time after dawn the next morning. From the
window of his room he could see, first, two bold escarp-
ments sloping down together like the letter V. Towards
the bottom, like liquid in a funnel, appeared the sea,
gray and small. On the brow of one hill, of rather
greater altitude than its neighbor, stood the church
which was to be the scene of his operations. The lonely
edifice was black and bare, cutting up into the sky from
the very tip of the hill. It had a square mouldering
tower, owning neither battlement nor pinnacle, and
seemed a monolithic termination, of one substance with
the ridge rather a structure raised thereon. Round the
church ran a low wall; overtopping the wall in general
level was the graveyard; not as a graveyard usually is, a
fragment of landscape with its due variety of chiaro-
scuro, but a mere profile against the sky, serrated with
the outlines of graves and a very few memorial stones.
Not a tree could exist up there; nothing but the monotonous gray-green grass.

—From *A Pair of Blue Eyes* by Thomas Hardy.

2 The girl was in the front room on the second floor,
peering through the blinds. . . . From between the slats
of the blinds she had a view of the road as it wended
across the meadow to the woods, and again where it
reappeared crossing the hill, half a mile away. It lay
yellow and warm in the summer sunshine. From the
long grasses of the meadow came the rhythmic click of
the insects. Occasional frogs in the hidden brook made
a peculiar chug-chug sound, as if somebody throttled
them. The leaves of the wood swung in gentle winds.

Through the dark green branches of the pines that grew in the front yard could be seen the mountains, far to the southeast, and inexpressibly blue.

—From "Three Miraculous Soldiers" by Stephen Crane.

53.2 **Carefully select details.**

a. **Include only those details that can be observed from your point of view.**

b. **Include only those details that contribute to your mental point of view—that one impression you wish to convey.**

c. **Select details that appeal to the senses: sight, sound, touch, taste, smell.**

Model Paragraphs

3 At last he heard from along the road at the foot of the hill the clatter of a horse's galloping hoofs. It must be the coming of orders. He bent forward, scarce breathing. The exciting clickety-click, as it grew louder and louder, seemed to be beating upon his soul. Presently a horseman with jangling equipment drew rein before the colonel of the regiment. The two held a short, sharp-worded conversation. The men in the foremost ranks craned their necks.

—From *The Red Badge of Courage* by Stephen Crane.

4 The Grocers'! oh, the Grocers'! nearly closed, with perhaps two shutters down, or one; but through those gaps such glimpses! It was not alone that the scales descending on the counter made a merry sound, or that the twine and roller parted company so briskly, or that the canisters were rattled up and down like juggling tricks, or even that the blended scents of tea and coffee were so grateful to the nose, or even that the raisins were so plentiful and rare, the almonds so extremely white, the sticks of cinnamon so long and straight, the other spices so delicious, the candied fruits so caked and spotted with molten sugar as to make the coldest lookers-on feel faint and subsequently bilious. Nor was it that the figs were moist and pulpy, or that the French plums

Comp.
53.2

blushed in modest tartness from their highly-decorated boxes, or that everything was good to eat and in its Christmas dress; but the customers were all so hurried and so eager in the hopeful promise of the day that they tumbled up against each other at the door, clashing their wicker baskets wildly, and left their purchases upon the counter, and came running back to fetch them, and committed hundreds of the like mistakes in the best humor possible.

—From "A Christmas Carol" by Charles Dickens.

5 It was a town of red brick, or of brick that would have been red if the smoke and ashes had allowed it; but as matters stood it was a town of unnatural red and black like the painted face of a savage. It was a town of machinery and tall chimneys, out of which interminable serpents of smoke trailed themselves for ever and ever, and never got uncoiled. It had a black canal in it, and a river that ran purple with an ill-smelling dye, and vast piles of building full of windows where there was a rattling and a trembling all day long, and where the piston of the steam engine worked monotonously up and down like the head of an elephant in a state of melancholy madness. It contained several large streets all very like one another, and many more small streets still more like one another, inhabited by people equally like one another, who all went in and out at the same hours, with the same sound upon the same pavements, to do the same word, and to whom every day was the same as yesterday and tomorrow, and every year the counterpart of the last and the next.

—From *Hard Times* by Charles Dickens.

53.3   Arrange the details.

a. **Arrange the details in the natural order that you see them or in some order that your reader can easily follow:** side to side, bottom to top, near to far, more prominent to less prominent, overall image to additional details, general impressions to special features, etc.

b. **In this arrangement you may change your point of view,** but you must warn your reader that you are doing so.

Comp.
53.3

Model Paragraphs

6 Imagine a small ditch such as a plow might make, with broken, irregular sides and at the bottom a trickling, muddy stream, and then magnify that in the imagination perhaps a million times, with scraggly but thick brushwood on the slopes, and you have some idea of the ravine of death where the "Lost Battalion" experienced its six-day nightmare. The ravine proper was perhaps 500 yards long, plugged at the upper end by another slope which made it actually not a ravine at all but a sort of gigantic V-shaped blind alley, the lower end of which sloped out into a flat stretch of marshy ground, interrupted quite some distance beyond by another wooded hill.

—From "The Lost Battalion" by Wilbur Forrest.

7 She put on her bonnet, and, leaving the house, descended the hill on the side towards Blooms-End, where she walked slowly along the valley for a distance of a mile and a half. This brought her to a spot in which the green bottom of the dale began to widen, the furze bushes to recede yet further from the path on each side, till they were diminished to an isolated one here and there by the increasing fertility of the soil. Beyond the irregular carpet of grass was a row of white palings, which marked the verge of the heath in this latitude. They showed upon the dusky scene that they bordered as distinctly as white lace on velvet. Behind the white palings was a little garden; behind the garden an old, irregular, thatched house, facing the heath, and commanding a full view of the valley. This was the obscure, removed spot to which was about to return a man whose latter life had been passed in the French capital—the centre and vortex of the fashionable world

—From *The Return of the Native* by Thomas Hardy.

53.4 **Use exact nouns and verbs instead of many adjectives and adverbs.** The overuse of adjectives and adverbs typifies amateur description. Look for nouns and verbs that include within themselves the same meaning as a noun with adjective modifiers or a verb with adverb modifiers.

Comp.
53.4

Instead of writing "The big airplane fell straight into the water" write "The Boeing 747 plunged into the ocean." When you do use adjectives and adverbs, select ones that are exact and colorful. (See 29.3–29.4.)

Model Paragraphs

8 The cliff called "Starved Rock," now pointed out to travellers as the chief natural curiosity of the region, rises, steep on three sides as a castle wall, to the height of a hundred and twenty-five feet above the river. In front, it overhangs the water that washes its base; its western brow looks down on the tops of the forest trees below; and on the east lies a wide gorge or ravine, choked with the mingled foliage of oaks, walnuts and elms; while in its rocky depths a little brook creeps down to mingle with the river. From the rugged trunk of the stunted cedar that leans forward from the brink, you may drop a plummet into the river below, where the catfish and the turtles may plainly be seen gliding over the wrinkled sands of the clear and shallow current. The cliff is accessible only from behind, where a man may climb up, not without difficulty, by a steep and narrow passage. The top is about an acre in extent.

—Francis Parkman

9 I am fond of loitering about country churches, and this was so delightfully situated that it frequently attracted me. It stood on a knoll round which a small stream made a beautiful bend, and then wound its way through a long reach of soft meadow scenery. The church was surrounded by yew trees which seemed almost coeval with itself. Its tall Gothic spire shot up lightly from among them, with rooks and crows generally wheeling about it. I was seated there one still sunny morning, watching two laborers who were digging a grave. They had chosen one of the most remote and neglected corners of the churchyard, where, from the number of nameless graves around, it would appear that the indigent and friendless were huddled into the earth.

—From "The Widow and Her Son" by Washington Irving.

Comp.
53.4

53.5 **Use comparisons to aid description.** Using comparisons is an excellent way to give your reader a mental picture of what you are describing. (See also 30.1–30.2.)

Observe the effectiveness of the comparisons in the following paragraphs.

Model Paragraphs

10 The water-turkey is the most preposterous bird within the range of ornithology. He is not a bird; **he is a neck** with such subordinate rights, members, belongings, and heirlooms as seem necessary to that end. He has just enough stomach to arrange nourishment for his neck, just enough wings to fly painfully along with his neck, and just big enough legs to keep his neck from dragging on the ground; and his neck is light-colored, while the rest of him is black.

—From "Morn Till Night on a Florida River" by Sidney Lanier.

11 He was a mongoose, rather **like a little cat** in his fur and his tail, but quite **like a weasel** in his head and his habits. His eyes and the end of his restless nose were pink; he could scratch himself anywhere he pleased, with any leg, front or back, that he chose to use; he could fluff up his tail till it looked **like a bottle brush,** and his war cry as he scuttled through the long grass was Rikk-tikk-tikki-tikki-tikk.

—From *The Jungle Book* by Rudyard Kipling.

12 Ichabod was a suitable figure for such a steed. He rode with short stirrups, which brought his knees nearly up to the pommel of his saddle; his sharp elbows stuck out **like grasshoppers' legs;** he carried his whip perpendicularly in his hand, **like a scepter,** and, as his horse jogged on, the motion of his arms was **not unlike the flapping of a pair of wings.** A small wool hat rested on the top of his nose, for so his scanty strip of forehead might be called; and the skirts of his black coat fluttered out almost to the horse's tail. Such was the appearance of Ichabod and his steed, as they shambled out of the gate of Hans Van Ripper, and it was altogether such an apparition as is seldom to be met with in broad daylight.

—From "The Legend of Sleepy Hollow" by Washington Irving.

Comp. 53.5

54 Character Sketch

A character sketch is a portrait of a *specific person.* The character sketch presents those characteristics that set the character apart as an individual personality and show what he is like.

The following suggestions will help you to write a clear and interesting character sketch:

54.1 Select a suitable character.

    a. Select someone you know well (a friend, a relative, public figure, etc.)

    b. Select someone who is interesting because of appearance, idiosyncrasies, or personality.

54.2 Select a title that includes the name of the character (My Uncle Cleve, "Willie" Green, My Youngest Brother, etc.).

54.3 Decide on the general impression you want to convey, such as laziness, sloppiness, greediness, diligence, neatness, generosity. Give the general impression of the person in the first sentence or two. Then add the details. See the excellent example by Charles Dickens on the next page.

54.4 Select the details carefully.

    a. Select the distinctive characteristics of the person that set him apart from others, especially from others of the same age, sex, or occupation.

    b. Select the most prominent characteristics (good or bad).

54.5 Reveal the character by any or all of the following methods.

    a. Describe his appearance: clothing, complexion, expression, hair, height, posture.

    b. Tell what he says or what he does.

    c. Tell what others say or think about him.

    d. Show how he reacts to people, things, or events.

    e. Show how others react to him.

    f. Put him in his environment—show him in typical surroundings.

Comp.
54.1

▶Note. No matter what methods you use, always avoid giving a description that could apply to just about anyone. Describe the characteristics of *one* specific person—make him an individual.

Scrooge

Oh! But he was a tightfisted hand at the grindstone, was Scrooge! A squeezing, wrenching, grasping, scraping, clutching, covetous old sinner! External heat and cold had little influence on him. No warmth could warm, no cold could chill him. No wind that blew was bitterer than he, no falling snow was more intent upon its purpose, no pelting rain less open to entreaty. Foul weather didn't know where to have him. The heaviest rain and snow and hail and sleet could boast of the advantage over him in only one respect—they often "came down" handsomely, and Scrooge never did.

Nobody ever stopped him in the street to say, with gladsome looks, "My dear Scrooge, how are you? When will you come to see me?" No beggars implored him to bestow a trifle, no children asked him what it was o'clock, no man or woman ever once in all his life inquired the way to such and such a place, of Scrooge. Even the blind men's dogs appeared to know him, and when they saw him coming on, would tug their owners into doorways and up courts, and then would wag their tails as though they said, "No eyes at all is better than an evil eye, dark master!"

But what did Scrooge care! It was the very thing he liked. To edge his way along the crowded paths of life, warning all human sympathy to keep its distance, was what the knowing ones call "nuts" to Scrooge.

—From *A Christmas Carol* by Charles Dickens.

Suggested Characters

Comp
54.5

A relative, a friend, a notorious (or notable) person in town, a historical figure, a character in a novel or play.

55 Type Sketch

A type sketch is the opposite of a character sketch. Instead of describing a specific individual, the type sketch paints a word picture of a general *type* of person. Usually the best way to bring the type sketch to life is to use *satire* or *sarcasm*—describing the person's vices instead of his virtues. Usually the title of the type sketch will reveal the sarcastic intent of the author: "The Spoiled Brat," "The Absent-Minded Professor," "The Grease Monkey," "The Bookworm," "The Tennis Nut," "The Tourist."

Follow these steps when writing a type sketch:

55.1 **Select your subject.**

a. Select a general type, not a specific person ("A Typical Golfer," *not* **"My Uncle George").**

b. Select a type of person that annoys or amuses you. You will then find it easier to think of the points to describe him.

c. Select a type that will be recognized by the reader.

55.2 **Don't waste time.** There is no need for a drawn-out introduction. Start with a broad statement that will create a general, overall impression of your subject.

55.3 **Decide how you will reveal the character of your subject.** Choose any or all of the following methods.

a. Describe the character's physical appearance.

(1) Use comparisons ("He looked like a bullfrog with the mumps . . .").

(2) Use vivid words (primarily vivid nouns and verbs).

(3) Use words that appeal to the senses.

b. Relate typical actions of the character.

(1) Place him in a typical setting.

(2) Relate an incident or an anecdote.

c. Give characteristic sayings which reveal the subject's character.

55.4 **Be selective in your choice of supporting details.**

    a. **Select the details that will evoke the emotional response that you desire in your reader.**

    b. **If you choose to emphasize one *specific trait* of the type in your sketch (gluttony, laziness, etc.), you should select only the details which illustrate that trait.**

    c. **Don't include too much physical description.** Remember that your purpose is to *reveal character*. Include a physical detail only if it illustrates a facet of the subject's character. Thus, describing the condition of a person's clothing (soiled, wrinkled) may do more to reveal the person's sloppy nature than would a detailed description of what he is wearing.

The Cynic

He "sitteth in the seat of the scornful" (Psalm 1:1). This sitting suggests a settled mood. The scorn is not an occasional thing, something that comes and goes, and never tarries long. It has come to stay. It has taken up its home there. There is an air of permanency about it. It is not a swift spasm of ill-feeling, born one moment and destroyed the next. It is a fixed habit. It is a residential feeling; it is a mood which knits the days together and runs throughout the life. The "seat of the scornful" is not a movable chair; it is an abode. This man has sat down to stay. He is not occasionally cynical; he *is* a cynic.

Now, what is a cynic? The etymology of the word introduces the features of a dog. And what is there dog-like about a cynic? A snarl. Who has not known the neighbour's dog which crouches just behind the garden gate and snarls at every passer-by? The passer-by may be a little child, or it may be an old man; it makes no difference, there is a snarl for both. It may be a tinker, soldier, sailor; it is all the same, every one is snarled at as he goes along the way. No matter how genial your presence, or how cordial your word, or how gracious your errand, there is a bitter snarl for you as you pass the gate.

Comp.
55.4

And that is the dog-like attitude which makes the cynic. He snarls at everything, and he sniffs and he sneers at everything. He is sarcastic and satirical. He is a disbeliever in the inherent worth of things. He has no confidence in the sincerity of others. He has a suspicion of every sort of courtesy, and he has a carping attitude to every social usage. He flings a mocking jibe at everything. He laughs at everything with bitter laughter. He suggests that there is a rotting decay at the heart of every beautiful thing. He cannot look at a flower without talking about the manure at its root. When others are admiring a lovely deed he hints at an unclean motive. Even a mother's love is only an animal instinct, a fierce and merely selfish passion at the very heart of her affection. The cynic penetrates the lovely in search of the unlovely, and he is always sure that he finds it. You can hear his cruel laughter in the loveliest garden. You can hear his mocking cry in the sunny noon, or under the light of the midnight stars. Whatsoever things are ugly, the cynic thinks on these things.

—From *Springs in the Desert* by J. H. Jowett. Copyright 1924 by George H. Doran Company. Reprinted 1976 by Baker Book House.

Suggested Topics

The truck driver, the librarian, the absent-minded professor, the tennis nut, the introvert, the road hog, the sports fan, the bookworm, the spoiled brat, the old grouch, the clumsy oaf, the gabby gossip, the neighbor's kid, the door-to-door salesman, the hypochondriac, the doting grandmother, the obnoxious salesclerk, the health-food nut, the incurable optimist (or pessimist), the practical joker.

Comp.
55.4

5 The Library

The library contains a wealth of information about almost any subject. To find information quickly and efficiently, first acquaint yourself with the general arrangement of your library—locate the on-line catalog or card catalog, the reference section, the indexes to periodical literature, and the book stacks. Then become familiar with their content and arrangement.

The Catalog

56.1 **An index to the entire library is contained in an on-line catalog or a card catalog.** The on-line catalog stores the index on computer; the card catalog stores it in a number of drawers. Both catalogs provide information by author, title, and subject. The cards in the card catalog may be alphabetized word by word or letter by letter. Compare the following group of words listed according to the two methods.

Word-by-Word	**Letter-by-Letter**
North Equatorial Current	Northeast
North Pole	North Equatorial Current
Northeast	Northern Hemisphere
Northern Hemisphere	North Pole
Northwest Territories	northwesterly
northwesterly	Northwest Territories

Abbreviations are usually alphabetized as if they were written out. That is, *St.* filed as *Saint, Dr.* filed as *Doctor,* etc. Names beginning with *Mc* or *M'* are usually alphabetized as if they were spelled *Mac.*

The card catalog usually contains at least three cards on each book: an *author* card, a *title* card, and a *subject* card. Books that treat more than one subject will have more than one subject card. Books that have more than one author will have more than one author card. Fiction books have no subject cards. Study the information on these sample cards.

Comp.
56.1

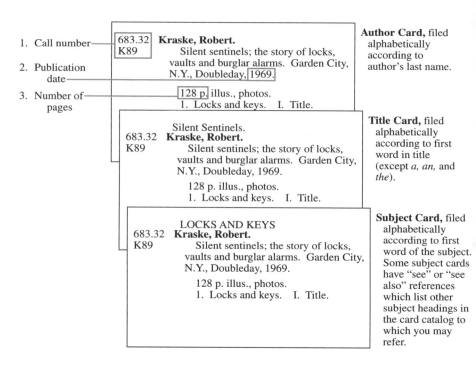

1. Call number
2. Publication date
3. Number of pages

683.32
K89

Kraske, Robert.
  Silent sentinels; the story of locks,
vaults and burglar alarms. Garden City,
N.Y., Doubleday, 1969.

128 p. illus., photos.
1. Locks and keys. I. Title.

Author Card, filed alphabetically according to author's last name.

Silent Sentinels.
683.32 **Kraske, Robert.**
K89   Silent sentinels; the story of locks,
     vaults and burglar alarms. Garden City,
     N.Y., Doubleday, 1969.

     128 p. illus., photos.
     1. Locks and keys. I. Title.

Title Card, filed alphabetically according to first word in title (except *a, an,* and *the*).

LOCKS AND KEYS
683.32 **Kraske, Robert.**
K89   Silent sentinels; the story of locks,
     vaults and burglar alarms. Garden City,
     N.Y., Doubleday, 1969.

     128 p. illus., photos.
     1. Locks and keys. I. Title.

Subject Card, filed alphabetically according to first word of the subject. Some subject cards have "see" or "see also" references which list other subject headings in the card catalog to which you may refer.

56.2   **Call number.** This is the number that locates a book on the shelves. The number 683.32 on the sample card is the *classification number* within the Dewey Decimal System. This book will be on the shelves with other books having to do with technology. Look for the shelves labeled 600–699. The number K89 indicates the order of this book within the group of books in the 683.32 classification. In some libraries you are not permitted to get books from the stacks yourself. You must write the call number on a slip of paper and present it at the library desk. A library worker will get the book for you.

56.3   **Publication date.** The date of publication may be important for you to note. For example, a book on space travel published before 1961 is now obsolete because most actual space exploration has taken place since that time.

56.4   **Number of pages.** The number of pages may indicate the value of the particular book for your research. A book on the Civil War containing only fifty pages would probably not be an adequate reference if you are writing a detailed term paper.

Look back at the sample cards. Notice that all three cards contain identical information. The only difference is the top line of each card.

The Reference Section

Your library has a reference room or a reference section where reference books are kept. Reference books are in such great demand that they must be accessible at all times; therefore, they cannot be removed from the reference room.

The reference room is usually the starting point for your research projects. It is there that you can get an overall view of the topic you have selected and can make a list of books (bibliography) that deal with your subject.

Reference books include *encyclopedias, dictionaries, biographical works, atlases, almanacs, books of quotations, yearbooks,* etc. You need to be familiar with the various reference works available in your library.

56.5 **Encyclopedias.** Encyclopedias contain summary articles on a wide range of subjects. These articles present an overall view of each subject. Sometimes an outline and a bibliography are included with the articles. For these reasons it is usually best to begin any research by consulting an encyclopedia.

The 32-volume *New Encyclopaedia Britannica* deserves special mention. It has four parts: the *Propaedia* (1 vol.), the *Micropaedia* (12 vols.), the *Macropaedia* (17 vols.), and an index (2 vols.). The *Propaedia* outlines all areas of knowledge and refers to the *Britannica* volumes that discuss each heading. The *Micropaedia* contains about 65,000 short, factual articles. The *Macropaedia* contains about 600 long (sometimes book-length) articles supported by excellent bibliographies. The index gives convenient access to the information in all parts of the encyclopedia.

Following is a list of other well-known encyclopedias:
Academic American Encyclopedia, 21 volumes
Collier's Encyclopedia, 24 volumes
The Encyclopedia Americana, 30 volumes
The World Book Encyclopedia, 22 volumes

Comp.
56.6

56.6 **Dictionaries.** Dictionaries contain an alphabetical listing of words in a language—with definitions, pronunciations, etymology, usage labels, and other helpful information, such as tables of weights and measures and guides to punctuation and capitalization. A good dictionary will give guidance concerning the usage of words. The fact that a word is listed in a dictionary does not mean that the word should be used. The listing merely indicates that some people are currently using the word or that the word was used in the past. Look for usage labels and usage notes to help you determine whether a word is correct to use, and if correct to use, under what circumstances. These are some common usage labels: *nonstandard, informal, slang, vulgar, obsolete, archaic, rare, poetic, dialect,* and *British.*

Some dictionaries, though useful for definitions and general aids, are of no help concerning **correct** usage. *Webster's Third New International Dictionary, Merriam Webster's Collegiate Dictionary* (previously titled *Webster's New Collegiate Dictionary*), and *The Random House Dictionary,* Second Edition Unabridged, fit this category. (See section 27.6 on page 116.)

At this time, the following dictionaries—in varying degrees of perscriptiveness—do give guidance concerning usage.

> *The American Heritage Dictionary of the English Language*
> *Oxford American Dictionary*
> *The Random House College Dictionary*
> *The Random House Dictionary,* First Edition Unabridged
> *Webster's New International Dictionary,* Second Edition Unabridged
> *Webster's New World Dictionary of the American Language*

56.7 **Special Dictionaries.** When you are searching for an exact word to express your thoughts, refer to *The Synonym Finder* by J. I. Rodale or to *Webster's New Dictionary of Synonyms.*

For geographical information *Webster's New Geographical Dictionary* is a good source. It contains more than 47,000 entries on ancient and modern place names with geographical and historical information.

For articles about people, places, and objects to which the Bible refers, *Unger's Bible Dictionary* is a good general source. It also has outlines of the books of the Bible and notes on important doctrines.

For information about the *correct usage* of words see the following:

The Careful Writer by Theodore M. Bernstein
A Dictionary of American-English Usage by Margaret Nicholson
A Dictionary of Modern English Usage by H. W. Fowler
Harper Dictionary of Contemporary Usage by William and Mary Morris
Modern American Usage by Wilson Follett

56.8   Biographical Aids. Information about the lives of prominent persons is recorded in biographical reference books. The *Dictionary of American Biography* and the *Dictionary of National Biography* are multivolume works containing biographies of men and women who are now dead. *Current Biography, Who's Who* (mostly British), and *Who's Who in America* contain biographies of living persons. *Current Biography,* issued monthly, provides more recent and more detailed information than that given in the current *Who's Who.* A good single-volume work is *Webster's Biographical Dictionary,* which has concise information about famous persons from the past and present. The following books by Kunitz and Haycraft contain biographies only of authors:

American Authors, 1600–1900
British Authors of the Nineteenth Century
The Junior Book of Authors
Twentieth Century Authors: A Biographical Dictionary of Modern Literature

56.9   Atlases. An atlas is a reference book made up primarily of maps; however, it also contains tables, charts, and illustrations that give much additional information about such things as population, principal crops, natural resources, and major industries. Familiarize yourself with at least one of the following atlases:

Gold Medallion World Atlas
The Harper Atlas of the Bible
National Geographic Atlas of the World
Rand McNally *Cosmopolitan World Atlas*
Reader's Digest *Atlas of the World*

Comp
56.10

56.10   Handbooks of Miscellaneous Information. An almanac is an annual publication that contains an amazing amount of miscellaneous information. It contains census figures;

251

ZIP code listings; election results; information about government, sports, and the arts; advancements in industry, technology, and education; and hundreds of other topics. Since the information in an almanac is not printed in any logical order, you will need to use the index. The two most widely used almanacs are *The World Almanac* and the *Information Please Almanac.*

Two other interesting and helpful handbooks of miscellaneous information are *Famous First Facts* by Joseph N. Kane and the *New Century Cyclopedia of Names.*

56.11 Books of Quotations. The following are well-known works that will help you locate quotations:
Dictionary of Quotations by Bergen Evans
Familiar Quotations by John Bartlett
A New Dictionary of Quotations by H. L. Mencken
The New Dictionary of Thoughts by Tryon Edwards

56.12 Reference Words on Literature. There are many reference books that help you locate Scripture verses, poems, short stories, novels, and so forth. The following are merely a few examples of those available:
The Exhaustive Concordance of the Bible by James Strong
Granger's Index to Poetry
A Guide to English Literature by F. W. Bateson
The Oxford Companion to English Literature
The Reader's Encyclopedia by William Rose Benét
Young's Analytical Concordance to the Bible by Robert Young

56.13 Other Specialized Reference Works. There are hundreds of other reference books on specific fields: music, religion, philosophy, art, history, science, sports, and so forth. The following are good references in these areas:
Dictionary of American History by James Truslow Adams
The Encyclopedia of Philosophy
The Encyclopedia of Sport
Encyclopedia of World Art
Grove's Dictionary of Music and Musicians
The McGraw-Hill Encyclopedia of Science and Technology
The New Schaff-Herzog Encyclopedia of Religious Knowledge

Comp.
56.11

56.14 The *Readers' Guide to Periodical Literature*. Frequently
when doing research, you will need to locate the most
recent thinking or the most recent developments concerning your subject. You then must turn to the various periodical indexes which serve the same purpose for magazines
that the card catalog does for books. These indexes tell you
in which magazines you may locate articles, stories, essays,
speeches, and poems that pertain to your subject. A good
general index is the *Readers' Guide to Periodical Literature,* published once a month. The *Reader's Guide* indexes
articles in 180 magazines. The information is indexed by
author and by subject. Stories are the only entries indexed
by title. In the front of each issue of the *Readers' Guide* is
a listing of the magazines that are indexed. Also in the
front is a listing of abbreviations used in the entries. Study
the following excerpt from the *Readers' Guide.*

SLOBOGIN, Kathy ——————————— Title of article
  Stress. il N Y Times Mat p48–50+ N 20 '77
SLOCUM, Jerald A. ——————————— Author entry
  FBO on floats. il Flying 101:46–9+ Ag '77
  Mooney the efficiency expert. il Flying ——— Title of magazine
  101:62–7 O '77
  Murphy wins again. il Flying 100 :68+ F '77 — Volume number
SLOCUM, Joshua
  Joshua Slocum's magnificent voyage; excerpt
  from My country. P. Berton. il Read Digest
  110:218–20+ F '77
SLOOPS ——————————————— Subject entry
         Materials ——————— Division of subject
  See Boats—Materials
SLOPES (physical geography)
  Slope profiles of cycloidal form. B. J. Bridge
  and G. G. Beckman. bibl il Science 198:610 — Description of article
  –12 N 11 '77
SLOTHS, Fossil
  Great late Pleistocene extinction: a slothful tale.
  D. E. Thomsen. il Sci N 112: 396–8 D 10 '77 — Page numbers
SLOW crockery cookery. See Cookery. ——— "See" cross reference
SLOW learning children
  Duck boy. M.H. Kingston. il N Y Times Mag — Name of author
  p54–5+ Je 12 '77
     See also ——————————— "See also" cross reference
  Learning disabilities
          Education
  Medicine pots—a motivation operation. L. L.
  Clark. il Sch Arts 76:32–3 F '77 ——————— Date of magazine

—From *Abridged Readers' Guide to Periodical Literature,* copyright ©
1977, 1978 by The H. W. Wilson Company. Material reproduced by
permission of the publisher.

Comp
56.14

The third entry in the excerpt above says that an illustrated article entitled "Joshua Slocum's Magnificent Voyage" is an excerpt from *My Country* written by P. Berton and can be found in volume 110 of *Reader's Digest* on pages 218–220 and on following pages of the February 1977 issue.

Dewey Decimal System

56.15 **Many libraries arrange nonfiction books according to the Dewey Decimal System.** This system uses a numbering scheme to indicate the subject matter contained in the various books. The Dewey Decimal System divides the fields of knowledge into ten main classes.

000–099	General works (reference materials)
100–199	Philosophy
200–299	Religion
300–399	Social sciences (economics, law, government)
400–499	Language
500–599	Pure sciences
600–699	Technology (engineering, aviation, inventions)
700–799	The arts (architecture, music, sports)
800–899	Literature
900–999	History (includes geography, travel books, and biography)

These ten main classes are divided into ten divisions. For example, the main class *Technology* is divided as follows:

600	Technology (Applied sciences)
610	Medical sciences, Medicine
620	Engineering and allied operations
630	Agriculture and related technologies
640	Home economics
650	Managerial services, Business services
660	Chemical and related technologies
670	Manufactures
680	Miscellaneous manufactures
690	Buildings

Comp.
56.15

Then the ten divisions are further divided into ten sections. For example, the division 640 *Home economics* is sectioned as follows:

640 Home economics
641 Food and drink
642 Food and meal service
643 The home and its equipment
644 Household utilities
645 Household furnishings
646 Sewing, clothing, personal grooming
647 Public households
648 Household sanitation
649 Child rearing and home nursing

Finally, the three-digit numbers are followed by a decimal and additional numbers indicating further subdivisions of the topic. For example, 646.4 stands for *Clothing construction,* which is a division of 646 *Sewing, clothing, personal grooming,* which is a division of 640 *Home economics,* which is a division of 600 *Technology.*

56.16 **Some libraries using the Dewey Decimal System do not classify books of fiction.** They label these books **F** or **Fic** and put them in a separate section. In this "fiction section" the books are arranged alphabetically by authors' last names. If there is more than one book by the same author, all of those books will be together and will be alphabetized according to the first word in the titles, excluding *a, an,* and *the.*

The following books are listed in the order in which they would appear on the shelves:

A Few Flowers for Shiner by Richard Llewellyn
How Green Was My Valley by Richard Llewellyn
None But the Lonely Heart by Richard Llewellyn
The Right Honorable by Justin M'Carthy
Christy by Catherine Marshall
Three Go Searching by Patricia St. John
Christmas Roses by Anne Douglas Sedgwick

The book by M'Carthy is placed before the one by Marshall because names beginning with *M'* or *Mc* are treated as if they were spelled *Mac.* The book by St. John is before the one by Sedgwick because names beginning with *St.* are treated as if they were spelled *Saint.*

Comp.
56.16

Library of Congress Classification System

56.17 **The Library of Congress Classification System is another system that is widely used, especially in large libraries.** You would do well to familiarize yourself with this system which you will encounter in college libraries and in many public libraries. This system uses letters of the alphabet and arabic numerals to provide millions of classification possibilities. A classification number may range in length from a single letter and numeral (T1) to two letters, four numerals, one decimal number, and a decimal letter and number combination (TH9745.5.F3U6). Main classes are marked with a single letter. The following are the main classes:

A   General Works (reference materials)
B   Philosophy; Psychology; Religion
C   Auxiliary Sciences of History (e.g. Archaeology; Biography)
D   History: General and Old World (Eastern Hemisphere)
E–F History: America (Western Hemisphere)
G   Geography; Maps; Anthropology; Recreation
H   Social Sciences
J   Political Science
K   Law
L   Education
M   Music
N   Fine arts
P   Languages and Literature
Q   Science
R   Medicine
S   Agriculture
T   Technology
U   Military Science
V   Naval Science
Z   Bibliography; Library Science

Subclasses are marked with two letters. The following example shows the subclasses of the main class *T Technology:*

Comp.
56.17

T   Technology (General)
TA   Engineering (General); Civil engineering (General)
TC   Hydraulic engineering
TD   Environmental technology; Sanitary engineering
TE   Highway engineering; Roads and pavements

TF	Railroad engineering and operation
TG	Bridge engineering
TH	Building construction
TJ	Mechanical engineering and machinery
TK	Electrical engineering; Electronics; Nuclear engineering
TL	Motor vehicles; Aeronautics; Astronautics
TN	Mining engineering; Metallurgy
TP	Chemical technology
TR	Photography
TS	Manufactures
TT	Handicrafts; Arts and crafts
TX	Home economics

Further subdivisions are marked with arabic numerals from 1 to 9999. The following example shows some of the subdivisions of the subclass *TT Handicrafts; Arts and crafts:*

TT	180–200	Woodworking; Furniture making; Upholstering
TT	205–267	Metalworking
TT	387–410	Soft home furnishings
TT	490–695	Clothing manufacture; Dressmaking; Tailoring
TT	697–910	Home arts; Homecrafts
TT	950–979	Hairdressing; Beauty culture; Barber's work

A further division of *TT 490–695 Clothing manufacture; Dressmaking; Tailoring* is *TT 500–565 Dressmaking and women's tailoring.* Still further divisions are *TT 540 Skirts, TT 545 Blouses,* etc.

57 The Research Paper

The research paper is a formal presentation of information gathered from various sources. The paper may be explanatory or persuasive, depending on the writer's purpose. The preparation of a research paper is an extremely profitable experience because the researcher learns to evaluate, select, and organize information about a topic of interest. The student receives great satisfaction since he becomes something of an expert on his particular subject.

Follow these steps in preparing your research paper:
1. Select and limit the subject.
2. Find sources and prepare the working bibliography.

Comp.
57

257

3. Prepare a preliminary outline.
4. Read and take notes. (Revise outline as necessary.)
5. Organize the notes.
6. Write the first draft. (Include footnote or endnote information.)
7. Rewrite the paper.
8. Edit the paper.
9. Type a trial list of your footnotes.
10. Type the paper.
11. Proofread the typed paper to ensure its accuracy.

57.1 Select and limit the subject.

a. Select a subject that interests you.

b. Select a subject about which you would like to become an authority.

c. Select a subject that has sufficient resource material available.

d. Select a subject that is not too broad to be adequately treated within the assigned number of pages. Subjects such as "Welfare" or "Social Security" are too broad to be covered in a research paper. However, "The Deficiencies of the Social Security System" would probably be about right. You may have to do some reading on a general subject like "Welfare" or "Social Security" before you can decide upon a limited subject.

e. Write out your purpose or thesis. This will help you locate materials and control your reading. Notice the following examples:

Statement of purpose: "The purpose of this paper is to discuss the deficiencies of the American Social Security System."

Thesis statement: "Although the original purpose of the Social Security System was to provide security for retired workers, the system today promotes insecurity and is in need of drastic reform."

**Comp.
57.1**

57.2 Find sources and prepare the working bibliography.

a. Read first in an encyclopedia to get an overall view of your subject. Look to see if a bibliography is included for your subject. If so, write down all references that look promising.

b. Consult the on-line catalog or card catalog to find books written on your subject.

c. Check the *Readers' Guide to Periodical Literature* and other periodical indexes to find magazine or journal articles that have been written on your subject.

d. Check the *Essay and General Literature Index* to find essays, articles, and speeches contained in collected works.

e. Consult published bibliographies in order to find sources that you may not find anywhere else. Probably the most direct way to find published bibliographies on your subject is to consult a bibliography of bibliographies, which contains bibliographies on all the various fields of knowledge. (See examples in section 57.20a.)

f. When you are preparing your working bibliography, make a card for every source that looks promising. It is good to have more sources than you think you will need. (If you do not find enough good sources, check with your instructor about changing topics.)

g. Take the time to fill out each card completely and accurately the first time.

h. Make out your cards according to the following general information.

(1) Use three-by-five-inch cards.

(2) Use a separate card for each source.

(3) Number each card in the upper right-hand corner—in consecutive order as you make out the cards. (You can use this "source number" on your note cards instead of writing out the author's name and the title of the source.)

(4) Record the library's call number.

(5) Record the location of the source, if necessary. (If working from an index, copy the name and year or volume of the index in which you found the source you are recording.)

Comp.
57.2

259

i. **Study these three basic bibliography cards, and refer to section 57.14 for examples of other sources.**

SAMPLE BIBLIOGRAPHY CARDS

FOR A BOOK

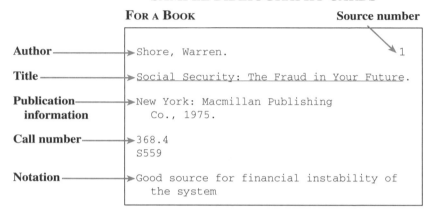

Author	Shore, Warren.
	Source number 1
Title	Social Security: The Fraud in Your Future.
Publication information	New York: Macmillan Publishing Co., 1975.
Call number	368.4 S559
Notation	Good source for financial instability of the system

FOR A MAGAZINE ARTICLE

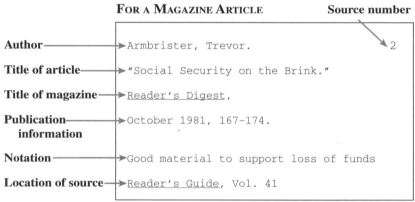

Author	Armbrister, Trevor.
	Source number 2
Title of article	"Social Security on the Brink."
Title of magazine	Reader's Digest,
Publication information	October 1981, 167–174.
Notation	Good material to support loss of funds
Location of source	Reader's Guide, Vol. 41

FOR AN ENCYCLOPEDIA ARTICLE

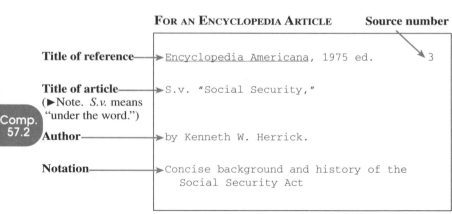

Title of reference	Encyclopedia Americana, 1975 ed.
	Source number 3
Title of article (▶Note. *S.v.* means "under the word.")	S.v. "Social Security,"
Author	by Kenneth W. Herrick.
Notation	Concise background and history of the Social Security Act

Comp.
57.2

260

j. Evaluate each source that you have located. (Often, if your time is limited, you will be able to find only some of the sources for which you have made bibliography cards.)

(1) Ask yourself several questions about each source: Is the author well qualified to write on the particular subject? Is the publisher well known and reliable? Is the date of the work significant? Does the work deal directly with your topic or only incidentally? Is the work well documented?

(2) You may look in an index such as the *Book Review Digest* to help you determine the value of your sources. The *Book Review Digest* indexes book reviews which appear in various periodicals and journals. Each book reviewed is entered with excerpts from as many reviews as are necessary to "reflect the balance of critical opinion" concerning the book.

(3) Make notations at the bottom of each card to remind you of the value of that particular source.

(4) Lay aside cards on any sources that are definitely inferior or unrelated to your purpose.

57.3 Prepare a preliminary outline.

a. List the ideas you think should be included in your paper. (In order to do this you may have to do a bit of reading on your subject.)

b. Look again at your statement of purpose (or thesis) and cross from your list any ideas that are not related to it.

c. Group your ideas under several main headings and make the preliminary outline. (You will need to decide whether to use a topical or a sentence outline. See 46.1 and 46.3i–j.)

d. Your preliminary outline will probably include only main headings and subheadings as in the example on the next page.

Comp.
57.3

THE INSECURITY OF THE AMERICAN

SOCIAL SECURITY SYSTEM

Thesis: Although the original purpose of the
Social Security system was to provide security
for retired workers, the system today promotes
insecurity and is in need of drastic reform.

 I. The original purpose of the Social Security
    system was to provide security for retired
    workers.

    A. Cash benefits would be available to
       retired or disabled workers.

    B. Medical care would be provided for the
       elderly.

    C. The unemployed would be provided for.

    D. The benefits would be secure because the
       money would be saved and invested in a
       trust fund.

 II. The Social Security system today promotes
     insecurity.

    A. There is no longer a trust fund in which
       tax monies are reserved for future pay-
       ments.

    B. Though a taxpayer may pay thousands of
       dollars into the system, he does not
       have a legally enforceable contract
       which entitles him to any benefits.

    C. Congress can choose to revoke benefits
       at any time.

    D. Taxpayers cannot count on a fair return
       on their tax dollars.

    E. Taxpayers are concerned that there may
       be no money in the system to meet their
       needs at retirement.

 III. The Social Security system is in need of
      drastic reform.

    A. Reforms are needed to separate the wel-
       fare elements from the insurance ele-
       ments of the system.

    B. Reforms are needed in the distribution
       of benefits.

C. Reforms are needed to keep benefits
   within a reasonable amount.
D. Reforms are needed to detect fraud
   within the system.
E. Reforms are needed to prevent the system
   from going bankrupt.

e. **You should make changes in the preliminary outline as often as necessary while you are taking notes. Insert new topics and remove topics as necessary.** The outline above will require considerable change before a paper based on it will be satisfactory.

57.4 **Read and take notes.**

a. **Use four-by-six-inch cards.**

b. **Write with ink.**

c. **Write on only one side of each card.**

d. **Write the source number in the upper right-hand corner.** This number, taken from the bibliography card, indicates the source from which the note was taken. Next to the source number indicate whether the note is summarized, paraphrased, directly quoted, or stated in your own words.

e. **Write the heading at the top of the card.** The heading is the point or subpoint from your preliminary outline to which the note pertains. Because the headings in a preliminary outline sometimes change, you may prefer to write the headings in pencil.

f. **Use a separate card for each note.** If you need several cards on the same point, write the same heading at the top of each card.

g. **While you are reading and taking notes, be on guard mentally.** Know your sources: Some writers are liberal, and some conservative; some publishers are liberal, and some conservative (see 57.21). Many writers whose sources you will use are not Christians. Some writers are Christians who have their highest confidence in the Word of God; other writers are Christians who believe the Bible but put too much confidence in the thoughts of scholarly men. Whenever you read,

Comp.
57.4

you must constantly ask yourself "Is this in line with the Scriptures?" (See Proverbs 3:5 and Psalm 119:128.) If a statement is not in line with the Scriptures, it is not correct no matter who says it or what scholarly "studies" may show. Writers are fond of saying "Studies show such and such to be true." Do not be intimidated by such statements, because often those studies show no such thing. The results of studies (especially those dealing with sociology or psychology) are often erroneous or misleading.

You must, of course, be wary of any writer who rejects revealed truth, but you must also be wary of Christian writers, because some of them accept uncritically the human ideas of philosophers, psychologists, sociologists, scientists, and even journalists and news commentators. These writers become so enamored of the supposed "authorities" that they use the ideas of the "authorities" as the foundation for their thinking instead of the eternal Word of God. After beginning on the wrong foundation, they mix in some Scriptures to try to make their system appear Christian. Such writers are not trustworthy, and anything they say must be regarded with extreme caution.

h. **Your notes may be précis, paraphrases, direct quotations, or a combination of the three.**

▶ Note. Any ideas which are not your own must be footnoted when they appear in your paper. Failure to give credit for another author's words or ideas is called *plagiarism*. Even if you do not quote the idea directly—if you paraphrase or summarize the author's words—you must still give proper credit in order to avoid plagiarism.

Since plagiarism is equivalent to stealing, it is a serious offense and must be scrupulously avoided. (See 57.10e for a sample plagiarism statement.)

Comp.
57.4

i. **If most of your note taking consists of writing précis and paraphrases, rather than of copying down direct quotations and disconnected bits of information, your paper will be much easier to write and will be a better paper.** (Of course, direct quotations are sometimes preferable and necessary.)

j. **Enclose direct quotations within quotation marks. Be sure to copy the punctuation, capitalization, and spelling exactly as it is in the original.**

k. **If you wish to omit certain words from a quotation because they are not essential to your purpose, use ellipsis points (dots) to show the omission.** Use three spaced dots to indicate an omission within a sentence. Use four dots (a period followed by three spaced dots) to indicate the omission of the last part of a sentence, the first part of the next sentence, or a whole sentence or paragraph. Leave a space before the first dot, unless it is a period, and a space after the last dot if a word follows.

l. **Record the number of the page from which the note is taken.** If the note is taken from more than one page, draw a vertical line to indicate where the information from each page ends. (See sample note on the next page.)

m. **If you make personal comments on a note card, enclose such remarks in brackets [ ] so that later you can distinguish your ideas from those of the person quoted.**

n. **As you take notes and become more familiar with your subject, you will add some points to your outline and drop some others.**

o. **If while taking notes you realize that your statement of purpose (or thesis) is inaccurate or does not really indicate the truth about your subject, do not hesitate to change it and your outline.**

p. **Occasionally during note taking, you should stop and sort the cards according to their headings to make sure that you do not neglect certain points and overemphasize others.**

q. **Remember there are four things that must appear on each card: (a) the source number, (b) the heading, (c) the note, (d) the page number. Study the sample note card on the next page.**

Comp.
57.4

SAMPLE NOTE CARD

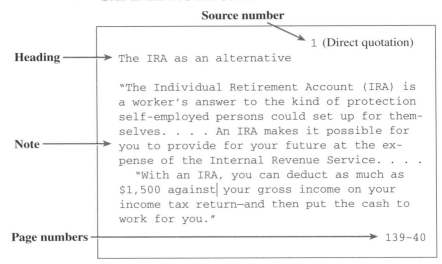

Source number

1 (Direct quotation)

Heading → The IRA as an alternative

"The Individual Retirement Account (IRA) is a worker's answer to the kind of protection self-employed persons could set up for them-selves. . . . An IRA makes it possible for

Note → you to provide for your future at the ex-pense of the Internal Revenue Service. . . .
    "With an IRA, you can deduct as much as $1,500 against| your gross income on your income tax return—and then put the cash to work for you."

Page numbers ────────────→ 139-40

57.5 **Organize the notes.**

a. **Make sure that the preliminary outline is accurate and that the points are in the best order.**

b. **Put the note cards in order according to the preliminary outline.**

57.6 **Write the first draft. (See 43.2.)**

a. **Place your outline, note cards, and bibliography cards before you.**

b. **Read through the note cards of each level of your outline before you start to write.**

c. **Write on every other line.**

d. **Acknowledge the sources of your information, whether you summarize, paraphrase, or quote directly.** Identify the sources by writing in parentheses the source number and the page number from the note card, for example, (2, 24). Place the notation at the end of the passage to which it refers, not before it. Later, you will remove these parenthetical identifications and replace them with note numbers which will run con-secutively to the end of the paper. Then you will pre-pare the corresponding footnotes or endnotes, which will tell exactly where you got the information that you used in your paper.

Comp.
57.5

e. Do not stop writing to look up additional facts. Write the whole paper; then look up any additional information.

57.7 **Rewrite the paper.** Look at the work as a whole. Do not be concerned about grammar, sentence structure, or mechanics at this point.

    a. Ask yourself the following questions.

        (1) Is the work *complete?* (Is everything on paper that needs to be there—no more and no less?)

        (2) Are all the parts in the right *order?*

        (3) Does the work have *unity?* (Do all the parts contribute to the single idea of the whole, or has some unrelated detail slipped in?)

        (4) Does the overall work have *coherence?* (Does the thought flow smoothly from one paragraph to the next? Are additional continuity devices needed? 44.5b)

        (5) Does the work have the proper *emphasis?* (Has each part been developed at a length proportionate to its importance in the composition?)

    b. Rewrite until you have satisfied the five questions above. (See 43.3, the last paragraph.)

57.8 **Edit the paper.**

    a. Check each *paragraph* for unity, coherence, and emphasis (sections 44.4–6).

    b. Check the *sentences* for correctness, clarity, and effectiveness (sections 13–26). Also check the grammar and mechanics.

    c. Check the *phrases* for accurate figures of speech and correct idiom. Eliminate jargon, triteness, and wordiness (sections 30–34).

    d. Check the *words.* Did you use vivid verbs and concrete nouns? Are your words appropriate to your audience (sections 28–29)? Are there any misspelled words?

Comp.
57.8

▶ Note. The following information in sections 57.9 and 57.10 conforms to the style set forth in Kate L. Turabian's *Manual for Writers of Term Papers, Theses, and Dissertations*, 5th ed. (Chicago: University of Chicago Press, 1987), hereafter referred to as "Turabian's *Manual*." Note also that in the following instructions the references to "inches" are given for computer users. The references to "spaces" are for work on a typewriter (or on a computer if you are using a fixed-width font, like Courier); but if you are using a proportionally spaced font, like New Century Schoolbook, you will need to follow the references to "inches."

57.9   Type a trial list of footnotes.

If you are doing footnotes, type a trial list of your notes before you type the body of your paper so that you will know how many lines your notes will require at the foot of each page. If you are doing endnotes, you may type the endnotes page now, or you may wait until you have typed the body of your paper. (See 57.10k.)

a. General information.

(1) Set the right and left margins of your paper at one inch. (If your instructor wants you to put your finished paper into a folder, add one-half inch to the left-hand margin.)

(2) Type your notes in numerical order.

▶Note. You must first go through your paper and insert the note numbers. (When you were writing your rough draft, you identified your sources with a parenthetical notation, but you did not number them. See 57.6d.) Begin with number 1 and number consecutively from one page to the next. Use arabic numerals.

(3) Indent the first line of each note six, seven, or eight spaces (0.60, 0.70, or 0.80 inches) from the left-hand margin (the same amount of indention as for the paragraphs in the text of your paper).

(4) Type the footnote numeral slightly above the line (never a full space above). Put no period after the numeral and leave no space between the numeral and the first word of the note.

Comp.
57.9

(5) Type to the right-hand margin as usual. Take runover lines back to the left-hand margin.

(6) Single-space each note, but double-space between notes.

(7) The following are examples of notes for basic sources. For sources not illustrated here, see Turabian's *Manual*, chapters 9 and 11.

Encyclopedia

¹World Book Encyclopedia 1984 ed., s.v. "Health," by Vivian K. Harlin.

Book

²Linda Meeks-Mitchell and Philip Heit, Health: A Wellness Approach (Columbus, Ohio: Merrill Publishing Co., 1987), 125.

Magazine

³Linda Williams, "America Goes Stair Crazy," Time, 18 December 1989, 83.

b. Do not give the complete information in a second reference to the same source. After a complete note has been given for a source, all later references to the same source should be done with "ibid." or with a shortened reference.

(1) Ibid. "Ibid." (for the Latin *ibidem*, "in the same place") should be used to refer to a single source cited in the immediately preceding note.

- "Ibid." may be used even though the note it refers to is not on the same page, as long as there are no intervening notes to another source.

- "Ibid." takes the place of the author's name, the title of the source, and as much else of the preceding note as is identical.

- If the second reference is to the same page as the preceding note, "ibid." is used alone. But if the reference is to a different page, the page number must also be given.

Examples: ¹⁰Ibid.   ¹¹Ibid., 57.

- Notice that "ibid." is not underlined.

Comp.
57.9

(2) **Shortened references.** A shortened reference should be used to refer to a source that has already been cited in complete form, but not in the immediately preceding note.

- A shortened reference to a work may include only the author's last name, the page number of the reference, and the volume number (if necessary).

- The title of the book or article must also be listed (sometimes in shortened form) when two or more works by the same author are cited. For information on when and how to shorten titles, see Turabian's *Manual*, sections 9.140–142.

- The following succession of notes illustrates the use of full and shortened references.

> [1]J. Gresham Machen, The Christian Faith in the Modern World(Grand Rapids, Mich.: Eerdmans, 1936), 243.

> [2]Homer Duncan, Humanism in the Light of Holy Scripture(Lubbock, Tex.: Missionary Crusader, 1981), 106.

> [3]Machen, 251.

[This reference to the same source as number 1 does not require the title because only one work by this author has been cited. Compare this one with note 8.]

> [4]J. Gresham Machen, Education, Christianity, and the State ed. John W. Robbins (Jefferson, Md.: Trinity Foundation, 1987), 2.

> [5]Ibid.

[This is a reference to the immediately preceding source, the same page. Compare this one with note 7.]

> [6]Erik von Kuehnelt-Leddihn,Leftism: From de Sade and Marx to Hitler and Marcuse (New Rochelle, N.Y.: Arlington House, 1974), 9.

> [7]Ibid., 98.

[This is a reference to the immediately preceding source, but to a different page. Compare this one with note 5.]

> [8]Machen, Christian Faith 157.

[This reference to the same source as number 1 requires the title because two works by this author have now been cited. Compare this one with note 3.]

57.10 Type the paper.

a. General information.

(1) Use 8½ by 11 inch white paper, preferably of 20-pound weight. Do not use erasable bond.

(2) Use standard type: pica or elite (preferably pica). Do not use any kind of "script" or other unusual style of type. If you are typing your paper on a computer, use 12-point Courier font.

(3) Use a fresh black ribbon.

(4) Interlineations, strikeovers, and crossing out of letters are not acceptable. Corrections made by a correcting typewriter or with correction fluid will be satisfactory if neatly done. Corrections should be few and should be made with such care that they will not be noticeable.

b. Responsibilities of the writer and the typist.

(1) The writer must submit a "clean" copy to the typist; that is, the copy should be accurate in every respect. Capitalization, punctuation, spelling, ellipses, interpolations, and indentions should be clearly indicated.

(2) The typist must produce an exact copy of the draft received from the writer.

(3) The typist is expected to follow all of the instructions given here and other standard typing procedures. See Turabian's *Manual,* sections 5.18–37, for instructions on typing ellipses, block quotations, and interpolations.

(4) The typist is responsible for the correct hyphenation of words at the ends of lines when word division is necessary to maintain the proper right-hand margin.

(5) The typist should proofread the paper before returning it to the writer.

Comp.
57.10

(6) The writer of the paper is responsible for the accuracy of the typing, whether he typed the paper himself or whether someone else typed it. The writer must proofread the paper and return it to the typist if any corrections need to be made.

(7) The typist is expected to retype any pages that are not accurate.

(8) Before typing begins, an explicit agreement should be reached between the writer and the typist concerning the things mentioned here and concerning the cost of the typing.

c. Order of pages in the paper.

(1) Title page
(2) Blank page
(3) Outline page(s)
(4) Body of the paper
(5) Appendix (if required)
(6) Endnotes page(s) (if endnotes are specified by your instructor)
(7) Bibliography page(s)

d. Title page. (See the example on page 306.)

(1) Center everything on the page if the paper is not to be bound. If your teacher wants you to bind your paper (put it into a folder), you will need to shift the center of your page one-half inch to the right.

(2) Type the entire title in upper case.

(3) If your title is longer than forty-eight spaces, type it in two or more double-spaced lines, in inverted pyramid form.

(4) Follow your teacher's instructions for the placement of your name, the date, the course number, and so forth. (Usually there is a two-inch margin at the top of the page and at least a two-inch margin at the bottom of the page.)

(5) Although this page is *counted* in the pagination of the front matter, its page number does not appear; that is, the number is not *typed* on the page.

Comp.
57.10

e. Blank page.

(1) This page is included to prevent the text of the following page from showing through the title page.

(2) This page is not counted in the pagination and has no page number.

(3) On this page, your instructor may wish to have you sign a pledge stating that you have avoided plagiarism in your paper. The following is an example.

```
    In this paper, every OPINION from someone else
has been indicated by a reference number placed at
the end of that information.  I realize that the
mere presence of a reference number does not avoid
plagiarism.  If I have used the exact words,
phrases, clauses, or sentences of someone else, I
have enclosed that information in quotation marks.
If I have paraphrased the opinions of someone
else, I have not enclosed the paraphrased portions
in quotation marks; but I have stated those
opinions in my own words and have placed a refer-
ence number at the end of the paraphrased portion.
    ALL FACTUAL INFORMATION (common knowledge or
uncontested knowledge), though not credited with a
reference number, has been stated in my sentence
structure.  I have not used anyone else's organi-
zation of the facts.
    This paper is my own work.  No one has helped
me in the preparation or writing of this paper.
    Signed: _____
```

f. Outline page. (See the example outline on pages 262–263.)

(1) The margins at the left and right of the page should be at least one inch. (The left-hand margin will be one and one-half inches if your instructor requires you to bind your paper.)

(2) Center the title on the thirteenth line (two inches) from the top edge of the page.

(3) Do not use the word *Outline* as the title.

Comp.
57.10

(4) If the title is longer than forty-eight spaces, type it in two or more double-spaced lines, in inverted pyramid form.

(5) Triple-space between the title and the first line of your thesis statement.

(6) At the left-margin, type the word *Thesis* (in upper- and lower-case letters). Underline the word *Thesis,* and put a colon after it. Space twice and type the thesis statement the full width of the page, observing the margins. Single space the lines.

(7) Do not include an introduction or a conclusion in your outline.

(8) Double-space between the purpose statement and the first main point (roman numeral I) in the body of your paper.

(9) Indent the first roman numeral four spaces from the left-hand margin. Align the succeeding roman numerals by the periods.

(10) Start the first word of each point on the third space after the period. (Strike the space bar twice and begin typing.)

(11) Follow this scheme of notation and indention:

I.

    A.

       1.

          a.

            (1)

               (a)

(12) Single-space the lines within each major division. Double-space before beginning a new major division (that is, before each division beginning with a roman numeral: I, II, III, etc.).

(13) The outline is to be a sentence outline. Every point in the outline should be a grammatically complete sentence. (This method helps to assure unity and logical connections in a research paper.)

▶ Exception: The main points (I, II, III, etc.) may be stated as topics rather than as sentences, but those topics must be grammatically parallel (all nouns, for example).

(14) Number the outline page(s) with small roman numerals (ii, iii, iv, etc.), centered at the bottom of each page, on the seventh line above the edge. This placement will leave a one-inch margin below the page number. Begin numbering with number ii. Leave one blank line between the last line of text and the page number. (Of course, if the outline does not fill the page, there will be more than one blank line between the last line of text and the page number.)

(15) If the outline requires more than one page, begin typing the text of each additional page on the seventh line (one inch) from the top edge of the page. The page numbers (small roman numerals) continue at the bottom of the page. (See 14 above.)

(16) Before you type this page, make sure that you have altered your preliminary outline to reflect any changes you may have made in the order or content of your paper while it was in process.

g. First page of the body of the paper.

(1) The margins at the left and right of each page should be at least one inch. (The left-hand margin will be one and one-half inches if your instructor requires you to bind your paper.)

(2) Center the title on the thirteenth line (two inches) from the top edge of the page. Type the entire title in upper case. Do not underline the title or put quotation marks around it.

(3) If the title is longer than forty-eight spaces, type it in two or more double-spaced lines, in inverted pyramid form.

Comp. 57.10

(4) Triple-space between the title and the first line of the text.

(5) Double-space the text except for block quotations, which you should single-space.

(6) Indent the first line of each paragraph six, seven, or eight spaces (0.60, 0.70, or 0.80 inches).

(7) On this page and throughout the body of your paper, make sure to place the note numbers **after** the passage to which it refers, not before. If there is any punctuation at that point, put the number outside every punctuation mark except the dash.

(8) Center the arabic numeral one (1) at the foot of the page on the seventh line (one inch) above the bottom edge of the page. Do not use a period or parentheses or hyphens with the number.

(9) Leave one blank line between the last line of text and the page number. An extra blank line may be left if necessary to avoid having a footnote number in the last line of text. (Most word processing programs automatically leave one blank line and adjust for another if necessary.) Of course, if you are doing endnotes, a note number in the last line of text is no problem.

h. Succeeding pages of the body of the paper.

(1) Center the arabic numeral (2, 3, 4, etc.) on the seventh line (one inch) from the top edge of the page. Do not use a period or parentheses with the number.

(2) Double-space between the page number and the first line of the text; that is, begin typing the text on the ninth line from the top edge of the page. (Most word processing programs adjust the text automatically to allow for page numbers, but on the second and following pages, you may need to add a hard return to maintain double-spacing between the page number and the first line of text.)

(3) All other considerations are the same as for the first page of the body.

i. Block quotations.

(1) Quotations set off from the text are called *block* quotations.

(2) Prose quotations of two or more sentences that require four or more typewritten lines should be typed as a block quotation, not run into the text. (For quotations of poetry, see Turabian's *Manual*, sections 5.3–6.)

(3) Double-space before and after a block quotation.

(4) Single-space the quotation.

(5) Indent the quotation four (4) spaces (0.40 inches) from the left-hand margin. Type to the right-hand margin as you do for the text.

(6) If the quoted matter begins a paragraph in the source from which it is taken, indent the first line of the block quotation an additional four (4) spaces—a total of eight (8) spaces (0.80 inches) from the left-hand margin.

(7) If the quoted matter does not begin a paragraph in the source from which it is taken, do not give it paragraph indention. The first line should begin flush, four (4) spaces (0.40 inches) from the left-hand margin.

(8) The initial letter of a block quotation is capitalized or not capitalized depending on the context in which it appears.

(a) If the quotation is made a syntactical part of the sentence that introduces the quotation, the initial letter of the quotation should be lower cased, even if the quotation in the original source is a complete sentence beginning with a capital letter.

(b) If the sentence that introduces the quotation ends with terminal punctuation or with a colon, the initial letter of the quotation should be capitalized, even if the quotation in the original source does not begin with a capital letter.

Comp. 57.10

(9) Do not use quotation marks at the beginning or at the end of a block quotation. But if something within the quotation calls for quotation marks, use quotation marks according to the usual rules.

(10) Omission of words, sentences, or paragraphs from quoted matter must be indicated by ellipsis points (spaced dots). Leave a space before and after each ellipsis point. Use *three* spaced dots *within* a sentence.

(11) Use *four* dots *at the end* of a sentence if at that point something is omitted and the quotation continues. The omission may consist of words, sentences, or paragraphs. The first of the four dots is the period, placed immediately after the last word. If the sentence is a question or an exclamation, the period is replaced with a question mark or an exclamation mark.

(12) It is seldom, if ever, necessary to use ellipsis points at the beginning or at the end of a quoted passage.

► Note. For examples and additional information concerning ellipses and block quotations, see Turabian's *Manual,* sections 5.16–38.

j. **Footnotes. (Skip to the next section if you are doing endnotes.)**

(1) If you are using a typewriter, estimate the space that will be needed for the footnotes.

(a) Whenever the first note number appears in the text, stop and refer to the trial list of footnotes (which you prepared earlier according to section 57.9). Count the number of lines in the corresponding footnote and subtract that number from 60 (line 60 is the bottom margin). Then subtract two more to allow for the line of separation. (See item 2 below.) The number you arrive at will be the number of the line at the end of which you must stop typing in order to allow room for the footnote.

As each succeeding footnote number appears in the text, stop and count the number of lines in the footnote and subtract that number from the previous total. Then subtract one more for the space between footnotes.

Comp.
57.10

(b) If you have footnotes on the first page, you must use the number 58 for your calculations in order to leave room for a blank line and the page number, which must go on line 60.

(c) For information on how to prepare a guide sheet for estimating space for footnotes, see Turabian's *Manual,* sections 14.15–16.

(2) Single-space after the last line of text and type a line twenty spaces (two inches) in length beginning at the left-hand margin of the page. Use the underlining key. Double-space after the line before typing the footnotes.

(3) A footnote must begin at the bottom of the page on which the reference occurs, but a lengthy note may be continued at the bottom of the next page if necessary.

(4) If the text on the last page fills only part of the page, put any footnotes for that page immediately below the text (in the usual manner), rather than at the bottom of the page.

(5) If you have a sequence of short footnotes, run them across one line rather than down the page. When you do this, you must leave at least three (3) spaces between notes, and you must be sure that all those notes are completed on one line:

[1]McCracken, Wordsworth, 34.

[2]Ibid., 38. [3]Ibid.

(6) If you are using a computer, you may use the footnote feature of your word processing program. This special feature will automatically place footnotes at the bottom of a page and adjust the text accordingly. Refer to your program manual for specific instructions.

k. Endnotes page. (See the example on page 307.)

Comp. 57.10

(1) Type the word NOTES (not ENDNOTES) on the thirteenth line (two inches) from the top of the page.

(2) Triple-space between the heading and the first note.

(3) Turn back to section 57.9 and follow the directions for typing a trial list of footnotes. The only difference in footnotes and endnotes is that **foot**notes are typed at the **foot** of the pages in the body of the paper and **end**notes are typed in a continuous list at the **end** of the paper.

▶ Exception: For endnotes, you may type the note numbers on the line followed by a period and two spaces, instead of slightly above the line (superscript) as in footnotes.

(4) On the first page of the notes, center the page number (an arabic numeral) on the seventh line (one inch) above the bottom edge of the page. The numbering is continuous with the preceding pages.

(5) For any succeeding pages, center the page number on the seventh line (one inch) from the top edge of the page. Double-space and resume typing the entries on the ninth line.

l. Bibliography page. (See the example on page 308.)

(1) The bibliography page is an alphabetical list of all the sources actually used in writing the paper. Include only those sources that you have quoted or referred to in your paper.

(2) Arrange your bibliography cards in alphabetical order according to the first word that appears on the card. This will be either the author's last name or the first word of the title (excluding *a, an,* or *the*). If you have done your bibliography cards correctly, you can simply copy the information directly from them.

(3) Type the heading on the thirteenth line (two inches) from the top of the page.

(4) Use the heading WORKS CITED if only printed sources are used. Use the heading SOURCES CONSULTED if your bibliography includes sources such as interviews, sound recordings, video recordings, computer programs, and radio or television broadcasts.

Comp.
57.10

(5) Triple-space between the heading and the first entry.

(6) Single-space each entry, but double-space between entries.

(7) Begin the first line of each entry flush with the left-hand margin; indent runover lines five (5) spaces (0.50 inches).

(8) Type to the right-hand margin as usual.

(9) If you have two or more sources by the same author, do not repeat the author's name for the entries after the first. In place of the author's name, type an unbroken line (eight spaces or 0.80 inches long) followed by a period.

(10) Center the page number (an arabic numeral) on the seventh line (one inch) above the bottom edge of the page. The numbering is continuous with the preceding pages.

(11) For any succeeding pages, center the page number on the seventh line (one inch) from the top edge of the page. Double-space and resume typing the entries on the ninth line.

57.11 Proofread the typed paper.

a. Compare the typed copy with your final manuscript to make sure that nothing was omitted.

b. Proofread every page, checking the correctness of every letter of every word and every punctuation mark.

c. The instructor will hold the writer, not the typist, accountable for the final form of the paper. The writer must catch all typographical errors and return the paper to the typist for corrections. Typographical errors will be graded as writer errors.

Comp.
57.11

TECHNICAL INFORMATION CONCERNING FOOTNOTES AND BIBLIOGRAPHY

57.12 **Explanation of footnote forms.** The first time you refer to a source, give the complete bibliographical information as explained here.

BOOKS

a. Single volume books. A typical footnote reference to a book includes four main parts: (1) author's name, (2) title of the work, (3) facts of publication, and (4) page number(s). Following are specifics about those four main parts of a footnote entry. (For information concerning additional items that are often necessary in a footnote, see the examples in section 57.14.)

(1) **Name of author(s).**

- Give the name(s) in the usual order (not reversed).

- Include the first name and middle initial (or first and second names) unless it is well known that the author uses his initials only (e.g., T. S. Eliot, C. S. Lewis, H. G. Wells). The name should appear as it does on the title page.

- If a work has more than three authors, cite only the first author's name given on the title page, and then follow the name with "et al." (for the Latin et alii, "and others"). Do not put a comma between the author's name and "et al." (See 57.14, example 4.)

- Omit titles indicating a scholastic degree or official position (Ph.D., M.A., doctor, professor, president, pastor, and so on).

- Sometimes the author is a corporate body (e.g., a committee, an institution, a government body, a city). (See 57.14, example 8.)

- If authorship cannot be determined, begin the entry with the title of the work. (See 57.14, example 9.)

(2) **Title of the book.**

- Give the full title of the book as it appears on the title page. Retain the exact spelling, but capitalize the words according to the usual rules of capitalizing titles. (See section 41.4.) This instruction includes capitalizing the first word of a subtitle.

• If there is a subtitle, put a colon between it and the title even though there may be no punctuation in the original.

• Underline the entire title (and subtitle, if any).

(3) **Facts of publication.** Give the place of publication, the publishing agency, and the date—all within parentheses. Place a colon after the place, and a comma after the publishing agency.

(a) *Place of publication.*

• If several cities are given, it is necessary to list only the first one.

• If the city is not well known or if there is more than one city by the same name, add the state. Use the standard abbreviation for the state. (See 57.16.)

• If the place of publication is not given, write "n.p." (for "no place").

(b) *Publishing agency.*

• Use the full name of the publisher as it is given on the title page, except for the following: omit an initial "The" and the abbreviations "Inc." or "Ltd."

• Abbreviate "Company" to "Co." and "Brother" or "Brothers" to "Bro." or "Bros."

• If no publisher's name is given, write "n.p." (for "no publisher").

• If neither place nor publisher is given, use one "n.p." to stand for both.

(c) *Date of publication.*

• If there is more than one copyright date listed on the copyright page, use the latest one.

• If a different date from the copyright date appears on the title page with the publisher's imprint, use that date instead of the copyright date.

Comp. 57.12

> - Ignore any other date listed in addition to the copyright dates. Those dates refer to new printings, not to new editions.
> - If no date is given anywhere, use "n.d." (for "no date").

(4) **Page number(s).**

> - To refer to a single page, follow this example: "35."
> - To refer to more than one page, follow this example: "35–36."
> - For the proper method of writing continued numbers see Turabian's *Manual,* section 2.67.

SAMPLE REFERENCE FOR A PUBLISHED BOOK

[1]Arthur S. Trace, Jr., <u>Reading Without Dick and Jane</u> (Chicago: Henry Regnery Co., 1965), 79.

b. Multivolume books.

(1) If the reference is to a multivolume work as a whole, the total number of volumes must be given. (See 57.14, example 16.)

(2) If the reference is to only one of the volumes in the set, the number of the particular volume must be given. (See 57.14, examples 17–19.)

(3) If all the volumes have the same title, the total number of volumes must be included (see 57.14, examples 16–17); but if the volumes are separately titled, the total number of volumes may be omitted. (See 57.14, examples 18–19.)

(4) If the set has an overall title and the individual volumes have different titles, give both the overall title and the title of the volume referred to. Underline both titles. (See 57.14, examples 18–19.)

(5) Use arabic numerals for volume numbers even if the book shows them as roman numerals.

(6) Study carefully examples 16–19 in section 57.14.

Comp.
57.12

PERIODICALS

c. Professional journals. A professional journal contains articles on subjects related to a particular branch of knowledge usually written by members of the profession. These are some examples: *Journal of Music Theory, Journal of Law and Education, Policy Review, Bibliotheca Sacra, American Historical Review, Human Life Review.* A typical entry for a professional journal includes six parts in the order given here.

(1) **Name of author(s).**

- Do the same as for a published book. (See 57.12a.)

(2) **Title of the article.**

- Enclose the title in quotation marks.

(3) **Title of the journal.**

- Omit an initial "The," even if it is actually a part of the title.
- Underline the title of the journal.

(4) **Volume number.**

- Include the volume number immediately after the title of the journal.
- Use an arabic numeral to indicate the volume number, even if the journal itself uses a roman numeral.

(5) **Date.**

- Give the date as listed on the journal (e.g., Spring 1994, August 1995).
- Enclose the date in parentheses.

(6) **Page number(s).**

- The page number follows a colon and is used without the abbreviations "p." or "pp."
- For the proper method of writing continued numbers, see Turabian's *Manual,* section 2.67.

SAMPLE REFERENCE FOR
A PROFESSIONAL JOURNAL

Comp
57.12

²John T. Norman, Jr., "ERA: Equal
Rights for Abortion?" Human Life Review 10
(Spring 1984): 31.

d. General magazines. A general magazine is a popular periodical that treats various areas of general interest. These are some examples: *Reader's Digest, Newsweek, Science Digest, Sports Illustrated, Life, Atlantic.* A typical entry for a general magazine includes five parts in the order given here.

(1) **Name of author(s).**

- Do the same as for a published book. (See 57.12a.)

(2) **Title of the article.**

- Enclose the title in quotation marks.

(3) **Title of the magazine.**

- Omit an initial "The," even if it is actually a part of the title.
- Underline the title of the magazine.

▶ Note. Do not use a volume number after the title as you do for a professional journal, even though the magazine may have a volume number listed.

(4) **Date.**

- Do not put the date in parentheses as you do for a journal.
- For weekly magazines, the day precedes the name of the month as in this example: 25 August 1995.

(5) **Page numbers.** Do the same as for a published book. See 57.12a(4).

SAMPLE REFERENCE FOR
A GENERAL MAGAZINE

      [3]George Russell, "Summitry: A Most Exclusive Club," <u>Time</u>, 18 June 1984, 35–36.

e. Newspapers. A typical entry for a newspaper includes six parts in the order given here.

(1) **Name of author(s).**

- Do the same as for a published book. (See 57.12a.)

(2) **Title of the article.**

- Enclose the title in quotation marks.

(3) **Name of the newspaper.**
- Omit an initial "The," even if it is actually part of the name.
- Underline the name of the newspaper.
- If the name of the city is not a part of the name of the newspaper, include the name of the city before the name of the newspaper. Underline the name of the city as if it were a part of the name of the newspaper.
- If the city is not well known or if the name of the city is the same as that of another well-known city, put the abbreviated name of the state in parentheses after the name of the city. Do not underline the name of the state.

   Example: Richmond (Ind.) Palladium-Item

(4) **Date.**
- The date of the newspaper must be included.

(5) **Section number (or letter).**
- If the newspaper has more than one section, the section number (or letter) must be included.

(6) **Page number.**
- The page number may be omitted if the newspaper has only one section, but it is always helpful to include it.

SAMPLE ENTRY FOR A NEWSPAPER

⁴Keith Herndon, "Farms Down to a Record Low in State," Atlanta Constitution, 23 May 1984, sec. B, p. 1.

▶ Note. For examples of footnotes for various other sources, such as encyclopedias, interviews, lectures, and so on, see section 57.14.

57.13 Explanation of bibliographical entries.
The form for bibliographical entries differs from the form for footnotes in several respects.

a. **Author's name(s).**

- For alphabetizing, authors' last names are put before their first names: Doe, John (*not* John Doe).

- Even if there are three or more authors, all the authors are listed. But only the first author's name is reversed: Doe, John, J. W. Brown, Fred Green, and James Fox.

b. Punctuation.

- Periods, instead of commas, are used after (and occasionally within) each of the three basic parts of an entry: author's name, title, and facts of publication. Compare the footnote and bibliographical entries in section 57.14.

- Parentheses are removed from around the facts of publication.

  ▶ Exception. Parentheses are retained around the date in references to periodicals when the date follows the volume number. (See section 57.14, example 20.)

c. Page references.

- Page references are omitted except for an item that is a part of a larger work (e.g., an essay in a book or an article in a periodical).

- Any page numbers that are given should be inclusive (that is, the first and last page of the selection should be given), unless the pages are not consecutive. If the pages are not consecutive, only the first page of the selection should be given.

57.14 Sample footnotes and corresponding bibliographical entries.

▶ Note. For a complete listing of footnote and bibliographic forms, refer to Kate L. Turabian's *Manual for Writers of Term Papers, Theses, and Dissertations,* 5th ed. (Chicago: University of Chicago Press, 1987), pages 175–203.

In all of the following examples, "N" indicates a footnote entry, and "B" indicates a bibliographical entry.

SINGLE-VOLUME BOOKS

1. One author

N.   [1]Jonathan Hughes, <u>American Economic History</u> (Glenview, Ill.: Scott, Foresman & Co., 1983), 127.

B.   Hughes, Jonathan. <u>American Economic History</u>. Glenview, Ill.: Scott, Foresman & Co., 1983.

2. Two authors

N. [2]E. Adamson Hoebel and Everett L. Frost, <u>Cultural and Social Anthropology</u> (New York: McGraw-Hill Co., 1976), 325-326.

B. Hoebel, E. Adamson, and Everett L. Frost. <u>Cultural and Social Anthropology</u>. New York: McGraw-Hill Co., 1976.

3. Three authors

N. [3]Ronald A. Anderson, Ivan Fox, and David P. Twomey, <u>Business Law</u>, 12th ed. (Cincinnati: South-Western Publishing Co., 1984), 537.

B. Anderson, Ronald A., Ivan Fox, and David P. Twomey. <u>Business Law</u>. 12th ed. Cincinnati: South-Western Publishing Co., 1984.

4. More than three authors

N. [4]Clair Wilcox et al., <u>Economies of the World Today</u>, 3d ed. (New York: Harcourt Brace Jovanovich, 1976), 113.

B. Wilcox, Clair, Willis D. Weatherford, Jr., Holland Hunter, and Morton S. Baratz. <u>Economies of the World Today</u>, 3d ed. New York: Harcourt Brace Jovanovich, 1976.

5. Editor, compiler, or translator as author (when no author appears on the title page)

N. [5]John Gage, ed. and trans., <u>Goethe on Art</u> (Berkeley and Los Angeles: University of California Press, 1980), 32.

B. Gage, John, ed. and trans. <u>Goethe on Art</u>. Berkeley and Los Angeles: University of California Press, 1980.

Comp.
57.14

6. Editor, compiler, or translator with an author

N. [6]John Locke, _An Essay Concerning Human Understanding_, ed. by Peter H. Nidditch (Oxford: Clarendon Press, 1975), 35.

B. Locke, John. _An Essay Concerning Human Understanding_. Edited by Peter H. Nidditch. Oxford: Clarendon Press, 1975.

7. Anthology (article, essay, or other component part by one author in a work edited by another)

N. [7]Noah Webster, "On the Education of Youth in America," in _Essays on Education in the Early Republic_, ed. Frederick Rudolph (Cambridge: Harvard University Press, Belknap Press, 1965), 48.

B. Webster, Noah. "On the Education of Youth in America." In _Essays on Education in the Early Republic_, ed. Frederick Rudolf, 41–77. Cambridge: Harvard University Press, Belknap Press, 1965.

8. Corporate author

N. [8]American Council on Education, _American Universities and Colleges_, 9th ed. (Washington, D.C.: American Council on Education, 1964), 8.

B. American Council on Education. _American Universities and Colleges_. 9th ed. Washington, D.C.: American Council on Education, 1964.

9. No author given

N. [9]_The Chicago Manual of Style_, 13th ed., rev. and enl. (Chicago: University of Chicago Press, 1982), 441.

B. The Chicago Manual of Style. 13th ed., rev. and enl. Chicago: University of Chicago Press, 1982.

10. Named author of preface, introduction, or foreword

N.   [10]Otto Jespersen, Analytic Syntax, with a Foreword by Samuel R. Levin (New York: Holt, Rinehart and Winston, 1969), 23.

B. Jespersen, Otto. Analytic Syntax. With a Foreword by Samuel R. Levin. New York: Holt, Rinehart and Winston, 1969.

Or if reference is to preface, introduction, or foreword

N.   [10]Samuel R. Levin, foreword to Analytic Syntax, by Otto Jespersen (New York: Holt, Rinehart and Winston, 1969), vii.

B. Levin, Samuel R. Foreword to Analytic Syntax, by Otto Jespersen. New York: Holt, Rinehart and Winston, 1969.

11. Book in a series

N.   [11]Aubrey Gwynn, Roman Education from Cicero to Quintilian, Classics in Education, no. 29 (New York: Teachers College Press, 1926), 85.

B. Gwynn, Aubrey. Roman Education from Cicero to Quintilian. Classics in Education, no. 29. New York: Teachers College Press, 1926.

12. Edition other than the first

N.   [12]Joseph Machlis, The Enjoyment of Music: An Introduction to Perceptive Listening, 3d ed. (New York: W. W. Norton & Co., 1970), 65.

Comp. 57.14

291

B. Machlis, Joseph. <u>The Enjoyment of Music:</u> <u>An Introduction to Perceptive</u> <u>Listening</u>. 3d ed. New York: W. W. Norton & Co., 1970.

13. A reprint

N. [13]J. Gresham Machen, <u>The Virgin</u> <u>Birth of Christ</u> (New York: Harper & Row Publishers, 1930; reprint, Grand Rapids, Mich.: Baker Book House Co., 1965), 43.

B. Machen, J. Gresham. <u>The Virgin Birth of</u> <u>Christ</u>. New York: Harper & Row Publishers, 1930; reprint, Grand Rapids, Mich.: Baker Book House Co., 1965.

14. A paperback book

N. [14]Theodore M. Bernstein, <u>The Care-</u> <u>ful Writer: A Modern Guide to English</u> <u>Usage</u> (Saddle Brook, N.J.: American Book—Stratford Press, 1965; New York: Atheneum, 1977), 72-73.

B. Bernstein, Theodore M. <u>The Careful</u> <u>Writer: A Modern Guide to English</u> <u>Usage</u>. Saddle Brook, N.J.: American Book—Stratford Press, 1965; New York: Atheneum, 1977.

15. Pamphlets (same as books)

N. [15]Donald W. Emery, <u>Sentence Analy-</u> <u>sis</u> (New York: Holt, Rinehart and Winston, 1961), 12.

B. Emery, Donald W. <u>Sentence Analysis</u>. New York: Holt, Rinehart and Winston, 1961.

Comp.
57.14

MULTIVOLUME BOOKS

16. Multivolume work referred to as a whole

N. ¹⁶Lewis Sperry Chafer, ed., <u>Systematic Theology</u>, 8 vols. (Dallas: Dallas Seminary Press, 1947-48).

B. Chafer, Lewis Sperry, ed. <u>Systematic Theology</u>, 8 vols. Dallas: Dallas Seminary Press, 1947-48.

17. Volume in a multivolume work with a general title only

N. ¹⁷James Newman, <u>The World of Mathematics</u>, vol. 2 (New York: Simon and Schuster, 1956), 2 : 809.

B. Newman, James. <u>The World of Mathematics</u>. Vol. 2. New York: Simon and Schuster, 1956.

18. Separately titled volume in a multivolume work (one author)

N. ¹⁸Winston S. Churchill, <u>A History of the English-Speaking Peoples</u>, vol. 2 of <u>The Birth of Britain</u> (New York: Dodd, Mead and Co., 1956), 37.

B. Churchill, Winston S. <u>A History of the English-Speaking Peoples</u>. Vol. 2 of <u>The Birth of Britain</u>. New York: Dodd, Mead and Co., 1956.

19. Separately titled volume in a multivolume work (general editor and individual editor or author)

N. ¹⁹Albert C. Baugh, ed., <u>A Literary History of England</u>, 2d ed., vol. 4, <u>The Nineteenth Century and After (1789-1939)</u>, by Samuel C. Chew and Richard D. Altick (Englewood Cliffs, N.J.: Prentice-Hall, 1967), 1350.

293

B. Baugh, Albert C., ed. <u>A Literary History of England</u>. 2d ed. Vol. 4, <u>The Nineteenth Century and After (1789–1939)</u>, by Samuel C. Chew and Richard D. Altick. Englewood Cliffs, N.J.: Prentice-Hall, 1967.

PERIODICALS

20. Professional journals

N. [20]David S. Shields, "Happiness in Society: The Development of an Eighteenth-Century American Poetic Ideal," <u>American Literature</u> 55 (December 1983): 545.

B. Shields, David S. "Happiness in Society: The Development of an Eighteenth-Century American Poetic Ideal." <u>American Literature</u> 55 (December 1983): 541–559.

21. General Magazines

N. [21]George Gilder, "What Ronald Reagan Doesn't Know about His Own Achievements," <u>National Review</u>, 29 June 1984, p. 23.

B. Gilder, George. "What Ronald Reagan Doesn't Know about His Own Achievements." <u>National Review</u>, 29 June 1984, pp. 22–25.

22. Newspapers

N. [22]Keith Herndon, "Farms Down to a Record Low in State," <u>Atlanta Constitution</u>, 23 May 1984, sec. B, p. 1.

B. Herndon, Keith. "Farms Down to a Record Low in State." <u>Atlanta Constitution</u>, 23 May 1984, sec. B, p. 1.

Comp.
57.14

ENCYCLOPEDIAS
23. Signed articles

N. [23]The World Book Encyclopedia, 1983 ed., s.v. "Nuclear Energy," by Alvin M. Weinberg.

B. The World Book Encyclopedia, 1983 ed. S.v. "Nuclear Energy," by Alvin M. Weinberg.

24. Unsigned articles

N. [24]The World Book Encyclopedia, 1983 ed., s.v. "Nobel Prizes."

B. The World Book Encyclopedia, 1983 ed. S.v. "Nobel Prizes."

CD-ROM
25. Book

N. [25]William Harrison, Description of Elizabethan England (1577), World Literary Heritage [CD-ROM] (Irvine, Calif.: Softbilt, 1994).

B. Harrison, William. Description of Elizabethan England (1577). World Literary Heritage [CD-ROM]. Irvine, Calif.: Softbilt, 1994.

26. Magazine

N. [26]Charles Lane, "Picked Pocket," New Republic, 19 December 1994, 12–14, MAS Full Text Elite, Disc 1 [CD-ROM], EBSCO Publishing, 1995.

B. Lane, Charles. "Picked Pocket." New Republic, 19 December 1994, 12–14. MAS Full Text Elite, Disc 1 [CD-ROM]. EBSCO Publishing, 1995.

Comp.
57.14

27. Newspaper

N.   [27]Robin Toner, "Senate Approves Welfare Plan That Would End Aid Guarantee," <u>New York Times</u>, 20 September 1995, national ed., A1, <u>New York Times Ondisc</u>, [CD-ROM], UMI-Proquest, December 1995.

B. Toner, Robin. "Senate Approves Welfare Plan That Would End Aid Guarantee." <u>New York Times</u>, 20 September 1995, national ed., A1. <u>New York Times Ondisc</u> [CD-ROM]. UMI-Proquest, December 1995.

28. Encyclopedia

N.   [28]<u>New Grolier's Encyclopedia</u>, 1993 ed., s.v. "Depression of the 1930s" [CD-ROM] (Danbury, Conn.: Grolier Electronic Publishers, 1993).

B. <u>New Grolier's Encyclopedia</u>, 1993 ed. S.v. "Depression of the 1930s" [CD-ROM]. Danbury, Conn.: Grolier Electronic Publishers, 1993.

29. Essay

N.   [29]Charles Augustin Saint-Beuve, "What Is a Classic (1837)," trans. E. Lee, <u>World Literary Heritage</u> [CD-ROM] (Irvine, Calif.: Softbilt, 1994).

B. Saint-Beuve, Charles Augustin. "What Is a Classic (1837)." Translated by E. Lee. <u>World Literary Heritage</u> [CD-ROM]. Irvine, Calif.: Softbilt, 1994.

30. No written source available

N.   [30]Pixel Multimedia (Tel Aviv) and Aaron Witkin Associates (London), <u>The Dead Sea Scrolls Revealed</u>, interactive ed. [CD-ROM] (Jerusalem: Logos Research Systems, under exclusive license of Israel Antiquities Authority, 1994).

B. Pixel Multimedia (Tel Aviv) and Aaron Witkin Associates (London). <u>The Dead Sea Scrolls Revealed</u>, interactive ed. [CD-ROM]. Jerusalem: Logos Research Systems, under exclusive license of Israel Antiquities Authority, 1994.

ON-LINE SERVICES
31. Book

N. [31]William J. Mitchell, <u>City of Bits: Space, Place, and the Infobahn</u> [book on-line] (Cambridge, Mass.: MIT Press, 1995, accessed 9 November 1995); available from http://www-mitpress.mit.edu:80/City_of_Bits/Pulling_Glass/index.html; Internet.

B. Mitchell, William J. <u>City of Bits: Space, Place, and the Infobahn</u> [book on-line]. Cambridge, Mass.: MIT Press, 1995. Accessed 9 November 1995. Available from http://www-mitpress.mit.edu:80/City_of_Bits/Pulling_Glass/index.html. Internet.

32. Magazine

N. [32]Anita Malnig, "Do We Trade Quality For More Flexibility?" <u>MacWEEK</u>, 24 October 1995 [magazine on-line]; available from http://www.zdnet.com/~macweek/mw_09-25-95/sr3.html; Internet; accessed 24 October 1995.

B. Malnig, Anita. "Do We Trade Quality For More Flexibility?" <u>MacWEEK</u>, 24 October 1995 [magazine on-line]. Available from http://www.zdnet.com/~macweek/mw_09-25-95/sr3.html. Internet. Accessed 24 October 1995.

Comp.
57.14

33. Newspaper

N.   [33]John Gallagher and David Everett, "Conference Shoves Jobs to the Forefront," Detroit Free Press, 16 March 1994, Free Press Business Writers Edition: Metro Final Chaser, sec. NWS, p. 1A [newspaper on-line]; CompuServe; accessed 9 November 1995.

B. Gallagher, John, and David Everett. "Conference Shoves Jobs to the Forefront." Detroit Free Press, 16 March 1994, Free Press Business Writers Edition: Metro Final Chaser, sec. NWS, p. 1A [newspaper on-line]. CompuServe. Accessed 9 November 1995.

34. Encyclopedia

N.   [34]Encyclopedia Britannica, 1995 ed., s.v. "British North America Act" [encyclopedia on-line]; available from http://www.pf.eb.com; Britannica Online; accessed 24 October 1995.

B. Encyclopedia Britannica, 1995 ed. S.v. "British North America Act" [encyclopedia on-line]. Available from http://www.pf.eb.com. Britannica Online. Accessed 24 October 1995.

35. Interview

N.   [35]Brian R. Benzanson, Sells Printing Company, New Berlin, Wisconsin; interview by Peter Leppik, 23 October 1995; Internet; accessed 24 October 1995.

B. Benzanson, Brian R. Sells Printing Company, New Berlin, Wisconsin. Interview by Peter Leppik, 23 October 1995. Internet. Accessed 24 October 1995.

Comp.
57.14

SPECIAL FORMS
36. The Bible

▶ Note. Neither the Bible nor its individual books are underlined or put in quotation marks. Always identify the version being quoted or cited.

N.   [36]1 Cor. 13:1-13 KJV.

B.   The Bible (King James Version).

37. Sermons

N.   [37]Jim Schettler, "Three Steps to Knowing God's Will," sermon preached at Pensacola Christian College Campus Church, 25 July 1993.

B.   Schettler, Jim. "Three Steps to Knowing God's Will." Sermon preached at Pensacola Christian College Campus Church, 25 July 1993.

38. Interviews

N.   [38]E. W. Hopkins, Jr., First Mutual Savings Association, Pensacola, Florida, interview by author, 20 September 1995.

B.   Hopkins, E. W., Jr. First Mutual Savings Association, Pensacola, Florida. Interview by author, 20 September 1995.

39. Lectures

N.   [39]John Reese, History 102 class lecture, Pensacola Christian College, 7 March 1994.

B.   Reese, John. History 102 class lecture. Pensacola Christian College. 7 March 1994.

Comp. 57.14

40. Tape recordings

N. [40]Max Rafferty, "Should the Schools Teach Patriotism?" no. 14, tape on file in Pensacola Christian College Library.

B. Rafferty, Max. "Should the Schools Teach Patriotism?" no. 14. Tape on file in Pensacola Christian College Library.

41. Compact discs

N. [41]Wolfgang Amadeus Mozart, _Symphony no. 38 in D Major_, Vienna Philharmonic, James Levine, Polydor compact disc 423 086-2.

B. Mozart, Wolfgang Amadeus. _Symphony no. 38 in D Major_. Vienna Philharmonic. James Levine. Polydor compact disc 423 086-2.

42. Videotapes

N. [42]_Making Grammar Practical and Interesting_, 45 minutes, A Beka Book Publications, 1979, videocassette.

B. _Making Grammar Practical and Interesting_. 45 minutes. A Beka Book Publications, 1979. Videocassette.

43. Television programs

N. [43]WPMI, "Rejoice in the Lord," 8 July 1984.

B. WPMI. "Rejoice in the Lord." 8 July 1984.

44. Radio programs

N. [44]WPCS, "Radio Bible Class," 4 May 1984.

B. WPCS. "Radio Bible Class." 4 May 1984.

45. Secondary source of quotation

If you find it necessary to cite from the work of one author as found in the work of another, your footnote must include both the original source and the source in which you found the material.

If the content itself is of primary significance, use the following form.

N.   [45]Clinton Rossiter, <u>Seedtime of the Republic: The Origin of the American Tradition of Political Liberty</u> (New York: Harcourt, Brace, 1953): 55, quoted in Russell Kirk, <u>The Roots of American Order</u> (Malibu, Calif.: Pepperdine University Press, 1974), 48, n. 15.

B.   Rossiter, Clinton. <u>Seedtime of the Republic: The Origin of the American Tradition of Political Liberty</u>. (New York: Harcourt, Brace, 1953): 55. Quoted in Russell Kirk, <u>The Roots of American Order</u> (Malibu, Calif.: Pepperdine University Press, 1974), 48, n. 15.

If it is more significant for your purpose to emphasize the author who is doing the quoting, use the following form.

N.   [45]Russell Kirk, <u>The Roots of American Order</u> (Malibu, Calif.: Pepperdine University Press, 1974), 48, n. 15, quoting Clinton Rossiter, <u>Seedtime of the Republic: The Origin of the American Tradition of Political Liberty</u> (New York: Harcourt, Brace, 1953): 55.

Comp.
57.14

 B. Kirk, Russell. <u>The Roots of American</u>
<u>Order</u>, 48, n. 15. Malibu, Calif.:
Pepperdine University Press, 1974.
Quoting Clinton Rossiter, <u>Seedtime</u>
<u>of the Republic: The Origin of the</u>
<u>American Tradition of Political</u>
<u>Liberty</u> (New York: Harcourt,
Brace, 1953): 55.

57.15 **Explanation of second or later footnote references.**
After a complete first-reference footnote has been given for
a particular source, all later references to the same source
should be shortened.

 a. "Ibid." Ibid. (for the Latin *ibidem,* "in the same place")
is used to refer to a single source cited in the immediately preceding footnote.

  (1) Ibid. may be used even though the reference it
refers to is not on the same page, as long as there
are no intervening references to another source.

  (2) Ibid. takes the place of the author's name, the title
of the source, and as much of the preceding reference as is identical.

  (3) If the second reference is to the same page as the
preceding reference, Ibid. is used alone. If the
second reference is to a different page, the page
number must also be given.

   Examples: [10]Ibid. [11]Ibid., 42.

  (4) The word "ibid." should not be underlined.

 b. Shortened references. A shortened reference is used to
refer to a source which has already been cited in complete form, but not in the immediately preceding footnote.

  (1) A shortened reference to a book includes only the
author's last name (unless more than one author by
the same last name has been cited), the title of the
book (in shortened form, if desired), the page
number of the reference, and the volume number (if
necessary).

Comp.
57.15

(2) A shortened reference to an article in a periodical or to any component part of a work (chapter, essay, and so on) includes only the author's last name (unless more than one author by the same last name has been cited), the title of the article or other component part of a work (in shortened form, if desired), and the page number of the reference.

(3) Follow these suggestions for shortening titles.

• Omit any subtitles, and use only the key words of the main title.

• Omit an initial "A," "An," or "The."

• Do not change the order of the words in the original title.

• Generally a title of two to five words does not need to be shortened, unless the words in the title are especially long.

• For examples of shortened titles, see Turabian's *Manual,* sections 6.150–153.

(4) The following succession of footnotes illustrates the use of full and shortened references.

[1]Joseph Machlis, <u>The Enjoyment of Music: An Introduction to Perceptive Listening</u>, 3d ed. (New York: W. W. Norton & Co., 1970), 65.

[2]David S. Shields, "Happiness in Society: The Development of an Eighteenth-Century American Poetic Ideal," <u>American Literature</u> 55 (December 1983): 545.

[3]George Gilder, "What Ronald Reagan Doesn't Know about His Own Achievements," <u>National Review</u>, 29 June 1984, p. 23.

Comp. 57.15

⁴Albert C. Baugh, ed., <u>A Literary History of England</u>, 2d ed., vol. 4: <u>The Nineteenth Century and After (1789–1939)</u>, by Samuel C. Chew and Richard D. Altick (Englewood Cliffs, N.J.: Prentice-Hall, 1967), p. 1350.

⁵Machlis, <u>Enjoyment of Music</u>, 70.

⁶Shields, "Happiness in Society," 558.

⁷Ibid., p. 543.

[The same work as the preceding note.]

⁸Gilder, "What Ronald Reagan Doesn't Know," 24.

⁹Shields, "Happiness in Society," 545.

¹⁰Chew and Altick, <u>Nineteenth Century</u>, 1348.

¹¹Ibid., 1341.

[The same work as the preceding note.]

¹²Ibid.

[The same page as the preceding note.]

57.16 Standard abbreviations for use in footnotes.

a. Abbreviations of states.

Ala.	Hawaii	Mass.	N. Mex.	S. Dak.
Alaska	Idaho	Mich.	N.Y.	Tenn.
Ariz.	Ill.	Minn.	N.C.	Tex.
Ark.	Ind.	Miss.	N.Dak.	Utah
Calif.	Iowa	Mo.	Ohio	Vt.
Colo.	Kans.	Mont.	Okla.	Va.
Conn.	Ky.	Nebr.	Oreg.	Wash.
Del.	La.	Nev.	Pa.	W. Va.
Fla.	Maine	N.H.	R.I.	Wis.
Ga.	Md.	N.J.	S.C.	Wyo.

Comp.
57.16

b. Abbreviations of books of the Bible.

Old Testament

Gen.	1 Kings	Eccles.	Obad.
Exod.	2 Kings	Song of Sol.	Jon.
Lev.	1 Chron.	Isa.	Mic.
Num.	2 Chron.	Jer.	Nah.
Deut.	Ezra	Lam.	Hab.
Josh.	Neh.	Ezek.	Zeph.
Judg.	Esther	Dan.	Hag.
Ruth	Job	Hos.	Zech.
1 Sam.	Ps. (*pl.* Pss.)	Joel	Mal.
2 Sam.	Prov.	Amos	

New Testament

Matt.	2 Cor.	1 Tim.	2 Pet.
Mark	Gal.	2 Tim.	1 John
Luke	Eph.	Titus	2 John
John	Phil.	Philem.	3 John
Acts	Col.	Heb.	Jude
Rom.	1 Thess.	James	Rev.
1 Cor.	2 Thess.	1 Pet.	

c. Example abbreviations for new editions.

Second Edition	2d ed.
Third Edition	3d ed.
Fourth Edition	4th ed.
New Edition	new ed.
New Revised Edition	new rev. ed.
Revised Second Edition	rev. 2d ed.
Second Edition, Revised	2d ed., rev.
Third Edition, Revised and Enlarged	3d ed., rev. and enl.
Revised Edition in One Volume	rev. ed. in 1 vol.
Fourth Edition, Revised by John Doe	4th ed., rev. John Doe

Comp.
57.16

57.17 **Prepare the title page according to the following example.** See page 272 for further details.

SAMPLE TITLE PAGE

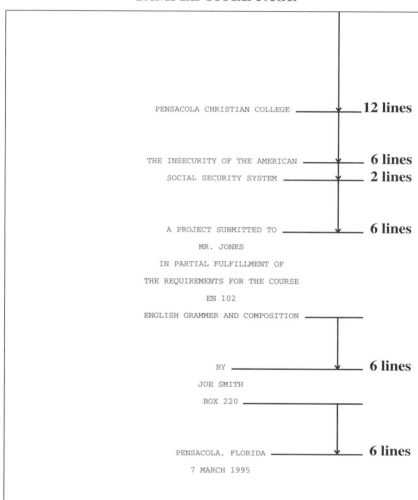

PENSACOLA CHRISTIAN COLLEGE — **12 lines**

THE INSECURITY OF THE AMERICAN — **6 lines**
SOCIAL SECURITY SYSTEM — **2 lines**

A PROJECT SUBMITTED TO — **6 lines**
MR. JONES
IN PARTIAL FULFILLMENT OF
THE REQUIREMENTS FOR THE COURSE
EN 102
ENGLISH GRAMMER AND COMPOSITION —

BY — **6 lines**
JOE SMITH
BOX 220 —

PENSACOLA, FLORIDA — **6 lines**
7 MARCH 1995

Comp.
57.17

57.18 Prepare an endnotes page according to the following example. See pages 279–280 for details.

SAMPLE ENDNOTES PAGE

NOTES

1. T. S. Eliot, <u>Essays on Elizabethan Drama</u>, quoted by Frank Kermode in <u>Voices and Visions: The Poet in America</u>, ed. Helen Vendler (New York: Random House, 1987), 297.

2. Kristian Smidt, <u>Poetry and Belief in the Work of T. S. Eliot</u> (Oslo, Norway: Kommisjon Hos Jacob Dybwad, 1949), 3.

3. Audrey F. Cahill, <u>T. S. Eliot and the Human Predicament</u> (Mystic, Conn.: Lawrence Verry, 1967), 65.

4. Smidt, 222.

5. Cahill, 66.

6. George Williamson, <u>A Reader's Guide to T. S. Eliot</u> (New York: Noonday Press, 1953), 163.

7. Ibid.

8. Elizabeth Drew, <u>T. S. Eliot: The Design of His Poetry</u> (New York: Charles Scribner's Sons, 1949), 119.

9. Ibid.

10. Balachandra Rajan, <u>The Overwhelming Question: A Study of the Poetry of T. S. Eliot</u> (Toronto: University of Toronto Press, 1976), 48.

11. Nancy Duvall Hargrove, <u>Landscape as Symbol in the Poetry of T. S. Eliot</u> (Jackson, Miss.: University Press of Mississippi, 1978), 106.

12. Grover Smith, <u>T. S. Eliot's Poetry and Plays: A Study in Sources and Meaning</u> (Chicago: University of Chicago Press, 1950), 122.

13. Nina Baym, ed., <u>The Norton Anthology of American Literature</u>, 3d ed. (New York: W. W. Norton and Co., 1989), 1821.

14. Ibid., 123.

11

Comp.
57.18

57.19 **Prepare the bibliography page according to the following example.** See pages 280–281 for details.

SAMPLE WORKS CITED PAGE

WORKS CITED

Baym, Nina, ed. <u>The Norton Anthology of American Literature</u>,
3d ed. New York: W. W. Norton and Co., 1989.

Cahill, Audrey F. <u>T. S. Eliot and The Human Predicament</u>. Mystic,
Conn.: Lawrence Verry, 1967.

Drew, Elizabeth. <u>T. S. Eliot: The Design of His Poetry</u>. New York:
Charles Scribner's Sons, 1949.

Hargrove, Nancy Duvall. <u>Landscape as Symbol in the Poetry of
T. S. Eliot</u>. Jackson, Miss.: University Press of Mississippi,
1978.

Rajan, Balachandra. <u>The Overwhelming Question: A Study of the Poetry
of T. S. Eliot</u>. Toronto: University of Toronto Press, 1976.

Smidt, Kristian. <u>Poetry and Belief in the Work of T. S. Eliot</u>.
Olso, Norway: Kommisjon Hos Jacob Dybwad, 1949.

Smith, Grover. <u>T. S. Eliot's Poetry and Plays: A Study in Sources
and Meaning</u>. Chicago: University of Chicago Press, 1950.

Vendler, Helen, ed. <u>Voices and Visions: The Poet in America</u>. New
York: Random House, 1987.

Williamson, George. <u>A Reader's Guide to T. S. Eliot</u>. New York:
Noonday Press, 1953.

12

Comp.
57.19

308

57.20 Selected list of reference works.

a. Bibliographies of bibliographies

> Besterman, Theodore. *A World Bibliography of Bibliographies.* 4th ed., rev. and enl. 5 vols. Lausanne: Societas Bibliographica, 1965–66.
>
> *Bibliographic Index, The: A Cumulative Bibliography of Bibliographies.* New York: H. W. Wilson Co., 1938– .
>
> Sheehy, Eugene P., comp. *Guide to Reference Books.* 10th ed. Chicago: American Library Association, 1986.

b. Subject indexes to books

> *American Book Publishing Record.* New York: R. R. Bowker Co., 1960– .
>
> *Book Review Digest.* New York: H. W. Wilson Co., 1905– .
>
> British Museum, Department of Printed Books. *Subject Index of the Modern Works Added to the Library, [in the Years] 1881–1900.* Edited by G. K. Fortescue. 3 vols. London: British Museum, 1902–3.
>
> *British National Bibliography.* London: Council of the B.N.B., British Museum, 1950– .
>
> *Cumulative Book Index: A World List of Books in the English Language* 1928/32– . New York: H. W. Wilson Co., 1933.
>
> *Essay and General Literature Index: Works Indexed 1900–1969.* New York: H. W. Wilson Co., 1972.

c. Subject indexes to periodicals

> *American Journal of Nursing Index.* New York: American Journal of Nursing Co.
>
> Association of Christian Librarians. *Christian Periodical Index.* Houghton, N. Y.: Houghton College Press, 1956– .
>
> *Computer Literature Index.* Phoenix: Applied Computer Research, 1980– .
>
> *Congressional Quarterly Index.* Washington, D.C.: 1940?– .
>
> *Cumulative Index to Nursing Literature.* Glendale, Calif.: Glendale Adventist Hospital, 1956– .

Comp.
57.20

Education Index. New York: H. W. Wilson Co., 1929– .

Education USA Index. Arlington, Va.: National School Public Relations Association, 1977?– .

General Science Index. New York: H. W. Wilson Co., 1978– .

National Geographic Index. Washington, D.C.: National Geographic Society, 1947– .

New York Times Index. New York: New York Times, 1913– .

Reader's Guide to Periodical Literature. New York: H. W. Wilson Co., 1900– .

Social Sciences and Humanities Index. New York: H. W. Wilson Co., 1907– .

d. Biographical aids

Biography Index. A Cumulative Index to Biographical Material in Books and Magazines. New York: H. W. Wilson Co., 1947– .

Current Biography. New York: H. W. Wilson Co., 1940– .

Dictionary of American Biography. 20 vols. with supplements. New York: Charles Scribner's Sons.

Dictionary of National Biography. Edited by Leslie Stephen and Sidney Lee. 22 vols. with 10 supplements. London: Oxford University Press.

Hyamson, Albert M. *A Dictionary of Universal Biography of All Ages and of All Peoples.* 2d ed., entirely rewritten. New York: E. P. Dutton, 1951.

Webster's New Biographical Dictionary. Springfield, Mass.: Merriam-Webster, 1988.

Who's Who: An Annual Biographical Dictionary. London: A. & C. Black, 1849– .

e. Literature

Abrams, M. H. *A Glossary of Literary Terms.* 6th ed. New York: Holt, Rinehart and Winston, 1993.

Bateson, F. W. and Harrison T. Mescrole. *A Guide to English and American Literature,* 3d ed. New York: Gordian, 1977.

Baugh, Albert C., ed. *A Literary History of England.* 2d ed. 4 vols. Englewood Cliffs, N.J.: Prentice-Hall, 1967.

Benét's Reader's Encyclopedia. 3d ed. New York: Harper & Row, 1987.

Dictionary of Literary Biography. 148 vols. Detroit: Gale Research, 1978– .

Harner, James L. *Literary Research Guide.* New York: Modern Language Association of America, 1989.

Harvey, Sir Paul. *The Oxford Companion to English Literature.* 5th ed. Ed. by Margaret Drabble. Oxford: Clarendon Press, 1985.

Holman, C. Hugh and William Harmon. *A Handbook to Literature.* 6th ed. New York: Macmillan, 1991.

Perkins, George; Barbara Perkins; and Philip Leninger, eds. *Benét's Reader's Encyclopedia of American Literature.* New York: Harper-Collins, 1991.

Reader's Companion to World Literature. Edited by Lillian H. Hornstein, Leon Edel, and Horst Frenz. New York: New American Library, 1973.

f. The fine arts

Apel, Willi. *Harvard Dictionary of Music.* 2d ed., rev. and enl. Cambridge: Harvard University Press, Belknap Press, 1969.

Baker, Theodore. *Biographical Dictionary of Musicians.* 5th ed. Revised by Nicolas Slonimsky. New York: Schirmer Books, 1965.

Chamberlin, Mary W. *Guide to Art Reference Books.* Chicago: American Library Association, 1959.

Encyclopedia of World Art. 17 vols. Palatine, Ill.: J. Heraty and Associates, 1959–87.

Gardner, Helen. *Art through the Ages.* 7th ed. Revised by Horst de la Croix and Richard G. Tansey. New York: Harcourt Brace Jovanovich, 1980.

Comp. 57.20

Osborne, Harold, ed. *The Oxford Companion to Art.* Oxford: Clarendon Press, 1970.

Sadie, Stanley, ed. *The New Grove's Dictionary of Music and Musicians.* 20 vols. London: Macmillan, 1980.

g. Religion

Hastings, James, ed. *Encyclopaedia of Religion and Ethics.* 12 vols. and Index. New York: Charles Scribner's Sons, 1908–27.

Schaff, Philip. *The New Schaff-Herzog Encyclopedia of Religious Knowledge.* Edited by Samuel M. Jackson et al. 12 vols. and Index. New York and London: Funk & Wagnalls Co., 1908–12.

Strong, James. *Exhaustive Concordance of the Bible.* New York: Hunt, 1894.

h. History

Adams, James Truslow, ed. *Concise Dictionary of American History.* New York: Charles Scribner's Sons, 1962.

American Historical Association. *Guide to Historical Literature.* Edited by George F. Howe et al. New York: Macmillan Co., 1961.

Langer, William L., ed. *An Encyclopedia of World History: Ancient, Medieval, and Modern, Chronologically Arranged.* 5th ed., rev. and enl. with Maps and Genealogical Tables. Boston: Houghton Mifflin Co., 1973.

Morison, Samuel Eliot. *The Oxford History of the American People.* New York: Oxford University Press, 1965.

i. Biological and physical sciences

Besançon, Robert M., ed. *The Encyclopedia of Physics.* 3d ed. New York: Chapman and Hall, 1990.

Clark, Randolph L., and Russell W. Cumley, eds. *The Book of Health: A Medical Encyclopedia for Everyone.* 3d ed. New York: Harcourt Brace Jovanovich, 1977.

Considine, Douglas M., ed. *Van Nostrand's Scientific Encyclopedia.* 7th ed. Princeton, N.J.: Van Nostrand Reinhold Co., 1989.

Gray, Peter, ed. *The Encyclopedia of the Biological Sciences.* 2d ed. New York: Van Nostrand Reinhold Co., 1970.

Lange, Norbert Adolph. *Lange's Handbook of Chemistry.* 14th ed. Edited by John A. Dean. New York: McGraw-Hill Book Co., 1992.

Parker, Sybil P., ed. *McGraw-Hill Encyclopedia of Science and Technology, The: An International Reference Work.* 7th ed. 20 vols. New York: McGraw-Hill Book Co., 1992.

Peterson Field Guide Series, The. Edited by Roger Tory Peterson. Boston: Houghton Mifflin Co., 1947– .

j. Other

Arlott, John, ed. *The Oxford Companion to World Sports & Games.* London: Oxford University Press, 1975.

Brock, Clifton. *The Literature of Political Science: A Guide for Students, Librarians, and Teachers.* New York: R. R. Bowker Co., 1969.

Hoselitz, Berthold F., ed. *A Reader's Guide to the Social Sciences.* Rev. ed. New York: Free Press, 1970.

Monroe, Paul et al. *A Cyclopedia of Education.* 5 vols. New York: Macmillan Co., 1911–13. Reprinted, Detroit: Omnigraphics, 1968.

Theodorson, George A. and Theodorson, Achilles G. *A Modern Dictionary of Sociology.* New York: Thomas Y. Crowell, 1969.

57.21 Conservative publishers and publications.

a. Book publishers with a conservative viewpoint

Crossway Books
Devin-Adair Publishers
The Human Life Press
Regnery Gateway
Ross House Books
Thomas Nelson

Comp
57.21

b. Periodicals written from a conservative viewpoint

Christian News
Conservative Chronicle
The Freeman

Human Events
Human Life Review
The Intercollegiate Review
Modern Age
National Review
New American
The Phyllis Schlafly Report
Policy Review
Reader's Digest
University Bookman
Wall Street Journal
World

58   Written Book Report

Written reports should include these four parts: the *introduction*, the *body*, the *conclusion*, and the *evaluation*. (The total length of your report should be 1½ to 2 handwritten pages.)

58.1   The Introduction

a. The first sentence should include the title of the book, the author's name, and the main idea of the entire book.

> <u>I Was a Slave in Russia</u> by John Noble is the personal account of an American who survived 9½ years of cruelty in the slave-labor camps in Russia.

b. Get your readers interested in what you are going to say—perhaps with a striking statement or quotation.

c. If the book has a setting (time and place of the action) you may include it.

d. One sentence (called the thesis sentence) should indicate the organization of your report. In the following example, three topics and their order of appearance are suggested.

> Mr. Noble tells of his surprising imprisonment, his long years of torture, and his eventual release.

58.2   The Body

a. For a biography, relate the chief incidents and tell their importance.

Comp.
58.1

b. **For a nonfiction book, tell the importance of the subject treated in the book and write a summary of several parts of the book.**

c. **For a fiction book, write a summary of the plot.** The plot is the sequence of actions which make up a story. The plot begins with a conflict involving the main characters. Sometimes the conflict involves two people. Other times the conflict involves the main character and a variety of people and circumstances. In some stories, conflict may be at work within the main character. In the story *Robinson Crusoe,* for example, the main character is in conflict with his hostile environment.

After you have stated the conflict, recount some key events that develop the conflict to the point at which one of the opposing forces is about to prevail over the other. This is called the climax.

d. **The body normally has the same number of paragraphs as are indicated by the thesis sentence in the introduction.**

58.3 **The Conclusion**

a. **For a biography,** the conclusion may be a statement concerning the main significance of the person's life.

b. **For a nonfiction book,** the conclusion may be a summation of the main points in the body.

c. **For a fiction book,** the conclusion follows the climax of the story and tells the events that resolve the conflict.

58.4 **The Evaluation**

a. **Give your thoughts about the book, whether they be favorable or unfavorable.** Were you satisfied and happy with the outcome or were you disappointed? If the work was written to meet a specific need, did the author succeed in meeting that need? Tell how the book influenced your thinking and your goals in life. Use examples from the book to support your statements.

Comp. 58.4

b. **The evaluation is as important as the body of your report.**

c. **The evaluation should be a good well-developed paragraph.**

► Note. As an introduction to critical analysis, it would be well to do some critical book reviews during the year instead of the usual book report as described here (see section 60).

Study the following example.

In his autobiography *They Call Me Coach,* John Wooden, former coach at UCLA and the greatest coach in the history of college basketball, reveals that the secret of his success is a sound philosophy based on consistent principles. Wooden shows how his philosophy—which works just as well in coaching as in everyday living—helped him be a success as a student, as a young coach in Ohio and Indiana, and as the coach of the world-famous UCLA Bruins.

Two men influenced John Wooden during his student days and helped him to develop his philosophy. The first of these men, Joshua Wooden, taught his son John to read the Bible every day, to value education and culture, to respect hard work and discipline, and to practice self-control, honesty, and integrity. These characteristics helped him be a success in high school both as a student and as an athlete. Later, at Purdue University, John was influenced by the wise coaching of Ward "Piggie" Lambert, who worked hard and expected his players to work hard as well. For four years John Wooden worked diligently to make good grades and to play good basketball. Because of his hard work, John did both. Piggie Lambert's expert coaching helped John develop his skills; as a result, John was named an all-American basketball player three times. Wooden seemed destined to spend most of his life on a basketball court.

The next time Wooden hit the court, however, he was a coach, not a player. After graduating from Purdue, John Wooden worked eleven years as a high school coach and as an English teacher in Ohio and Indiana. A versatile man, Wooden was called upon to coach basketball, baseball, and tennis. He even had to keep track of the money made from selling tickets and refreshments! Wooden never complained, but faced each new assignment with confidence and a strong desire to excel. After serving in the Navy during World War II, Wooden went

Comp.
58.4

to Purdue, returning after fifteen years to coach the team for which he had played so well. Wooden's success at Purdue established a reputation that spread across the United States; soon, offers to coach other teams began to come in. After carefully considering several offers, Wooden decided to go to California to coach the UCLA Bruins. College basketball would never be the same again.

At UCLA, Coach Wooden did not compromise his principles or abandon his philosophy. By emphasizing fundamentals, conditioning, team play, and discipline, Wooden turned a mediocre UCLA team with a losing record into a powerful UCLA team with a winning record (they won twenty-two out of twenty-nine games the year Wooden came to UCLA). From that victorious first season to the date of this book (1972), Wooden's teams had won eight NCAA championships (six of them in a row). Even when extraordinary players played for UCLA, Coach Wooden maintained that it was the team effort of the Bruins that led them to so many victories. Wooden's emphasis on team effort and strict discipline has paid good dividends: during Wooden's incredible career at UCLA, his teams won four out of every five games they played. It is very unlikely that such a record will ever be equaled.

They Call Me Coach is an invaluable book because it shows that lasting success must be based upon correct philosophy and that one must have definite principles by which to guide his actions. The heart of correct philosophy is revealed in this quotation from John Wooden: "It should be recognized that basketball is not the ultimate. It is of small importance in comparison to the total life we live. There is only one kind of life that truly wins, and that is the one that places faith in the hands of the Savior. Until that is done, we are on an aimless course that runs in circles and goes nowhere. Material possessions, winning scores, and great reputations are meaningless in the eyes of the Lord, because He knows what we really are and that is all that matters." Is it not interesting that even in the sports world, where everyone is doing everthing possible to attain success, that the one who bases his philosophy on Scriptural principles is the one who is eminently successful?

Comp.
58.4

59 Oral Book Report

59.1 **Two parts of an oral report.**

   a. Written Preparation This preparation should be made as explained in section 58 with one major difference: the *body* should be done in *topical outline* form. (This counts 50 points toward your grade.)

   (1) *Introduction* (10 points)
   - Write this word for word as you will say it in your report.
   - Attempt to capture the attention of your audience with a striking statement.

   (2) *Body* (25 points)
   - Write this in topical outline form (see section 46).
   - Have three main headings (I, II, III).

   (3) *Conclusion* (5 Points)
   - Write this word for word as you will say it in your report.

   (4) *Evaluation* (10 points)
   - Write this word for word as you will say it in your report.

   ▶ Note. The total length of the report will be 1½ to 2 pages.

   b. Oral Presentation (This counts 50 points toward your grade.)

   (1) The time limit is 2 to 3 minutes with a margin of 15 seconds. If your report is overtime or undertime, you will lose 5 points.

   (2) If you are not prepared on the day assigned, you will lose 10 points.

   (3) You will receive points for the following:
   - Posture (10 points)
   - Eye contact (10 points)
   - Enthusiasm, smoothness, and expression (10 points)

Comp.
59.1

- Preparation for oral delivery (10 points)
- Poise—going to and from the front of the room (5 points)
- Gestures and mannerisms—not distracting (5 points)

59.2 **Procedure for preparing an oral report**

a. **Prepare your outline. (See section 46.)**

b. **Write your introduction.**

c. **Write your conclusion.**

d. **Write your evaluation.**

e. **Revise your entire paper.**

f. **Write your final draft.**

g. **Make reminder cards (one card for each main point in your outline).**

h. **Memorize the introduction, conclusion, and evaluation.**

i. **Practice your report aloud several times. Keep practicing until you can give it smoothly within the time limit.**

Study the following example of written preparation for an oral report.

George Müller and His Orphans by Nancy Garton tells of a man whose life was a series of miracles. Because he built his life on a foundation of faith, George Müller was unusually blessed by the Lord. Mr. Müller's simple, childlike faith made him a mighty servant of the Lord and a great blessing to others. In revealing the secret of Müller's success, the book shows George Müller as a young man establishing his faith, as a mature Christian servant using his faith in his everyday life, and as an esteemed Christian leader sharing his faith with others.

    I. Establishing his faith
       A. Salvation
       B. Bible study
       C. Early Ministry

Comp. 59.2

II. Using his faith
    A. To get him through difficult times
        1. Death of his first wife
        2. Failure of health
    B. To build his orphans' homes
    C. To keep his homes open
III. Sharing his faith
    A. With his orphans
    B. On his world tours

George Müller died in 1898, but the work of his homes and the influence of his ministry continue to this day. His selflessness, his willingness to serve God, his perseverance, and his patience made him a unique individual; yet he was quick to point out that anyone who has faith in God will be as richly rewarded as he was.

In this book, Nancy Garton vividly depicts George Müller's exciting life of faith. Putting his faith to work, Mr. Müller would often stand over an empty table in an empty dining room and give thanks for the food that the Lord was going to provide. Then, after Müller had said *Amen,* someone would knock on the door—a baker who had baked too much bread, or a dairyman wondering what to do with some extra milk, or someone else the Lord had sent to feed Müller and his orphans. Müller never doubted for one instant that God would hear and answer his prayers . . . and God always did. Müller's victorious life is an encouragement to me, for it shows that God honors the faith of His people. As Müller himself said, "Surely, if such a one as I am . . . has his prayers answered, may not you also, at last, have your requests granted to you."

60   Critical Book Review

In the critical book review you tell whether you liked or disliked a book. More important, you explain *why* you liked or disliked it.

Here is how you might go about writing a critical book review:

Comp. 60.1

60.1   **Read the book carefully.** You cannot evaluate a book that you have merely skimmed. Read it and think about it. Get a good understanding of the author's purpose and of the plot.

60.2 **Evaluate the work.** Ask yourself these questions:

a. Purpose. What is the author's purpose? Did he fulfill that purpose?

b. Planning. Does the work show planning? Is the plot clear and well organized? Does the author include only what is necessary, or does he clutter the book with needless events and details?

c. Beauty. Does the language have depth, or does the author use trite expressions and clichés? Does the book have good descriptions or comparisons? Is symbolism used? Does the author use restraint and avoid an over-blown or gushy style? Does the author's style (the way he says things) fit the mood of the story?

d. Vitality. Is the book boring and lifeless, or is it vivid and alive? Is the language colorful and exciting? Do the characters come to life? Does the author make the characters seem real, or do they remain flat and color-less?

e. Accuracy. Is what the author says accurate and truth-ful? Does he accurately portray events? Are characters presented truthfully? Is the author consistent?

60.3 **Write the review.** The critical book review has four parts:

a. Introduction. This paragraph includes general infor-mation, such as the author and title of the book as well as what type of book it is (fiction, biography, informa-tion, etc.). Your introduction should also include your thesis statement, which reveals your attitude toward the book and gives the main ideas to be developed in the review. The thesis statement gives your evaluation of the book (favorable or unfavorable) and your reasons for giving such an evaluation. Compare these thesis state-ments:

Poor: "I didn't like this book. Something about it bothers me." (Vague; no reasons given.)

Better: "Despite an exciting plot, this book is not quite satisfying because it gives an inaccurate picture of life in the South before the Civil War." (Specific reason given.)

Comp.
60.3

321

Poor: "I think this is a good book. I really enjoyed it." (Vague. Why is it a good book? Why did you enjoy it?)

Better: "Every page in this book shows Mark Twain's mastery as a writer, but the things which make the book especially enjoyable are the lively dialogue, the vivid description, and the convincing characterization." (Specific reasons given why you liked the book.)

b. **Summary.** Give a *brief* summary of the work. Don't bore the reader by retelling every event in the story.

c. **Proof of thesis.** In the third paragraph, you must show that your evaluation is fair and accurate. Use the questions mentioned under point 2 as a basis for your evaluation. Prove your thesis by using examples from the work itself. If you accuse the work of being inaccurate, give an example of the author's inaccuracy. If you like the author's planning, show how the plot demonstrates his organization. If you praise the work's vitality, quote an especially vivid passage. Above all, be *specific.* Give *specific* details.

d. **Conclusion.** The concluding paragraph is a general restatement of the thesis. You may also predict whether or not the work will continue to be popular in the years to come.

Hemingway at His Best

In *The Old Man and the Sea,* Ernest Hemingway has returned to the stripped, lean, objective narrative so characteristic of him at his best. In his short novel of an aging but still resourceful Havana fisherman there is not a waste word, not a single intrusion of the author or of a bystander who might be Hemingway. The old man, sage, tempered, and set apart by his age, has been cursed with eighty-four days of bad luck. Not a fish in that time; so the young boy who was his helper has been ordered by his parents to another and a luckier boat, and the old man must go out alone to farther, deeper waters where the bigger marlin lie. The boy Manolin still helps him when the boats are ashore—helps him get his supper, picks up the fresh baits, and helps him carry the gear, the rolls of line in the basket, the harpoon and gaff, the mast with the furled sail, down to the waterside. So it is that the old man rows out in his skiff in the dark before dawn for the most taxing fight in his long life, a struggle with a giant marlin which is to break his luck for good.

Mr. Hemingway has stripped the story to the essentials of the old Cuban. Having no family, he has few wants; lust and liquor are behind him; in his little shack ashore he has but one meal a day and lives in that borderland between reverie and sleep. But on the sea it is different; he lives for fishing and he loves *la mar*— "the old man always thought of her as feminine and as something that gave or withheld great favors, and if she did wild or wicked things it was because she could not help them." To his fishing he brings the instinct and knowledge of a lifetime, great courage and cunning to make up for the youth he has lost.

The old man's response to the sea, the sureness with which he pierces its depth with line or sight, the incredible resourcefulness with which he hangs on to the giant marlin through days and nights, and the rage with which he tries to defend his prize from the sharks—these are the successive stages in a story which is beautiful in its description, and of clean thrusting power in its pursuit. Here is none of the braggadocio which made that other fisherman, Harry Morgan, something less than believable. The old man and the boy are perfectly tuned to Hemingway's purpose: their affection and utterance are true to themselves as their philosophy is true to the sea. I have put this book on the top shelf of Mr. Hemingway's work, and I am grateful for it.

Comp.
60.3

61 Letters

Friendly Letters

61.1 **Learn the five parts of a friendly letter.**

940 Guildford Drive
Halstead, Kansas 67056
May 9, 1995

a. Heading

Dear Cathy,

b. Salutation

_____

_____

_____

_____

c. Body

_____

Your friend,
Alice

d. Closing
e. Signature

a. The *heading* gives the complete address of the writer and the date of writing.

b. The *salutation* is followed by a comma.

c. The *body* is what you have to say. Indent each paragraph.

d. The *closing* is followed by a comma. Use such closings as *Sincerely yours, Your friend, With love.*

e. The *signature* is the name of the writer.

61.2 **Remember these guidelines when writing a friendly letter:**

a. Show good taste. Avoid extremes in stationery and ink color.

b. Be neat. Avoid blots and cross-outs. Maintain at least half an inch margins at the top, bottom, and sides of the letter.

c. Make the content of the letter interesting as well as informative.

Comp.
61.1

(1) Do not begin by saying "How are you? I hope you are all right. I am fine."

(2) Do not make a lengthy apology for not having written sooner.

(3) Be sure to answer any question that the other person asked, and comment on his letter.

(4) Do not overuse the pronoun I.

(5) Suit the letter to the receiver's age and interests.

(6) Include specific details, colorful description, narration, or dialogue whenever possible.

(7) Do not close by saying "Well, I can't think of anything else to say, so I guess I'll close for now."

61.3 **Social notes.** Friendly letters that contain a specific message to meet a specific social situation are called *social notes.* Courtesy requires that you write these notes to express your appreciation for a gift, favor, or hospitality.

a. Two kinds of social notes are the *thank-you note* and *bread-and-butter note*.

(1) The *thank-you note* should be written to thank someone for a gift or favor.

(2) The *bread-and-butter note* should be written to thank the hostess in the home where you have visited.

b. Observe the following courtesies when writing social notes.

(1) Write promptly.

(2) Be brief but sincere.

(3) In a thank-you note give specific reasons for your gratitude.

(4) In a bread-and-butter note mention some of the things that were done for you.

Comp. 61.3

(5) Write about something else as well.

Business Letters

61.4   **Learn the six parts of a business letter.**

2502 Cerney Place	
Hammond, Montana 59332	**a. Heading**
May 22, 1995	
The Honorable Robert A. Skinner	**b. Inside**
Secretary of Transportation	**Address**
Washington, D.C. 20590	
Dear Mr. Secretary:	**c. Salutation**
_____	
_____	**d. Body**
_____	
Very truly yours,	**e. Closing**
John Valier	
John Valier	**f. Signature**

a. The *heading* is the same as the heading of a friendly letter.

b. The *inside address* is the address of the person or company to whom you are writing. This is identical to the address used on the envelope.

c. The *salutation* is the greeting. It is followed by a colon.

    (1) Salutation for a person whose name is used in the inside address:

        Dear Mr. McDowell: Dear Miss Horne:
        Dear Mrs. Bates:

    (2) Salutation for a person whose name you do not know, but whose title you do know:

        Dear Sir: Dear Madam:

    (3) Salutation for a group or firm:

        Gentlemen:

d. The *body* is what you have to say.

Comp.
61.4

  e. The *closing* is followed by a comma. The following closings are standard for formal business letters.

   Truly yours,   Yours truly,
   Very truly yours,

  f. The *signature* is the full name of the writer. If you are typing the letter, you should type your name underneath your signature.

61.5 **Observe these rules when writing a business letter:**

  a. Use white, unlined, 8¹/₂-by-11-inch paper.

  b. It is best to type business letters. However, you may write them by hand if necessary, using either blue or black ink.

  c. Be neat. Avoid blots, erasures, and cross-outs. Maintain at least half an inch margins at the top, bottom, and sides of the letter.

  d. Write on only one side of the page.

  e. Be brief and to the point.

  f. Avoid using such expressions as *Permit me to state,* *Please find enclosed,* **and** *Thanking you in advance.*

61.6 **Some special types of business letters:**

  a. The *order letter* should include the following information: the description of the item, the quantity, the size, the color, the price, the catalog number, and the place you saw it advertised. Also tell how you are paying: cash, check, credit card, money order, or C.O.D.

  b. The *request letter* should be clear, specific, and courteous. Avoid vague and general statements. Give only the specific information necessary to fulfill your request, but be careful not to omit anything that is necessary. Routine requests for catalogs and prices may be limited to a one-sentence letter.

  c. The *complaint letter* should be neither angry nor sarcastic. Be courteous. Describe briefly but fully what the problem is. Include exact details. State clearly what action you think should be taken on the problem.

Comp.
61.6

  d. The *letter to a government official* should be written in a clear, friendly style. Since government officials are supposed to represent "we, the people," you as a good citizen should not hestitate to write letters expressing your opinion about bills, laws, government policy, or any other matter of current concern. Also, you can often get informative materials about government from your senator or congressman. Use the following chart for reference when writing letters of opinion or request to a state or federal official:

Forms of Address for Government Officials

Official	Envelope Address	Salutation*
Governor	The Honorable ___ ___ (full name) Governor of ___ (state) ___, ___ (capital city, state, and ZIP code)	Dear Governor ___:
Congressman	The Honorable ___ ___ (full name) House of Representatives Washington, D.C. 20515	Dear Mr. ___:
Senator	The Honorable ___ (full name) United States Senate Washington, D.C. 20510	Dear Senator ___:
Cabinet Official	The Honorable ___ (full name) Secretary of ___ (department) Washington, D.C. ___ (ZIP code)	Dear Mr. Secretary:
Supreme Court Justice	Mr. Justice ___ (last name) The Supreme Court Washington, D.C. 20543	Dear Mr. Justice: or Dear Justice ___:
Chief Justice	The Chief Justice The Supreme Court Washington, D.C. 20543	Dear Mr. Chief Justice:
President	The President The White House Washington, D.C. 20500	Dear Mr. President:
Vice President	The Vice President The United States Senate Washington, D.C. 20510	Dear Mr. Vice President:

*Note. Sir: or Dear Sir: is suitable for use with all of these officials.

e. The *letter of application* (also often called a cover letter) should persuade a potential employer to choose you from among many applicants for a job. This letter normally accompanies a resumé. (See samples on pp. 331–332.) The letter of application demands more care and attention than most other letters because much more is at stake: the quality of your letter may very well determine whether or not you get the job you want. The letter should therefore put you in the best possible light; it should make you look qualified and confident, but not boastful or pretentious. Make sure you use quality paper in either gray, cream, or another neutral color for both your letter and resumé. It is wise to call the company before you send in your letter to see if the company wants you to include references.

(1) Include the following in a letter of application:

- *Introduction.* Tell what position you are applying for and where you heard about the position.

- *Educational background.* Tell when you intend to graduate and what kind of education you have had.

- *Qualifications.* Mention any training you have received or any jobs you have had which qualify you specifically for the position.

- *References.* List the names and addresses of at least two people willing to write about your character and abilities only if the company *desires* references.

- *Conclusion.* Request an interview so that you can talk with your potential employer personally. Tell where and when you can be reached.

Comp. 61.6

(2) Rewrite and edit your letter. (See 43.3–4.)

• *Neatness and correctness.* A letter containing smudges, numerous erasures, and typographical errors creates a bad impression. Such a letter will quickly find its way into the wastebasket.

• *Tone.* Be dignified, but not stilted; be interesting, but not familiar. Do not try to make the employer feel sorry for you; on the other hand, do not write as though you would be doing the employer a favor by working for him.

• *Pertinence.* The letter does not necessarily have to be brief, but it *must* be to the point. Employers are too busy to waste their time on an unorganized, rambling letter.

• *Effectiveness.* For every opening, there are many applicants; your letter must convince the employer that you are the best choice and that it would be to *his* advantage to hire you. Your letter should stand out from the others, not because of personal eccentricity, but because of the quality and conviction of your writing.

▶ Note. Update your cover letter and resumé periodically. Each time you advance in your position or receive exclusive job training, your resumé will need to change. Entire books devoted to resumé and cover letter writing can be found in your local library.

Comp.
61.6

SAMPLE LETTER OF APPLICATION

6522 Raintree Road
Joliet, Illinois 60435
May 12, 1995

Clarke Professional Services
6709 Sherwood Drive
Chicago, Illinois 60609

Gentlemen:

I am responding to your May 10 *Chicago Sun-Times* advertisement which mentioned your need of a business manager, a position for which I am well qualified.

From 1990 to 1994 I attended Northwestern University; I received a B.S. degree in business management and maintained a high B average in my classes. About a fifth of my classes were devoted to computer training.

My experience has been valuable and extensive. During the summers of my college years I was the assistant payroll manager of the Bevins Construction Company in Joliet. During the school year, I worked as a part time computer operator for Datatronics, Inc., a computer firm in Evanston. After graduating, I became an assistant loan manager at First Fidelity Savings and Loan in Joliet, with twelve people under my supervision. I have done well in this position, but I would now like to move on to a larger firm.

May I have an interview at your convenience? You can reach me at 815-876-4355 from 8:30 to 4:30 on weekdays. I am looking forward to hearing from you.

Sincerely,

Michael D. Palmers

Michael D. Palmers

Enclosure

Comp.
61.6

SAMPLE RESUMÉ

Michael D. Palmers

Residence
6522 Raintree Road
Joliet, Illinois 60435
(815) 876–4355

Office
First Fidelity Savings and Loan
2232 Sharp Avenue, Suite 19
Joliet, Illinois 60435
(815) 876–4027

Career Objective
To obtain a position as a business manager in a company that will use current experience, encourage further training, and offer advancement opportunities.

Education
Northwestern University, Evanston, IL
B.S. May 1994
   Major: Business Management
   Minor: Computer Science

Career-Related Courses
   Systems Design
   Corporate Finance
   International Business

   Financial Management
   Business Statistics
   Business Communications

Experience
May 1994–present

First Fidelity Savings and Loan, Joliet, IL
Assistant Loan Manager
   • Supervised 12 employees.
   • Approved loans.

*1990–1994 (during
school year only)*

Datatronics, Inc., Evanston, IL
Computer Operator
   • Compiled and analyzed customer feedback reports.
   • Automated month-end inventory reports.

*1990–1994
(summers)*

Bevins Construction Company, Joliet, IL
Assistant Payroll Manager
   • Worked with personnel and payroll policies, accounting procedures, salary and benefit distributions, and tax laws.
   • Prepared cost comparisons and projected departmental expenses for the Controller.
   • Maintained employee absence and vacation records.

Activities/Interests
   • Counselor at Evanston Juvenile Justice Center
   • All-conference baseball player
   • President of Phi Delta Sigma fraternity

Comp.
61.6

62 The Narrative Essay

The narrative essay is a story that relates events to make a point. To develop the narrative, the writer uses one or more of the following methods: *descriptive details* which allow the reader to *see* the action, *dialogue* which permits the reader to *hear* the conversation of the characters, and *exposition* which explains to the reader the *relationship of events* in the story.

The narrative essay differs from an expository or argumentative essay. Those essays state their points explicitly, but the narrative essay conveys a message implicitly through the details and events in the story.

Follow these steps when writing the narrative essay:

62.1   Begin by reflecting on past experiences.

a. Think of a personal experience that you remember vividly.

(1) The experience may be something you instantly regretted.

(2) The experience may be something that had a lasting effect on you.

(3) The experience may reveal a truth learned from a daily routine.

(4) The experience may promote a positive character trait such as determination, punctuality, or honesty.

(5) The experience may relate an event that caused you to change your attitude toward a particular person, place, thing, or idea.

b. Although personal experiences work best, the narrative does not have to come from a personal experience. It may be someone else's experience or an event that you witnessed.

62.2   Write a sentence that summarizes the point that your narrative will make. Before you can plan the incidents to be included in your story, you must know what message you hope to convey.

Comp.
62.3

62.3   Write out a list of incidents that you want to include. Ask yourself these questions: What happened? When did it happen? Where did it happen? Why did it happen? What were your impressions? How did the event make you feel?

62.4 **Arrange the events in chronological order.** You should always arrange the incidents in chronological order even though you may decide later to insert some foreshadowing or flashbacks.

62.5 **Think about the characters in the story and perhaps make a list of details that indicate what each character is like.** This list will help you to make their actions and conversation accurate and realistic.

62.6 **Write a rough draft, simply telling the story from beginning to end.**

a. **Use first person pronouns (*I, me, my, mine, we, us, our, ours*) if the story is about you.** Use the third person pronouns (*he, him, his, she, her, hers, they, them, their, theirs*) and the persons' names if you are telling a story from another's point of view.

b. **Begin in a way that will immediately catch your readers' attention and suggest the point of the story.** Try one or more of these:

(1) Use description to set the scene for the action.

(2) Use dialogue to spark interest in the characters.

(3) Begin in the middle of the story to promote suspense.

c. **Make sure that every detail contributes in some way to the message you wish to convey.**

d. **Avoid merely *telling* about the events and characters; you must *show* the details and actions.** Use concrete nouns and active verbs instead of relying on adjectives. Use images that appeal to the senses.

e. **Start a new paragraph at each change of topic or speaker.**

f. **Use transitional expressions to help your reader keep track of the times, places, and activities.** (See section 44.5 for a list.)

g. **Do not just end the story at the end of the action.** Write an effective ending which emphasizes the message that you want to convey—without saying, "The point is. . . ."

Comp.
62.4

334

62.7 **Rewrite and edit your story.** (See section 45.6.)

62.8 **Write an interesting title that gives a hint of the message in your story.**

62.9 **Write the final draft.** (See section 45.7.)

Eyewitness

I only half-listened as Mrs. Murphy, my eighth-grade history teacher, spoke the crew members' names . . . "Gregory B. Jarvis, Sharon Christa McAuliffe, Ronald E. McNair, Ellison S. Onizuka, Judith A. Resnik, Francis R. Scobee, and Michael J. Smith." Why was everyone so excited? After all, living near the Kennedy Space Center at Cape Canaveral, we had seen our share of space shuttle launches. These very names, however, would soon teach me to value even the "routine" experiences of life.

At first, I had enjoyed our little field trips to the school parking lot where we watched the launches. They provided an interesting diversion from what I considered a tedious class. But eventually even "launch days" had become routine.

Mrs. Murphy asked, "What makes this launch special—different from the other launches we have seen?" I daydreamed about what I would wear to the class party this weekend.

"Does it have anything to do with that one lady— what's her name?" asked Ryan.

"Yes, it does. Christa McAuliffe, a school teacher from New Hampshire, will be on board the space shuttle today. She is the first civilian to participate in a shuttle mission." Mrs. Murphy turned and started out the door. "Ryan, bring the radio so we can listen to this launch while we are outside. Class, let's go!"

As I trooped outside with my classmates, the chilly morning air covered my arms with goose bumps and the wind tousled my hair. I shivered and tried to keep my hair out of my eyes. Convinced this launch would be just like all the others, I complained all the way to the parking lot.

"Mrs. Murphy, why can't we just watch this launch on TV tonight?" I challenged.

Comp. 62.8

335

Mrs. Murphy gave me the usual history-teacher response, "Because we are experiencing history in the making. Thirty years from now you can tell your children about this."

Refusing to enjoy myself, I stood with arms folded, gazing in every direction but up while the rest of the class joined in with the radio announcer's final countdown: "Six . . . Five . . . Four . . . Three . . . Two . . . One. WE HAVE LIFTOFF!!"

Everyone around me cheered and scanned the sky to see who could spot the blazing tail of the *Challenger* first.

"There it is!" someone yelled.

"Where? I don't see it."

"Over there." Mark's finger followed the flame.

"Come on, Melissa. If you don't look now, you'll miss it!" Allison grabbed my arm and urged me to join in the excitement.

Just as I reluctantly focused my eyes on the streak of fire ascending in the cloudless sky, the unimaginable happened. Two trails of smoke shot from the top of the shuttle and wildly streaked off in opposite directions. The *Challenger* had exploded! The cheering and clapping stopped. *Space shuttles are not supposed to explode. They never do. Surely those seven names are okay. Their families are watching. That teacher's students are watching. We are watching.* We turned imploring eyes toward Mrs. Murphy.

"Class, I don't know what to say. . . . I don't see how anyone could have survived. . . . Let's go inside."

Confused and shaken, we obediently returned to the refuge of our classroom. Some of my classmates wept softly; others sat in a daze. A huge lump formed in my throat. *What were the names? Who were the seven crew members?* I could not remember them all, but I knew one thing for certain: I had something that seven people had just lost—the opportunity to make every precious moment of my life count.

—Melissa Carney

Comp.
62.8

A Backpacker's Discovery

Our old church van, jokingly referred to as the "green machine," slowly bumped to a halt, and we tumbled out—a group of junior high "goofs" as our pastor lovingly referred to us. Like explorers embarking on an expedition, we were eager to begin this long-awaited backpacking trip to the Pictured Rocks of Michigan's Upper Peninsula. The five-hour drive up the interstate had only heightened our excitement. I had planned on a fun-filled week with my friends—it never occurred to me that backpacking could be a spiritual experience. I had no idea how God was going to use this week to reveal Himself to me.

For ten chaotic minutes we chattered, giggled, and checked our packs while our pastor tried to shout directions above the din. Exasperated, he finally started down the winding trail without us and we quickly hoisted our gear to follow him. Soon we were enveloped in a tunnel of dense foliage and arched treetops. We hiked merrily along thinking this trip would be a "breeze" until the path abruptly turned steep. By the time we reached the halfway mark of this "mini-mountain," my twenty-five pound pack felt as though it weighed two hundred pounds.

We finally reached the summit and took a short break. Peering through a narrow opening in the trees, I marveled at the view. Two shades of blue met at the horizon: the water, a crisp aquamarine, and the sky, a soft periwinkle. Lake Superior sparkled with the reflection of the sun's golden rays. The cries of gulls echoed off the water, and the waves gently lapped the shore. The beauty of this unspoiled wilderness compelled me to thank God for His wonderful creation.

The second day of the trip proved to be the most memorable. After breakfast and prayer, we packed our things and began our trek along jagged cliffs high above the water. At certain points along the trail, we could hear waves crashing into the rocks below. Hiking so close to the edge of the cliff filled us with excitement and suspense.

Comp.
62.8

The Pictured Rocks held true to their name. Up close, the water in the coves shimmered in the sunlight emanating brilliant shades of purple, teal, gray, and china blue. But when we hiked farther down the trail, the rocks formed an Indian's face with the trees fashioning his mohawk. At another site, named "Battleship Row," the shoreline jutted out forming a fleet of destroyers docked side by side in battle readiness.

That evening we set up camp at Chapel Rock (so named because it resembled a little church). Nearby, rapids surged into the frigid waters of Lake Superior. After a biting-cold swim in the lake, we retreated to the much warmer river. The bubbling current soothed our aching bodies like a whirlpool. Surrounded by this wild beauty, I realized that the God I know and love is the same God Who created the Pictured Rocks and all their splendor. Suddenly, I knew Him better.

At the end of the week, I no longer felt like an explorer, seeking to conquer and civilize new lands. I wanted this place to remain an untouched paradise. Reluctantly, I bid farewell to the Pictured Rocks. As a backpacker, I felt weary and sore. As a Christian, I felt closer to God—refreshed by His creation.

—Marie Thompson

63   The Argumentative Essay

The argumentative essay uses reasoning and evidence to change minds and to spur people to action. A well-written essay can defeat an opposing view, strengthen people's confidence in what they believe, and even encourage them to take a stand on an issue. The following suggestions will help you to write a well-organized and convincing essay.

63.1   Select a subject.

a. Select an arguable subject. (There must be an opposing view.)

Comp.
63.1

b. Select a subject that is of interest to you and to your audience.

c. Select a subject about which you already have some knowledge.

63.2 **Limit your subject.** (See 45.2.)

63.3 **Write a thesis sentence.**

    a. Determine your purpose. These are the usual purposes of an argument: (1) to offer a solution to a problem, (2) to defend a position, or (3) to refute a position held by others.

    b. State your thesis in a declarative sentence.

    (1) Make the subject of your argument the grammatical subject of the sentence; make your arguable point—your thesis—the predicate. (A thesis is simply the predication that one makes about a topic.)

    (2) Make the sentence a simple sentence or a complex sentence, but not a compound sentence.

    (3) These are some examples: "The whole-word method of teaching reading should be replaced with intensive phonics." "American sports players are paid far too much." "The reading of the classics is still important for high school students."

    c. Write an expanded thesis sentence. Writing an expanded thesis sentence will help you determine the divisions of support for your argument. Add the word *because* and fill out your thesis sentence with the subtopics that constitute the divisions of support for your thesis. For example, "The whole-word method of teaching reading should be replaced with intensive phonics *because* the whole-word method ignores the phonetic basis of our language, it limits one's reading vocabulary to memorized words, and it causes illiteracy."

    ▶ Note. Although the writing of an expanded thesis sentence will help you plan your argument, you may not always want to include the expanded portion at the beginning of your paper. (In your introduction, you may wish to include only the portion of the thesis sentence down to the word *because*.) Sometimes if you reveal the divisions of support at the very beginning, you lose the anticipation and interest of your audience, and may even prompt an antagonistic reader to summarily dismiss your argument.

Comp.
63.3

  d. Revise the thesis sentence. Realize that your thesis sentence may need to be qualified and altered somewhat as you gather evidence and learn more about your subject.

63.4   **Analyze your audience.**

  a. What is the age, economic status, religion, education, philosophy, vocation, and attitude of your audience?

  b. What do you think these readers believe about your subject?

  c. What do these readers need to know in order to understand and accept your thesis about this subject?

63.5   **Gather your evidence.** Keeping in mind what you learned from your audience analysis, gather the pertinent evidence (support). Follow the usual research methods for locating the evidence that you need for your argument. (See 57.2–5.)

63.6   **Evaluate the evidence.**

  a. What kind of evidence have you located (examples, statistics, analogies, comparisons, observable incidents, quotations from experts, cause and effect arguments)?

  b. Which kinds of evidence will most effectively accomplish your purpose with this audience?

63.7   **Make an outline of the reasons that you will use to support your argument.**

  a. You must include reasons to offset all of the significant objections that could be raised by the opposition. If you ignore significant arguments from the other side, you will probably lose the argument.

  b. You must state each reason in a carefully constructed sentence.

   (1) Word your sentences in such a way that you appear reasonable.

   (2) Word your sentences in such a way that the connection to your thesis is obvious.

Comp.
63.4

63.8 **Organize your argument.**

    a. Plan the introduction.

      (1) If you are offering a solution to a problem, make sure that you establish that a real problem exists. If you are defending a position or refuting a position, make it clear what that position is. Define any terms that need to be defined. If you are refuting an opposing view, be sure to explain the opposing view completely and fairly. Be respectful of the opposition so that you do not alienate those who do not agree with you at first.

      (2) Summarize the argument. (State your thesis and explain the theories, assumptions, and arguments which you intend to advance. Usually do not cite authorities in the introduction.)

    b. Plan the body of the argument.

      (1) Present your arguments one by one in descending order of importance. (It is usually best to place your strongest argument first.)

      (2) Fully develop each division of your argument.

         (a) Begin each division with a clear topic sentence.

         (b) Attack and refute the main arguments of the opposing view. Be as positive as you can in your refutation, but do not concede anything to the opposition. Usually emphasize the strength of your arguments rather than the weakness of your opponent's arguments. Do not attack your opponent: deal with the issues.

         (c) After refuting all the significant arguments of the opposition, continue with further evidence for your side of the argument.

         (d) If the argument is lengthy, end each division with a short summation.

Comp. 63.8

         (e) Begin each new division with a clear transition (word or sentence) to maintain a clear connection between the parts of your argument.

c. Plan the conclusion.

    (1) The conclusion should consist of a short summary of the evidence and a recommendation that your thesis be accepted.

    (2) Be sure, in your summary, to emphasize your strongest argument.

63.9 Write the rough draft. (See 43.2.)

63.10 Examine your argument and rewrite it.

  a. Check all the things under sections 45.5 and 63.7–8.

  b. Make sure that your evidence is *accurate, relevant, logical,* and *sufficient.*

  c. Make sure that you eliminate any fallacies of argument.

    (1) *Name-calling.* Avoid statements like this: "Only an *idiot* would accept such a foolish recommendation."

    (2) *Absolute statements.* Sometimes a writer makes a statement without considering that it can be proven false by a single exception. Avoid terms such as *everyone, always,* and *never.* Use qualifiers such as *generally speaking, frequently, most people.*

    (3) *Either/or* solutions. Do not limit a problem to a choice between two extremes. For example, a young man desperately wanting to marry a certain young lady might argue thus: "*Either* you marry me, *or* I will kill myself." Actually there are more choices available to the young man than marriage and suicide. He could, for example, remain unmarried or he could find someone else to marry.

    (4) *Faulty generalizations.* Avoid generalizations such as these: Television is worthless. All politicians are crooks. The Irish are big drinkers.

    (5) *False cause.* Avoid blaming an effect on the wrong cause as in the following example: "Public school teachers are failing to teach children how to read because the teachers' salaries are too low." The real cause has been shown to be the use of wrong methods.

Comp.
63.9

(6) *Begging the question.* Do not present assumptions as facts, as in the following example: "Congressman Jones does not care anything about children because he failed to attend the charity benefit for our local orphanage." He might have been sick or obligated elsewhere.

(7) *Ambiguous terms.* Some terms have different meanings to different audiences. For example, to a Christian audience the term *fundamentalist* may mean "one who believes in the basic doctrines of Christianity," but to a secular audience it may mean "one who is a terrorist." Do not use a term that has different meanings to different audiences without first defining the term.

(8) *False analogy.* An analogy is the comparing of two or more things to indicate that the things are similar in one or more respects. Every analogy proceeds from the similarity of two or more things in *some respects* to similarity in *some other respect.* Do not assume that because some things in an analogy are comparable that all things in the analogy are comparable. In order to analyze the accuracy of an analogy, you can arrange the points of comparison according to the following form:

> The things *a* and *b* have the attributes 1 and 2.
> The thing *a* also has the attribute 3.
> Therefore, *b* probably has the attribute 3.

An analogy will not be effective, unless the conclusion drawn from the points of similarity appears highly probable. Probability can be indicated by the **number** of attributes compared and by the **relevance** of the compared attributes. Of the two, relevance is the most important. Quantity alone will not suffice. One clearly relevant attribute of comparison is stronger than many irrelevant attributes of comparison. For instance, if a person argues that a curfew for teen-agers will reduce crime in his town because a curfew reduced crime in a similar town, he has suggested that everything that works for one town will work for another.

Comp
63.10

> Your opponent could point out the following irrelevant attributes of comparison implicit in this analogy: The other town was an isolated success story among many failures; the other town did not have problems with teen-age gangs before the curfew was imposed; the curfew in the other town occurred many years ago in significantly different circumstances; the other town did not actually reduce crime among *teen-agers;* and the police in the other town did not attribute the reduction in crime to the curfew.

63.11 **Edit the essay.** (See section 45.6.)

63.12 **Write a captivating title that states the problem.**

63.13 **Type the final draft according to an accepted standard.** (See section 36.)

The Anniversary of the Lifesaver Bomb

Ever since the Smithsonian Institution earlier this year tried to give us all a guilty conscience about the B-29 named *Enola Gay,* the press has inundated Americans with a torrent of breast-beating about dropping the atom bomb on Hiroshima. *Newsweek* magazine accompanied pages of ugly pictures with a poll reporting that Americans now think dropping the bomb on Japan was "wrong." But the poll demographics tell a different story. The senior citizens whose lives were on the line in World War II approve of the bombing, while those too young to remember the hardships of war have the luxury of sanctimonious second-guessing. Although the fiftieth anniversary of August 6, 1945, is supposed to make us all hang our heads in shame, we should be proud of the American war effort and thankful that so many American lives were saved by the mission of the *Enola Gay.*

For the men who fought in World War II, the atom bomb was a lifesaver in every sense of the word. Dropping the atom bomb on Hiroshima meant the difference between life and death to hundreds of thousands of America's best and brightest young men. Instead of dying a tortured death 5,000 miles away, those fine young American men could come home, grow up to live normal lives, marry, and raise families.

Comp.
63.11

What the Hiroshima bomb accomplished was the preemption of Gen. George Marshall's horrendous plan to defeat Japan: an island-by-island invasion at a projected cost of 500,000 American deaths. The first phase, called Operation Olympic, would have sent 650,000 Americans—starting November 1, 1945—to try to capture the island of Kyushu. Operation Olympic would have ended with an American slaughter because the Japanese were prepared to defend Kyushu with 540,000 troops and 5,000 kamikaze planes. The follow-up invasion, called Operation Coronet, was scheduled to start the drive toward Tokyo on March 1, 1946. U.S. plans projected an invasion force of 2 million men.

Marshall could not have had any illusions about the hideous human cost of such an island-by-island invasion. Iwo Jima had given us a preview. On February 19, 1945, 30,000 Marines landed on that little five-mile island, and five days later planted the U.S. flag, an event immortalized in the most famous war photograph in history. When the Iwo Jima battle ended a month later, the price we had paid for raising our flag was 26,000 casualties; of these, more than 6,800 died, including three of the six men in the photograph.

Japanese soldiers were tough fighters. Under orders not to be captured alive, only 1,000 were taken prisoner while 22,000 died defending Iwo Jima. With such high casualty figures, only a reckless disregard for American lives could cause a U.S. leader to send American troops to invade Japanese home islands. But that was Marshall's plan, even though he knew from the coded messages we had intercepted that Japan planned to defend its home islands with 2.3 million troops, another four million Army and Navy employees, and an armed militia of 28 million, all sworn to fight to the death.

Admiral William D. Leahy, Truman's military adviser, predicted that 30 to 35 percent of U.S. soldiers would be killed or wounded during the first 30 days of an invasion of Japan. The Hiroshima bomb

Comp
63.13

345

saved those lives, as well as those of about 400,000 Allied prisoners of war and civilian detainees whom Japan had planned to execute in the event of an American invasion.

President Harry "the buck stops here" Truman had no difficulty making the atom bomb decision. As he told reporters in 1947, "I didn't have any doubts at the time." His decision saved 250,000 to 500,000 American lives.

"I'd do it again," Truman said in 1956. In 1962, he added, "I knew I'd done the right thing."

Nor did other Americans at the time have any qualms about the loss of life in the country that had started the war with a sneak attack on Pearl Harbor. *Newsweek,* for example, cheered the fact that "perhaps 1 million persons were made homeless" by our firebombing of Tokyo.

Many argue today that we should not have dropped the bomb because "Japan was already seeking to surrender." In an interview with veteran journalist Philip Clarke in 1962, Truman answered, "The bombs were dropped after Japan had been warned that we had discovered the greatest explosive in the history of the world and then we asked them to surrender. They did not do it." In fact, Japan did not even surrender after the first bomb was dropped at Hiroshima. It took the second bomb at Nagasaki, three days later, to induce Japan to surrender.

Instead of being haunted by the ghosts of Hiroshima, Americans today should remember the American heroes of Iwo Jima, Guadalcanal, Midway, and Okinawa, and rejoice that the survivors of those bloody battles lived to come home to America instead of being killed on the beaches of Japan.

Schlafly, Phyllis. "The Anniversary of the Lifesaver Bomb." *Conservative Chronicle*, 23 August 1995, 22. Reprinted by permission of Copley News Service.

Comp.
63.13

Self-Control, Not Gun Control

Disarm Americans. Force every law-abiding citizen to surrender all firearms and America will at last be a safer place to live. Sounds absurd doesn't it? But the anti-gun lobby, fueled by misinformation—and the FBI's unprecedented political support of gun control—is effectively eroding Americans' constitutional right to keep and bear arms.

Passage of the Brady Bill was strategically important. Brady II, which will require federal licensing and registration of all guns, has been submitted to Congress. We can expect more restrictive legislative initiatives to follow.

Meanwhile, Americans are fearful, almost desperate, as they are assailed with reports of an exploding crime wave.[1] Proponents of gun control promise safety and protection in exchange for our civil liberties. That's not a new promise, but it is an empty one. All totalitarian regimes disarm their citizens.

Routinely, superficial theories are offered to explain the orgy of violent crime in our nation. The fundamental reason is ignored. Self-control—not gun-control is the key to preventing anarchy in America.

Personal accountability has virtually been abandoned in our social structure and is conceptually absent for an entire generation of young Americans. Amid a web of informational overload, one message is paramount. The moral standards, and internal restraints inherent in historic Western culture are obsolete. Human behavior has been officially unleashed. And if, in a hedonistic tantrum, one goes beyond the ever increasing limits of acceptable conduct, one need not look far for absolution. Society, biology, psychology, racism, sexism—anything—except the individual is now responsible.

It is as natural, and in their hands as deadly, for such a deviant to use a knife, a hatchet, a club. The Gainesville student murders are a case in point. Gruesome details of rape, stabbing, and decapitation were revealed after Danny Rolling, a career criminal, pleaded guilty to murdering five college students.

Comp
63.13

Rolling suffers, we are told, from "intermittent explosive disorder, a rare condition characterized by aggressive, violent outbursts and sometimes by remorse."

A glance at our criminal justice system shows there are minimal or often no consequences for criminal behavior. Criminals are routinely characterized as victims. Through plea bargaining, psychiatric defenses, prison furloughs, and early parole, they are put back on our streets. Seventy percent of all violent crimes are committed by only six percent of all criminals.

Demands to reform our criminal justice system are valid. But it's a long road back to sane procedures and substantive justice. Instilling self restraint and responsible behavior will not be instantaneous or easy. It is, however, our best hope.

Moreover, is it beneficial, is it moral, to surrender the right to effectively protect our children— ourselves? By capturing the moral high ground with their assertion: "If gun control saves just one life, then it's worth it," proponents of gun control are often successful in evading the alternative. "Existing gun control laws have already cost innocent lives."

In October 1991, 23 people were murdered in Luby's cafeteria in Killeen, Texas. The assailant reloaded his two pistols five times before the police arrived. Texas law, which prohibits carrying firearms, insured that all the victims would be unarmed and defenseless. Most of us remember the Luby's massacre. It was national news, and is often cited as proof of the need for still more comprehensive gun control.

Shoney's in Anniston, Alabama, just two months later, was the scene of another violent encounter involving two criminals with stolen pistols who forced employees and 20 customers into the walk-in refrigerator of the restaurant. You probably don't remember the Shoney's episode. Most people have never heard about it. It never made the national news. (National coverage is rare when guns are used to save lives.) Unlike Texas, the only people killed this time were the two criminals. Thomas Glen Tarry, a courageous citizen who was legally armed under Alabama law, fatally shot both outlaws, and saved the lives of 20 innocent people.[2]

In a landmark study on crime control, criminologist Gary Kleck explains that "Victim gun use in crime incidents is associated with lower rates of crime completion and of victim injury than any other defensive response, including doing nothing to resist." According to Professor Kleck, "victim gun use may be one of the most serious risks a criminal faces."[3] Fear of confronting an armed citizen is a deterrent that also benefits the roughly 50 percent of American families who don't own firearms. If Janet Reno and her allies prevail, only criminals will be armed.

Far from vigilantism, the right to keep and bear arms is affirmed in our Constitution, and is rooted in centuries of responsible citizenship.

But while the constitutionality of gun control laws is being argued, empirical evidence has shown they simply don't work. Already, there are over 20,000 gun control laws in the United States. A 1982 National Institute of Justice report concluded that such laws had no impact in reducing criminal violence.[4]

To remove guns from law-abiding citizens presumes that guns are to blame for violent crime, and shifts responsibility from the individual to an object. It has been said before. It's worth repeating: guns don't kill people; people do.

—Catherine Farmer

Reprinted by permission of The Foundation for Economic Education from *The Freeman,* February 1995.

1. For countervailing perspective on crime trend see, Rich Henderson, "Crime Story," *Reason,* June 1994, p. 14.

2. David B. Kopel, "The Violence of Gun Control," *Policy Review,* Winter 1993, p. 7.

3. Professor Gary Kleck, "Crime Control Through the Private Use of Armed Force," *Social Problems,* February 1988, pp. 16, 2.

4. Kopel, p. 16.

Comp.
63.13

*I*NDEX

A

Index

Index

Index

H

Had better, better, 144
Had of, 148
Had ought, 148
Handbooks of miscellaneous information, 251–252
Hanged, hung, 148
Hardly, in double negative, 86
Have, of, 148
Have, subjunctive forms of, 76
Heading of a letter, 324, 326
Heighth, 148
Helping verbs
  defined, 15
  list of, 7, 16
Here, sentences beginning with, 6, 8, 56
Hisself, 19
Historical events, capitalization of, 165
Honorable, abbreviation of, 160
Hopefully, 148
Hung, hanged, 148
Hyperbole, 134
Hyphen
  with certain prefixes and suffixes, 182
  with compound adjectives before a noun, 182
  to divide word at end of line, 162, 182
  with numbers and fractions, 182

I

I, capitalization of, 168
Ibid., 302
-ics, number of words ending in, 57
Idioms
  in dictionaries, 125
  use of, 135–136
i.e., 161
Ill, comparison of, 84
Illicit, elicit, 146
Illiteracies, 129
Illogical comparison, 85
Illogical subordination, 94–95
Illusion, allusion, 142
Illustrations in dictionaries, 124
Immigrate, emigrate, 146
Imminent, eminent, 146
Imperative mood, 76
Imperative sentence
  defined, 5
  punctuation of, 5, 169
  subject of, 5, 9
Implied reference of pronouns, 100
Imply, infer, 148
Improprieties, 130–131
In, into, 148
Inc., omission of, 283
Incidents, paragraph developed by, 191–192

Incomplete construction (*See* Elliptical clause)
Indefinite pronoun
  agreement with, 58–59
  defined, 19
  as subject, 58–59
  used as adjective, 21
Indention
  on bibliography page, 281
  of block quotations, 158, 277
  of footnotes, 158, 268–269
  of outline, 274
  of paragraphs, 158, 276
Independent clause, 4, 33
Independent element, 26
Independent elements, diagramed, 54–55
Indicative mood, 76
Indirect object
  case of, 79
  compound, 12
  defined, 10
  diagramed, 42
  distinguished from object of preposition, 10
  pronoun as, 79
Indirect question, punctuation of, 169
Indirect quotation, punctuation of, 179
Infer, imply, 148
Infinitive
  complement of, 79
  defined, 21, 28
  subject of, 79
  used as adjective, 21
  used as adverb, 23
Infinitive phrase, 31–32
  dangling, 99
  diagramed, 46–47
  used as adjective, 32
  used as adverb, 32
  used for conciseness, 109
  used to correct monotonous style, 112
  used as noun, 31–32
Inflected forms of words, 121–123
Informal usage (*See* Standard informal usage)
Inside address, 326
Inside of, 149
Intensive use of compound personal pronouns, 19
Interjection
  capitalization of, 168
  comma with, 173
  defined, 3, 26
  diagramed, 54
Interrogative pronoun
  defined, 19
  used as adjective, 21
Interrogative sentence
  defined, 5
  punctuation of, 5, 169
  subject of, 8
Into, in, 148
Intransitive verb, 14
Introduction of an essay, 206–207

Introductory phrases or clauses, commas with, 174
Inverted sentence, 8, 111
Irregardless, 149
Irregular adjectives, 84
Irregular adverbs, 84
Irregular comparison, 84
Irregular verbs, 62–63
Isn't, agreement with subject, 59
It, sentences beginning with, 8–9
It, you, they, reference of, 100–101
Italics (underlining)
  for foreign words and phrases, 182
  for names of ships, aircraft, etc., 181–182
  for titles of books, magazines, plays, etc., 181–182
  for words, letters, and numbers referred to as such, 182

J, K, L

Jargon, 136–137
Joint possession, 183
Junior
  abbreviation of, 160
  capitalization of, 164

Kind of, 149
Kind of a, 149
Kinds of dictionaries, 114–115
Kinds of pronouns, 18–19
Kinds of sentences, 4–5, 37–39

Lab, 141
Languages, capitalization of, 165
Lay, lie, 66
Lay, principal parts of, 66
Learn, teach, 149
Leave, let, 149
Less, fewer, 147
Let, leave, 149
Letter
  business, 326–332
  friendly, 324–325
Letters, italicized, 182
Levels of usage, 127
Library
  card catalog, 247–249
  fiction books, 255
  nonfiction books, 254–255
  reference section, 249–254
Library of Congress System, 256–257
Lie, lay, 66
Lie, principal parts of, 66
Like, as, as if, 149
Limiting the subject
  for an essay, 204–205
  for a research paper, 258
Linking verbs
  chart of, 7
  defined, 15
  list of, 11, 15–16
  with subject complements, 11, 78

Index

Index

Index